ETHNIC VARIATIONS IN DYING, DEATH, AND GRIEF

SERIES IN DEATH EDUCATION, AGING, AND HEALTH CARE

HANNELORE WASS, CONSULTING EDITOR

ADVISORY BOARD

Herman Feifel, Ph.D.

Jeanne Quint Benoliel, R.N., Ph.D.
Balfour Mount, M.D.

Bard—*Medical Ethics in Practice*
Benoliel—*Death Education for the Health Professional*
Bertman—*Facing Death: Images, Insights, and Interventions*
Brammer—*How to Cope with Life Transitions: The Chanllenge of Personal Change*
Cleiren—*Bereavement and Adaptation: A Comparative Study of the Aftermath of Death*
Corless, Pittman-Lindeman—*AIDS: Priciples, Practices, and Politics, Abridged Edition*
Corless, Pittman-Lindeman—*AIDS: Priciples, Practices, and Politics, Reference Edition*
Curran—*Adolescent Suicidal Behavior*
Davidson—*The Hospice: Development and Administration, Second Edition*
Davidson, Linnolla—*Risk Factors in Youth Suicide*
Degner, Beaton—*Life-Death Decisions in Health Care*
Doty—*Communication and Assertion Skills for Older Persons*
Epting, Neimeyer—*Personal Meanings of Death: Applications of Personal Construct Theory to Clinical Practice*
Haber—*Health Care for an Aging Society: Cost-Conscious Community Care and Self-Care Approaches*
Hughes—*Bereavement and Support: Healing in a Group Environment*
Irish, Lundquist, Nelson—*Ethnic Variations in Dying, Death, and Grief: Diversity in Universality*
Klass, Silverman, Nickman—*Continuing Bonds: New Understandings of Grief*
Leenaars, Maltsberger, Neimeyer—*Treatment of Suicidal People*
Leenaars, Wenckstern—*Suicide Prevention in Schools*
Leng—*Psychological Care in Old Age*
Leviton—*Horrendous Death and Health: Toward Action*
Leviton—*Horrendous Death, Health, and Well-Being*
Lindeman, Corby, Downing, Sanborn—*Alzheimer's Day Care: A Basic Guide*
Lund—*Older Bereaved Spouses: Research with Practical Applications*
Neimeyer—*Death Anxiety Handbook: Research, Instrumentation, and Application*
Papadatou, Papadatos—*Children and Death*
Prunkl, Berry—*Death Week: Exploring the Dying Process*
Riker, Meyers—*Retirement Counseling: A Practical Guide for Action*
Samarel—*Caring for Life and Death*
Sherron, Lumsden—*Introduction to Educational Gerontology, Third Edition*
Stillion—*Death and the Sexes: An Examination of Differential Longevity, Attitudes, Behaviors, and Coping Skills*
Stillion, McDowell—*Suicide Across the Life Span—Premature Exits, Second Edition*
Vachon—*Occupational Stress in the Care of the Critically Ill, the Dying, and the Bereaved*
Wass, Corr—*Childhood and Death*
Wass, Corr—*Helping Children Cope with Death: Guidelines and Resources, Second Edition*
Wass, Corr, Pacholski, Forfar—*Death Education II: An Annotated Resource Guide*
Wass, Neimeyer—*Dying: Facing the Facts, Third Edition*
Weenolsen—*Transcendence of Loss over the Life Span*
Werth—*Rational Suicide? Implications for Mental Heath Professionals*

IN PREPARATION

Lair—*Sharing the Journey*

ETHNIC VARIATIONS IN DYING, DEATH, AND GRIEF:
Diversity in Universality

Edited by

Donald P. Irish
Kathleen F. Lundquist
Vivian Jenkins Nelsen

Taylor & Francis
Publishers since 1798

USA	Publishing Office	Taylor & Francis 325 Chestnut Street, Suite 800 Philadelphia, PA 19106
	Distribution Center	Taylor & Francis 7625 Empire Drive Florence, KY 41042
UK		Taylor & Francis 11 New Fetter Lane London EC4P 4EE

On pages 7 and 8, material from the *Star Tribune* (Minneapolis/St. Paul) used with permission.

On page 9, material from the *New York Times.* Copyright © 1990 by the New York Times Company. Reprinted with permission.

On pages 60 and 61, material from "The Rites for Cousin Vit." From "Blacks," © by Gwendolyn Brooks, The David Company, Chicago, 1987, and the Third World Press, Chicago, 1991. Reprinted with permission.

On page 129, material reprinted with permission of Charles Scribner's Sons, an imprint of Macmillan Publishing Company from A DICTIONARY OF BUDDHISM by T. O. Ling which the text is taken from A DICTIONARY OF COMPARATIVE RELIGION, edited by S. G. Brandon. Copyright © 1970 S. G. Brandon.

ETHNIC VARIATIONS IN DYING, DEATH, AND GRIEF: Diversity in Universality

This book was set in Times Roman by Taylor & Francis. The editors were Jean Atcheson and Joyce Duncan; the production supervisor was Peggy M. Rote; and the typesetter was Wayne Hutchins. Cover design by Michelle Fleitz. Printing and binding by Braun-Brumfield Inc.

A CIP catalog record for this book is available from the British Library. ∞ The paper in this publication meets the requirements of the ANSI Standard Z39.48-1984(Permanence of Paper)

Library of Congress Cataloging-in-Publication Data

Irish, Donald P.
   Ethnic variations in dying, death, and grief: diversity in
universality / Donald P. Irish, Kathleen F. Lundquist, Vivian
Jenkins Nelson.
     p. cm.
   "Sponsored by the Minnesota Coalition for Death Education and Support, Inc."
   Includes bibliographical references.

    1. Death—Cross-cultural studies. 2. Terminal care—Cross-cultural studies
I. Lundquist, Kathleen F. II Nelson, Vivian Jenkins. III. Minnesota Coalition
for Death Education and Support. IV. Title.
   [DNLM: 1. Attitudes to death. 2. Cross-Cultural Comparison.
3. grief. BF 789.D4 I68e]
R726.8.I75 1993
393—dc20
DNLM/DLC
for Library of Congress   92-48746
                                                                         CIP

ISBN 1-56032-277-2 (case)
ISBN 1-56032-278-0 (paper)
ISSN 0275-3510

Contents

PART 1: CROSS-CULTURAL AND PERSONAL PERSPECTIVES

             and Understanding of Grief   13
             Paul C. Rosenblatt

             Death and Life   14
             "Grief" Across Cultures   14
             Learning to Deal with Grief Cross-Culturally   16
             Conclusion   18
             References   19

CHAPTER 2   One Woman's Interracial Journey   21
             Vivian Jenkins Nelsen

             The Assassination of a Young President   21
             Childhood Learnings about Death   23
             Deaths Experienced in Youth   24
             Experiencing Deaths as an Adult   26

CHAPTER 3   Personal Reflections on Death, Grief, and Cultural
             Diversity   29
             Kathleen F. Lundquist and Vivian Jenkins Nelsen

             Death Awareness   30
             Grief Awareness   36
             Multi-Cultural Awareness   42

PART 2: DYING, DEATH, AND GRIEF AMONG SELECTED ETHNIC COMMUNITIES

             Hosea L. Perry

             Illustrative Episode   51
             Introduction   53
             Vestiges of Africa and Slavery   54
             African American Funeral Patterns in Transition   56
             Some Psychological Insights   59
             Insights from African American Literature, Drama,
                 Poetry, Music   60
             Conclusion   63
             References   64

PART 3: REFLECTIONS AND CONCLUSIONS

Contributors

Tobin Gonzales Barrozo, Ph.D., *Associate Chancellor, State University, 555 Park Street, St. Paul, MN 55103*

Dr. Barrozo is a native of Montana. He received his B.A. degree from San Francisco State University and his Ph.D. degree from Stanford University, majoring in philosophy at both institutions. Before coming to Minnesota, he served as provost and vice-president for academic affairs at Metropolitan State College, Denver. Prior to those roles, he was an interim vice-president and an associate dean for academic affairs at William Paterson College, New Jersey and, later, president of Metropolitan State University in the twin cities of Minnesota.

Bruce Thowpauo Bliatout, Ph.D., *Director, International Health Center, 12710 SE Division, Portland, Oregon 97236*

An American of Hmong ancestry, Dr. Bliatout was born in Laos, where he received his earliest education. He received his B.A. degree in sociology and a Master of Public Health degree from the University of Hawaii. He was granted a Master of Public Health in hygiene and pursued doctoral work in public health at Tulane University. His Ph.D. degree is from Century University.

His first professional position was as director and administrator of the Refugees of Indochina Culture Education, a mental health project with the Institute of Behavioral Sciences in Honolulu. Relocating, he became director of the Southeast Asian Refugee Federation and then refugee coordinator for Portland, Oregon.

Martin Brokenleg, Ed.D., *Associate Professor of Native American Studies, Augustana College, Sioux Falls, South Dakota 57197*

Dr. Brokenleg has taught at Augustana College for the past 18 years. He was granted his B.A. degree by South Dakota State University, his Master of Divinity degree by the Episcopal Theological Seminary, and his D.Ed. degree from the University of South Dakota. He is a member of the clergy and an enrolled member of the Rosebud Sioux tribe.

Jorge L. Chinea, M.A., *Coordinator of Hispanic Studies, Mankato State University, Mankato, Minnesota 56001*

Professor Chinea was born in Puerto Rico, but in 1967 his family moved to New York City's Spanish Harlem. A former board member of the Puerto Rican Family Institute in the city, he later attended Bronx Community College. He received his B.A. and M.A. degrees in Latin American/Caribbean Area History from the State University of New York at Binghamton. He has taught at John Jay College of Criminal Justice–CUNY, Macalester College, and Metropolitan State University, St. Paul, Minnesota. He is completing his doctoral dissertation in Latin American History at the University of Minnesota.

Barry D. Cytron, Ph.D., *Rabbi, Adath Jeshurun Congregation, 3400 DuPont Avenue South, Minneapolis, Minnesota 55408*

Rabbi Cytron was ordained by the Jewish Theological Seminary (New York city), following receipt of his B.A. and M.A. degrees from Columbia University. His Ph.D. at Iowa State University focused on Christian-Jewish Studies; and he served as rabbi at Tifereth Israel Synagogue in Des Moines. His current congregation is a large progressive one. He also teaches Jewish studies at the University of St. Thomas and Macalester College in St. Paul.

Farah Gilanshah, Ph.D., *Assistant Professor of Sociology, University of Minnesota-Morris, Morris, Minnesota 56267*

Dr. Gilanshah was born in Tehran, Iran. She received her B.A. degree in sociology from the National University of Tehran. Her M.A. and Ph.D. degrees were awarded by the University of Minnesota. She taught at the University of Wisconsin–La Crosse, Lander College-South Carolina, and Miami University of Ohio before coming to the University at Morris.

David Middleton, M.A., *Director, Connors Elder Care, and Corporate Grief Counselor, Jefferson Hospice (Madison), 7115 Century Avenue, Middleton, Wisconsin 53562*

David Middleton was a counseling intern for the Wellness Center at Augustana College. He was ceremonially adopted as a brother by Martin Brokenleg and has extensive experience with members of the Rosebud Sioux youth and elders. He has specialized in Native American issues, grief therapy, counseling, and philosophy. His M.A. in counseling was granted by the University of South Dakota, Vermillion.

Hosea L. Perry, M.A., M.S.W., *Department of Sociology/Social Work, Winona State University (Retired), Winona, Minnesota 55987*

Professor Perry was born in Georgia. He received his B.A. degree from Allen University–South Carolina, his M.A. degree from North Carolina Central University, and his M.S.W. degree from the University of Iowa. His degree work focused on social policy, aging, and race relations. Included in his teaching specialties has been cross-cultural perspectives on death and dying. He began his teaching career at Florida A & M University. Thereafter he served the Department of Social Services at Mobile State Junior College, and as assistant professor at Barber-Scotia College in North Carolina.

Paul C. Rosenblatt, Ph.D., *Professor of Family Social Sciences, 290 McNeal Hall, University of Minnesota, 1985 Buford Avenue, St. Paul, Minnesota 55108*

Dr. Rosenblatt came to the University of Minnesota in 1969. Previously he was a faculty member at the University of Missouri–Columbia and the University of California–Riverside. He has also been a visiting professor at Northwestern University. Of his major publications, three deal with loss: *Grief and Mourning in Cross-Cultural Perspective,* published in 1976, *Bitter, Bitter Tears: Nineteenth Century Diarists and Twentieth Century Grief Theories,* which appeared in 1983, and *Farming Is In Our Blood: Farm Families in Economic Crisis,* which was issued in 1990.

Joanne M. Spears, M.A., *Great Plains Institute of Theology, 1824 Catherine Drive, Bismarck, North Dakota 58501*

Joanne Spears received her B.A. degree from Arizona State University and her master's degree from Union Theological Seminary, New York City. She is currently translating the Bible for children.

Ken Truitner, M.A., *International Institute of Minnesota, 1694 Como Avenue, St. Paul, Minnesota 55108*
    Ken Truitner received his B.A. degree in English from Berkeley and an M.A. degree in linguistics from the University of California–Los Angeles. He taught linguistics at Fresno State University before coming to Minnesota, where he served as a teaching associate in the Department of American Indian Studies, University of Minnesota. He was education supervisor at the International Institute of Minnesota for 17 years.

Nga (Nita) Truitner, M.S.W., *Supervisor, Community Resources Division, Hennepin County, Minneapolis, Minnesota 55415*
    Nita Truitner was born in Vietnam, graduating from Saigon University with a B.A. degree in English. She earned her M.S.W. degree at the University of Minnesota, serving also as a case worker with the International Institute. Since 1985 she has been employed by Hennepin County. She has been an officer of the Vietnam Buddhist Association of Minnesota since 1976 and a volunteer director of Vietnamese Social Services since 1988.

Juan L. Turner, M.S.N., *White Sands Beach Post Office, Montego Bay, Jamaica, West Indies*
    "Jo" Turner, now retired, served as a nursing instructor for 15 years with the Minneapolis Community College.

Marcial Vásquez, M.Div., *Pastor, La Puerta Abierta, Faith United Methodist Church, 1530 Oakdale Avenue, West St. Paul, Minnesota 55118*
    Rev. Vásquez was born in Belize. He served for six years as a missionary in Guatemala before being a pastor in Chicago for a time before coming to Minnesota.

Barbara Younoszai, Ph.D., *Chair, Modern Language Department, Hamline University, St. Paul, Minnesota 55104*
    Dr. Younoszai received B.A. degrees in political science and Spanish, and an M.A. degree in Spanish from the University of California–Berkeley. Her Ph.D. degree, as a Danforth Foundation Scholar in Spanish and Latin American studies, was granted by the University of Minnesota. She was a Fulbright Research scholar in Spain and served twice as a faculty advisor to the Minnesota Student Project for Amity among Nations, for Argentina and Mexico. She co-taught an off-campus academic program in which students from several colleges resided and worked in an isolated Mexican mountain village. The students experienced and shared in the community's responses to deaths that occurred during their stay in the pueblo. She has explored the theme of death in Latin American literature, especially in Mexican writings.

Foreword

Death is an irremediable feature of human existence. It is natural, therefore, to reflect on its meaning. Is there "life" after death? Is there "life" before birth? How may we comfort the dying? And what can be said to those who will for a time survive?

Three distinct perspectives must be taken into account. The person dying must prepare for this, the final event of living. The family member, friend, or lover must reconcile the fact of their survival with the absence in their life of another. Those responsible for care of the dying or arrangements following a death must consider how they may help without undue intrusion.

A polyglot "tower of babble" or a cauldron ever-threatening to boil over: these are metaphors of our society. Every American and Canadian has roots that reach across vast oceans or lay deep in the soil of North America. Every major city is a delicatessen of the food, lifestyles, and seasonings from every region of the earth. The air is punctuated with sounds and music warm and resonant to some, and strange and unintelligible to others. A gesture may be an expression of warmth in one social setting and an insult in another. Each person presents her- or himself to others as an enigma. So persistent is this a feature of our experience that it is hardly noticed.

We are multi-ethnic societies. The authors of the articles within this volume elucidate for health professionals and those responsible for last rites the profound variety in thinking about death and dying.

Examples of different cultures provide insights to understand and appreciate the book's contents. Regarding sensitivity to cultural differences, it might be asked: "If death is an inevitable, universal characteristic of human existence, do not all human beings react essentially in the same way?" The question is a reasonable one; and, on one level of understanding, the answer is yes. On a visceral level, every person may fear death, and sadness over the loss of a loved one is unavoidable. Fear and sadness are universal human emotions.

Beyond these basic emotions, however, there are habits of mind and sentiments that are the products of growing up in a particular culture. The philosopher Wittgenstein wrote of language as if it represented a "form of life." He knew that human beings think of themselves, their place in society, and their world differently. The logic of different languages mirrors differences in worldviews. Different cultures and the great world religions they embody are lenses through which reality is viewed. A lens with an amber tint reveals a world different from a world seen through a lens of different hue. To think that all human beings experience reality the same way is ethnocentric.

A reflection on the meaning of death is as inescapable as death itself. Dying and the grief of others are occurrences that take us to the core of our being. At those times there are moments of clarity on the "big questions," and the meaning and purpose of living take form in our minds. The authors remind us that dying and grief are intensely personal, yet these experiences and feelings cannot be separated from who we are and from the cultures that nourish and surround us.

Tobin Gonzales Barrozo

Preface

This volume has three aims. First, it is directed especially to those professional persons who regularly work in occupations related to death and dying. There is a need to recognize, understand, and adapt to the needs of clientele with cultural patterns that deviate from the standard and dominant patterns in the United States and Canada.

The second function advances the first. Illustrative episodes and in-depth presentations of selected ethnic patterns and materials for personal reflection about death and dying and multicultural issues are included.

A third goal is manifest in the fact that each of the ethnic chapters has been prepared almost exclusively by representatives who share the cultural traditions they describe. Thus, they speak for themselves.

The creation of this volume has been greatly aided by the Minnesota Coalition for Death Education and Support, incorporated in 1979, and the book is published under its auspices.

Donald P. Irish
Kathleen F. Lundquist
Vivian Jenkins Nelsen

Acknowledgments

This project was developed under the aegis of the Minnesota Coalition for Death Education and Support (MCDES). The co-editors express their appreciation to the members of the Board of MCDES for their encouragement, financial aid, and steadfast support throughout the preparation of this volume. Special gratitude is due Louise Quinn Kroese, its president during that time, Gail Noller, treasurer, and the chairs of the Education Committee, Adele Cole and Diane Barrett.

Boyd Koehler, Augsburg College reference librarian, ably aided us with his very conscientious editing of much of the manuscript. Diane Clayton, Hamline University reference librarian, and student Paulette Susens helped with bibliographic searches. Hamline library staff member Laura McDermott and student Caroline Tajbakah located much of the population data. Judith Hamilton, initially, and Stanley Thomas Moses later, both helped us greatly with word processing and computer work under great time pressures.

The manuscript was perused in its entirety by numerous professional colleagues in diverse disciplines. Their responses through personal correspondence appear in Chapter 12. Individuals who critiqued particular chapters only and assisted us with their content are credited therein.

Initially we were a fine foursome. We remain grateful to Richard Lundy, Lakota Native American, for his participation with us and the contributions he made during the early months of our collaborative efforts. We much regret that he could not continue.

Ron E. Wilder, acquisition editor for Taylor & Francis, and his assistant Carolyn Baker were from the beginning enthusiastic about our endeavor and lent their full support to its completion. We are very appreciative also of the very conscientious and thoughtful editing performed by Jean Atcheson and Joyce Duncan. Michelle Fleitz creatively utilized her talents for the cover and interior art work. All three were graciously responsive to our suggestions. Although we had no contact personally with behind-the-scenes Washington staff, Peggy M. Rote, as production supervisor, and Wayne Hutchins, as typesetter, certainly were patient and responsive to our numerous copy changes.

The members of our families were very supportive and forbearing during the lengthy process needed to prepare this volume.

D.P.I.
K.F.L.
V.J.N.

Introduction

Multiculturalism and the Majority Population

Donald P. Irish

The United States and Canadian societies have traditionally been predominantly white in race and Christian in religion. Thus, the professional personnel who have daily been involved in the treatment of the dying and the nurture of the bereaved will most commonly have been related to white Roman Catholics and mainline Protestant patients and clients. The specialists themselves—physicians, nurses, clergy, social workers, hospice and hospital chaplains, and funeral directors—as trained professionals have usually also been members of the dominant groups. For both reasons, these practitioners have tended to be better acquainted with the beliefs about life and death, related rituals, patterns of emotional response, and attitudes toward the body that prevail within the majoritarian cultures.

This volume, therefore, is intentionally focused upon ethnic groups about which our professional personnel are less well informed and/or with which they have had little or no experience. The editors have deliberately omitted any chapters covering the most common and conventional societal patterns related to dying, death, and bereavement.

Until recent years, the training of medical, nursing, social work, and religious professionals included virtually no consideration of the knowledge and skills needed to relate appropriately and most helpfully to patients, clients, or parishioners who were facing death or experiencing grief. The sensitivity of dealing with the traditionally taboo subject of death delayed its inclusion within the curricula and training programs. The additional subtleties that are introduced when concern is directed toward patterns found among "minority groups" increase the need for sensitizing professional workers in the field of death and dying to multi-cultural differences.[1]

Contrary to popular myth, the United States and Canada have never functioned as well-stirred "melting pots," although there has been considerable intermixture among those of originally European nationalities. There has never been a thorough melding of cultural and racial differences to create homogeneity, nor do we assume that such a fusion would be desirable.

Both countries, like many others, are still mainly multi-ethnic, and not yet fully multi-cultural. Some minority cultural groups have survived for centuries within multi-ethnic societies in spite of dominant pressures upon them to assimilate. Others were exterminated; yet others managed to survive but have been socially marginalized.

Many minority peoples in the contemporary world are developing a heightened group consciousness. Currently, this trend is particularly visible in Yugoslavia and other parts of Europe, South Africa, French Canada, and among the indigenous people of the Western Hemisphere. They are organizing themselves within and among their communities and are seeking respect, equal participation in the larger national and world societies, and control over their own destinies. The international community is manifesting interest in their demands. Their issues can no longer be ignored.

---

[1]The terms "majority" and "minority" are used here to indicate power relationships within a society, not numerical magnitudes within a population. For the entire world, those of the white race constitute a distinct *minority* numerically; "people of color" are the vast *majority*. However, in times past and present, as, for example, in South Africa, white numerical minorities have maintained power over non-white majorities, controlling the circumstances under which the latter lived. In the United States and Canada, white majorities have dominated, discriminated against, and even pursued genocidal practices toward their non-white minorities, the indigenous peoples, the "First Nations," and those who came to the New World as slaves.

Although a distinction between the terms "multi-ethnic" and "multi-cultural" is not clear in common parlance, we suggest a differentiation, by degree but not in kind. A multi-*ethnic* society may be one comprised of identifiable cultural groups (by race, religion, language, national origin, or other distinguishable traits) that exist quite separately from and subordinate to a majority population. Such groups are not appreciably assimilated and may even resist the process. They do not receive equal respect from the majority and they lack equal access to opportunities within the society. In their experiences, African Americans, Native Americans, many Hispanics, and possibly other groups as well may fall into the former category. They represent what has been called "diversity without equality." A multi-*cultural* society likewise contains groups within it that are distinguishable by their sharing of common cultural traits. However, they are able to share fully, or almost fully, in the wider culture's opportunity structure and resources and are not depreciated by the dominant group. They represent "diversity with equality," or almost equality. Jews, Quakers, and others may be positioned toward the other end of the spectrum.

OBJECTIVES WITHIN THE CONTENT

This efflorescence of "identity" needs among many minority peoples, sometimes accompanied by a resurgent nationalism, is provoking within the majority, dominant populations attitudes and actions that are anti-immigrant, anti-alien, anti-differentness. Such concerns are further heightened during times of economic distress and external threats. There is a very real need for programs and resources to counter these trends and to enhance the fairness of institutions in societies that value equality of opportunity and political freedom.

This volume focuses upon just one of the major arenas: the health-care system and its personnel. The material has several objectives:

1. to bring into focus the increasingly salient and urgent problems within our multi-ethnic societies in relation to aspects of dying, death, and grief (Introduction);

2. to present genuine examples of occasions when health-related institutions and professional practitioners have confronted cultural issues while serving their clientele, sometimes sensitively, at other times not (the illustrative episodes throughout the book);

3. to encourage readers to reflect upon their own personal attitudes about and experiences with death, grief, and cultural differences (Chapter 3);

4. to incorporate extended information about several contrasting ethnic patterns of handling seven aspects related to death, dying, and grief, presented by representatives of those cultures (Chapters 1–2, 4–11);

5. to include reflections by professional practitioners in the health-care institutions with regard to cultural differences and their own occupational settings and practices (Chapter 12); and

6. to share our insights into the implications of these materials for the policies and practices of health-care institutions and personnel, mainly by asking a series of questions (Conclusions).

The Seven Aspects

Each author of the ethnic patterns identified here was asked to address seven aspects that provide a framework of themes for their presentations.

1. An experiential quality or "feel" for those participating in the dying, death, and bereavement features of the culture.

2. A consideration of the philosophy and theology of death and dying within their tradition, the meaning of life and death, the nature of soul and personality, the role of belief in an afterlife, relationship to a deity, and related matters.

3. An indication of how "death education" takes place within their communities—how children and youth learn about death and dying, appropriate bereavement behavior, taboos, values, and attitudes.

4. A discussion and description of actions, rituals, and emotional expressions that reflect the values of their culture *just prior* to an expected death, while death is being awaited.

5. A presentation and characterization of actions, rituals, and emotional expressions that are manifested immediately *following* a death, including treatment of the body, funeral ceremonies, and body disposal.

6. A report on actions, rituals, and expressions that are expected to be shown *later on,* as, for example, at anniversaries of a death.

7. An elucidation of the adaptations that have occurred within their traditions because of "acculturation," indicating accommodations necessitated by living within their contemporary setting, along with a discussion of how their present patterns are distinguished from those of the majority-dominant group.

SITUATIONS PERSONALLY ENCOUNTERED

An Arizona physician friend recounted recently in conversation how a colleague who was not very patient-centered proceeded to explain in considerable detail numerous technical procedures that would be used to extend the life of a dying Tohono O'odhan (Pápago Indian). When the doctor finished, the patient's response was, "But Indians don't care for life support!"

In contrast, a sensitive, discerning physician contacted the author for assistance with an infant patient who would quite probably die without some serious surgery. The operation itself would be life-threatening. The young parents were Native Americans who were not fluent in English. The doctor wished to be sure that the adults were fully aware of the situation so that they could give informed consent to the surgery, knowing the risks involved if they chose that course. He also wanted them to thoroughly understand his professional and personal concerns for their child, lest they hold him culpable or view him as insensitive if the child were to die. A Native American speaker of their language was located who could interpret both the medical facts and the doctor's concerns to the parents. By this means the twin cultural barriers of language and a different view of medical treatment were surmounted to protect the interests of both family and child as well as the physician's own integrity.

A nurse friend reported that when a Native American patient in her hospital requested that a shaman visit her in her room, she was told that only priests, rabbis, and ministers were allowed to make such visits.

The author was called upon to make arrangements with a funeral home for the body of a four-year-old Iranian girl to be shipped by plane back to her home, accompanied by her parents. The child had fallen into a pool at a neighbor's home and drowned. However, when the time for departure came the airline refused to accept the parents as passengers because, in terms of American culture, they were "hysterical" and "creating a scene," which was thought might become a problem for other passengers.

A metropolitan hospital in an area with a substantial Hispanic population each season sets out attractive flower beds of marigolds bordering the walks leading to the main entrance. However, these orange blossoms may heighten the anxiety of people of Mexican origin who are visiting, because that color is one of the symbols of death in their traditional culture.

A sociology colleague of the author, who is of Hispanic origin, was asked for "long distance" help by a Salvadoran woman whose son, a refugee in the United States, had been murdered; she wanted a photograph of the corpse to keep as a memento. He was able to arrange for a photograph to be taken and conveyed to the grief-stricken parent in El Salvador. To display a picture of the deceased shortly after death, on a gravestone or atop the coffin, is a common practice in several cultures.

MEDIA REPORTS ON DYING, DEATH, GRIEF, AND ETHNICITY

Community lore dealing with dying, death, and grief attests to the great need for sensitivity and understanding, both within institutions and on the part of individual practitioners. Media attention has frequently been focused on these concerns. It is not our intention to pinpoint the institutions or personnel involved, so the following examples are simply summaries of documented situations, to assure anonymity and/or confidentiality.

Native Americans

A Chippewa woman accused a county hospital of denying her the right to practice her religion. Hospital guards had stopped her from burning sage in her room. (In some Native American ceremonies sage is burned and the smoke is fanned with an eagle feather to purify people or objects.) She was praying for strength to deal with the possibility that she might not be able to walk again. The guards forced the woman to her knees, although she had recently had spinal fusion surgery and was under physician's orders to remain prone. Hospital officials contended that the issue was not one of religion but of fire hazard. Further, the hospital had a firm no-smoking policy. The patient said that her religious ceremony did not fit that policy, and she filed suit in district court. At another hospital in the same city, staff members had permitted tribal medicine men to perform ceremonies as long as health and safety were not endangered.

Beginning in 1987, an urban community in the upper Midwest formed a "hearse project" to meet the needs of many Native Americans who spent their lives in the city but wished to be buried at home on reservations. Poor families had found the cost of long-distance transportation of bodies to be prohibitive. Tribes donated three older vehicles, and 15 volunteer drivers were secured. The service was able to assist several hundred families before frequent delays and mishaps caused it to unravel four years later. The only Native American funeral director in the urban community, it was contended, had not cooperated fully with the project, which brought about some of the problems. There was a lack of money to pay a coordinator and to maintain a hearse. The only reliable income came from those families on public assistance. The director of Catholic Indian Ministries averred that "it was really a clash of cultures—the urban economic life and culture and the tradition of living off the land and living without dollars." The uniqueness of Native American funerals presents a challenge because the culture has different rituals and often different time considerations. However, as 1992 began the Urban Indian Hearse Project was "back on the road" once more.

A young man from the Pine Ridge reservation in South Dakota shot himself in Minnesota. His mother and the woman friend who was the mother of his three children became involved in a legal struggle over where his body should be buried: in Minnesota according to the woman, in South Dakota according to his mother. The case pitted Oglala Sioux tribal law against that of Minnesota, with little legal precedent for guidance. A Minnesota judge ruled that the man should be buried in the state where he had died and his children were living, but the Pine Ridge tribal court already had decided that he should be buried in South Dakota. The women and the three children planned a traditional Sioux wake, followed by a Catholic service. But no matter which party "won," some of the tribal customs could not be observed.

Such incidents represent the backdrop against which the "First Nations" people frequently play their roles in many segments of society. It is most unlikely that all our societal institutions, including the so-called caring professions, have been insulated fully from such misunderstandings and insensitivities. Our societies are indeed multi-ethnic, but they have not yet become multi-cultural.

Hmong and Southeast Asians

The coming of thousands of Southeast Asians to the United States in the past two decades has introduced many new cultural patterns, with their accompanying stresses to which the dominant society must respond.

Hmong men from Laos have been subject to what has been defined as a "sudden unexpected nocturnal death syndrome." Numerous immigrant Hmong men in their prime have died in their sleep. Causal factors remain uncertain, but perhaps the strains involved in the transition from their culture to another, very different one may have been involved in their deaths.

In Fresno, California, in 1990 a measles outbreak brought the deaths of 10 Hmong children. During one month alone, 75 percent of the measles cases were within the Hmong community. Fifteen Southeast Asian physicians and nurses with interpreters were then enlisted to combat the attack with a door-to-door campaign promoting vaccination. Success was achieved within four to five weeks, and an epidemic was avoided. About the same time, physicians and Hmong leaders in Saint Paul, Minnesota, indicated that Hmong families were less likely to have their children immunized or to seek Western medical help when illness struck.

A Hmong immigrant man worried that his recent hip surgery, which had inserted a piece of metal in his bone, would leave a curse on his descendants. The man contended that "if you have any type of metal in your body and you die, your grandchildren will be born with some type of deformity or problem. They might have some kind of bone disease or infection that makes the bone come out."

One metropolitan county hospital has adapted its maternity ward practices to the Hmong traditional culture by arranging for the women to give birth in a squatting position rather than lying prone on a table with stirrups and related equipment.

Sensitivity to cultural differences within the health-care system is manifestly evident in some hospitals. Staff meetings and conferences at medical centers are trying to understand and adapt to the gap between modern medical care and Hmong values. In a lengthy article by Jean Hopfensperger (1), attention is drawn to several institutions in Minnesota's Twin Cities.

[M]any of the 15,000 Hmong immigrants to the Twin Cities fear that modern medicine conflicts with their spiritual convictions. Many arrive at health clinics with little grasp of science or English but with a profound belief that sickness and recovery depend on the spiritual realm. Western medical providers arrive at the same clinics with their own cultural baggage. Their impatience, quickness to recommend surgery, and air of cultural superiority often alienate Hmong patients, who then go without needed treatment. . . .

Many traditional Hmong families continue to rely on shamans, or spiritual leaders, to diagnose and cure illness. [One shaman explained]: "Every human being has twelve spirits. . . . The spirits represent the eye, the mouth, the nose, the hand, the body parts. If those spirits wander around and go into another body, it can cause a person to get sick, and then they would call a shaman. The shaman would come in and perform a ritual ceremony to barricade the road so the spirits can't wander around. . . . That way they have nowhere to go, so they have to go back to the body and the person can get better." . . .

These beliefs lead many Hmong to refuse, or hesitate to accept, certain medical practices. Surgery and blood tests can release one's spirits, which then must be located and lured back. Removing an organ can prevent a person from reincarnating, because reincarnation requires an intact body. Autopsies on elders are taboo for the same reason.

Reference is made in the same article to Dr. Patricia Walker, who was reared in Southeast Asia and is conversant with their languages. She sees many Hmong patients at the international clinic she operates. Dr. Walker reports on Hmong beliefs and responses:

Hmong believe in karma, spirits, animism, as well as natural causes—things they can see. . . . And they have a completely different concept of time and urgency. Once I wanted to do a thyroid scan on a woman. She said, "I will do that in two years." That was her polite way of saying she didn't want it.

In another case a man learned that his infant daughter had pneumonia. First, he called a shaman. The shaman told him his daughter was sick because she had heard something she didn't like while in the womb. The shaman recommended that the father sacrifice a cow, which he did. Then he took his daughter to a physician.

The article provides additional insights:

Cultural conflicts peak in life-threatening situations, when quick decisions are needed. . . . [Physicians] spent five hours trying to convince a husband that his wife needed immediate surgery to remove a growth on her uterus. Without the surgery, she could have died.

[Dr. Walker recalled that] the patient was getting more and more short of breath. I was saying, "We have to put a tube down her lungs to breathe for her." Her husband is saying, "We will not do this." The moral issue for me is, "Do I allow her to die because her husband says so? . . . I would have had to forcibly remove him to do what I thought was needed.

Dr. Walker was able to convince the family to allow the surgery. The woman recovered and the family was grateful. If the result had been the patient's death, however, the entire clan might have avoided the hospital thereafter.

The events recounted above concern Native Americans and Southeast Asians, two culture groups that are among the numerically smaller ones within North American society. They have parallels, of course, both unhappy and satisfying, among other minority groups as well, but space limitations preclude the inclusion of sets of similar experiences often encountered by African Americans and Hispanics.

Many of the situations reported in this introduction probably resulted more from ignorance of cultural differences than from knowing intent. Some may have happened because of good intentions accompanied by a narrowness of vision. Some of the problems have arisen from the nature of an ethnic group's own belief system, when confronted with the dominant society's value perceptions. For example, Amish children are more subject to measles, mumps, and rubella because their parents' religious beliefs lead them to avoid the use of vaccines. Many other instances of "hurt" occur because of insufficient sensitivity on the part of professional personnel. Yet others result from institutional practices that have perpetuated discriminatory patterns of treatment, reflecting long-standing priorities and prejudices within the dominant society toward others who are different.

PROFESSIONAL RECOGNITION
OF MULTICULTURAL NEEDS

The presence, frequency, and severity of certain diseases are known to be related to ethnicity and race. A report (Leary, 1990) indicates that medical personnel are increasingly aware of these factors and their implications for care:

[R]ace and ethnicity can and should be factors in evaluating symptoms while reaching a diagnosis and in determining the treatment and how the patients fare. . . .

Because of the country's sensitivity to racial issues, there has been a reluctance to address race or ethnicity in medicine except in the most obvious cases. . . .

[Well-]known health problems, although often considered ethnically neutral, may express themselves in different ways and vary in incidence among ethnic groups, requiring different approaches in treatment. . . .

"It has become almost impossible to properly deliver medical care without considering the ethnic background of the patient, including the effect of both genetic and socioeconomic factors," said [Dr. Robert Murray, Jr., Professor of Medicine, Howard University]. . . .

Citing mounting evidence that knowledge of a patient's background can improve care, Dr. Arthur Caplan, director of the Center for Biomedical Ethics at the University of Minnesota, said, "You must take into account race and ethnicity. You can't ethically treat patients without considering it."

U.S. society remains unsure of how to handle the idea of equality, and medicine reflects their uncertainty, Caplan said. With some exceptions, he added, medicine generally has ignored ethnic differences in the name of equality, which has led to considering the norm as being white and middle class.

"Failure to acknowledge the racial or ethnic background of a patient is itself a kind of discrimination," said [Dr. Richard] Williams [Adjunct Professor, UCLA Medical School]. . . .

Dr. Reuben Warren [of the Federal Centers for Disease Control, Atlanta] believes that most ethnically related health problems in this country have environmental and cultural causes. . . . "There are many things that ethnic minorities share in common that influence poor health, and most of them are social and economic," Warren said. . . . "In health, you have to take ethnic background into account . . . but always in the context of environment."

SOME CROSS-CULTURAL CAVEATS

The demographic trends and related cultural developments in many areas of the United States and Canada lend added validity and importance to the need for a heightened awareness of diversity by professional practitioners in all our social institutions. For reasons of both principle and pragmatism, the recognition of the implications of these changes must affect the way professionals feel and act in relation to dying patients and their loved ones. Individual readers will need to inform themselves about the population they serve and then adjust their policies, practices, and programs accordingly. We have selected only a few of the many possible minority cultural groups that exist in the U.S. and Canadian societies. Readers will need to transfer whatever sensitivities and insights they gain from learning about a specific entity and keep these in mind as cautions when relating to people from other ethnic backgrounds than their own, avoiding any advance presumption of what an appropriate response, diagnosis, or treatment might be.

There are variations within ethnic groups, too, as well as among them. The features presented in the coming chapters cannot be generalized to all segments of a given community. The Lakota Indians do not represent all Native Americans or "First Nations," because there are many tribal groups with contrasting cultures. Likewise, one cannot assume that Conservative Jewish practices apply in detail to Orthodox or Reform Jews. Asian Americans and Hispanics also manifest great variation: as do Hmong in contrast to other Southeast Asian immigrants, Mexican Americans in comparison with those of Cuban background, and so on. Other groups not included here also have their own idiosyncratic beliefs and practices.

We urge our readers to utilize the devices presented in Chapter 3 to aid them in reflecting upon their own attitudes toward and experiences with multicultural features of their lives and upon their individual experiences with dying, death, and bereavement.

REFERENCES

Hopfensperger, J. (1989, August 25). Twin Cities doctors work to bridge gap with Hmong. *Minneapolis Star Tribune,* pp. 1A, 12A

Leary, W. E. (1990, September 25). Uneasy doctors add race-consciousness to diagnostic tools. *The New York Times,* p. B5(N) or C1(L).

Part One

Cross-Cultural
and Personal Perspectives

Chapter One

Cross-Cultural Variation in the Experience, Expression, and Understanding of Grief

Paul C. Rosenblatt

New anthropological studies of dying, death, and grief suggest that there is no one grief theory or one psychology of ego defenses that applies to everyone. Majority-culture American social scientists and human service practitioners may have been unintentionally ethnocentric in ways that have made it difficult to understand and deal with the realities of people from other cultures. American theory, research, and practice have reified Western culture and elevated it to the status of universal truth (cf. Good, Good, & Moradi, 1985; Lutz, 1985). Western cultural concepts such as "dying" and "grief" originated in the context of its culture. It now seems that realities differ so greatly from culture to culture that it is misleading and ethnocentric to assume that Western concepts apply generally.

In talking about the troubles of people from other cultures, we should put quotation marks around the terms we use from our own culture. "American" terms that describe emotion, such as *grief, depression,* and *anxiety,* are highly suspect. Even physical health terms like *ulcers* and *hypertension* should be questioned (Good, Good, & Moradi, 1985). These are categories from American culture, based on American beliefs and the way Americans think, categorize, and understand. People from other cultures understand and classify their experiences and perceptions differently and place them in the context of their own beliefs about the origins of events, the nature of the person, the proper way to behave, the meaning of losses, and much more.

It is easy, in looking at the emotions and experiences of people from other cultures, to adopt a superficially helpful but nonetheless ethnocentric stance that implies, "Of course, our understandings are the right ones, but we will communicate with you in your own terms while still remaining assured that our way of thinking is correct." We will never understand people whose language or culture is different from ours if we translate what they say into our own terms and assume the transcendent reality of those terms.

DEATH AND LIFE

Perhaps our fundamental assumption in terminal care is that we know what dying, death, and life are. That assumption is not supported by recent cross-cultural research. In many cultures people are counted as dead whom most Americans would consider alive, and people are counted as alive whom most Americans would consider dead. On the island of Vanatinai, southeast of Papua New Guinea, for instance, people are thought of as dead whom we would consider merely unconscious, so it is possible for a person to die a number of times (Lepowsky, 1985). Among extremely poor women in northeastern Brazil, children are counted as dead whom we would consider merely ill (Scheper-Hughes, 1985). Counting somebody as dead whom we would consider alive generally leads to what we would consider neglect. But in Vanatinai or northeastern Brazilian culture, what people do makes perfect sense to them.

On Vanatinai, as in many cultures, the dead, in some sort of ghostly or spiritual manifestation, are considered to be capable of actively affecting the lives of the living and to be open to interaction with the living (cf. Rosenblatt, Walsh, & Jackson, 1976; Rosenblatt, 1983). Many Americans, too, believe that they have an ongoing relationship with the spirits of deceased people who were important to them in life (Rosenblatt & Elde, 1990). We should not presume, however, that spiritual contacts have the same character or meaning from one culture to another. Even if one's beliefs bear a resemblance to those of people one is trying to help, there may be crucial differences.

"GRIEF" ACROSS CULTURES

What people who have experienced a loss believe, feel, and do varies enormously from culture to culture (Rosenblatt, 1988). For the impoverished northeastern Brazilian mothers studied by Scheper-Hughes, for example, most infant and child deaths were understood as inevitable and as a function of the individual child's will to live. In consequence, infants and children were typically not mourned more than a few days. The dead children are still counted as part of the nuclear family, however, and mothers expect to join these children in heaven.

"Muted Grief"

In Bali, the gods will not heed one's prayers if one is not calm. Emotional control in bereavement is highly prized there (Wikan, 1988). Emotional agitation is perceived as a threat to health, making one more vulnerable to the sorcery of malevolent people. Thus, a bereaved Balinese will work very hard, with the help of supporters who joke, tease, and distract, to treat death lightly, redefining it as not bad or even desirable (Wikan, 1988). In Balinese culture, people differentiate between surface feelings and underlying feelings. Not all cultures where losses are quickly redefined make that distinction.

The Ifaluk, a Pacific atoll people, differentiate among losses that are inevitable or justified and losses that are illegitimate frustrations, especially those that are caused by and rectifiable by others (Lutz, 1985). Among the Ifaluk, different losses call for different self-talk about the loss, different behaviors on the part of the bereaved, different forms of response from potential supporters, and different feelings and expressions of feeling. Among the Ifaluk the expectation is that, after a good cry, the bereaved will return to ordinary functioning. One is supposed to forget the person who died. Continued grieving is seen as a failure to replace the person who died and is defined as "pathological."

"Excessive Grief"

Not only does the cross-cultural literature supply examples, like the northeastern Brazilians, the Balinese, and the Ifaluk, of culturally normal and expected grief that by U.S. standards is quite attenuated, but the literature also offers examples of extreme grief. Wikan's (1988) exploration of grief in the slums of Cairo, Egypt, reveals a culture that expects that a major loss—for example, a parent's loss of a young adult child—will cause years of muted depression, constant suffering, and remaining in bereavement. Such a consequence is culturally normal. The social support given the Egyptian bereaved actively encourages suffering and a dwelling on pain and the gravity of one's loss.

Somatization

One striking difference between grief and other dysphorias of Americans in the dominant culture and those of people in many other cultures is that the dominant American dysphoria is psychologized whereas in many other cultures it is somatized. In China and in many other societies, "somatization (the presentation of personal and interpersonal distress in an idiom of physical complaints . . .) [is] the predominant expression of difficulties in living" (Kleinman, 1986, p. 51). People "experience serious personal and social problems but interpret and articulate them, and . . . come to experience and respond to them, through the medium of the body" (Kleinman, 1986, p. 51). They experience physical pain, weakness, and discomfort. When grief is associated with somatization, the physical complaints may at times be a distraction from thoughts of loss, but they also may lead to obsessive connection with the loss.

Some metaphors of somatization may "make sense" to Americans. Physical pain seems an appropriate index of emotional pain from a loss. Neurasthenic weakness seems an appropriate index of how much the loss of a spouse or other person significant in a person's life may weaken one's sense of grounding and one's practical help system. *Men,* a Chinese term for something pressing on or depressing the chest and heart (Kleinman, 1986), may also be interpretable in Western idiom as heart-breaking. There are also somatization patterns that do not make sense to a Westerner. We may be too quick to ignore connotations, meanings, and feelings associated with somatization that do not fit Western idiom.

"Violent Grief"

In quite a few cultures, anger and aggression are part of mourning (Rosenblatt, Walsh, & Jackson, 1976). Dominant American culture does not define most losses as matters for anger or aggression. This may leave Americans ill-prepared to deal with people for whom anger and aggression are culturally normal in bereavement. Among the Kaluli of Papua New Guinea, the grief of men may be transformed into anger and action through attempts to redress the loss resulting from a death (Schiefflin, 1985). Many deaths are thought to be caused by somebody, even deaths that would be the standards of the dominant American culture be called accidental or natural. There are even situations where, if a person with whom he is on friendly terms reminds a Kaluli man of a past loss it is legitimate to injure the "reminder"; and the "reminder," whether injured or not, will pay compensation to the person whose grief was set off by the reminder. The pattern of injury and compensation does not, in the understandings of the Kaluli as described by Schiefflin, represent wrongs redressed but a pattern of reciprocity and legitimating another's feelings that ties people closer together.

LEARNING TO DEAL
WITH GRIEF CROSS-CULTURALLY

Normal grief and the normal understanding of death and life in other cultures may be quite odd, viewed by the standards of one's own culture. To work effectively with the dying and with bereaved people from other cultures, therefore, it is necessary to step outside one's own culture and presuppositions.

A first step outside one's own culture is to find educational sources. However, even people who are from the same culture as the grieving person may prove unhelpful. They may be ethnically different; they may be from a very different social stratum; they may not have had much experience of death, grief, and mourning in their own culture; they may be unwilling to confide things that would be embarrassing or taboo. Written sources are also risky to use. Even skilled anthropologists have made major errors in reporting on death, grief, and mourning in other cultures. A text that is accurate may still not apply to the actual individual one is trying to help. As in our own culture, there are substantial individual differences in other cultures. Nonetheless, those sources may be helpful in providing a starting point in freeing one from ethnocentrism.

Another source of understanding is the person or people we are trying to help. Whether they are American men who strive to control their tears or immigrants from the many cultures where people fear that the act of naming the deceased calls up a dangerous ghost, we must be constantly sensitive to their taboos and leanings. Our active curiosity and genuine interest are of the utmost importance. Asking someone to help us understand things in the way that people in their culture understand and experience them is a powerful way to learn what we need to learn. Learning their terms and working at using them properly can be helpful. We should not presume to teach them to feel "grief." It is not merely a matter of working among subtly different translations of the same terms. It is a matter of coming to grips with what may be vastly different concepts and vastly different explanatory systems and interpretative approaches. Those who live in the dominant U.S. culture will never experience, for example, dealing with witchcraft as a cause of death, seeing the next baby born in the community as the reincarnation of the deceased, dealing with the deceased as a god, fearing being haunted by the ghost of the deceased because the proper death ceremonies cannot be performed in the United States, fearing the wind because it brings dangerous spirits—and on and on. We must be skeptical of what people tell us, but we must also be ready to leave our own culture to share in a world that is surprisingly different from our expectations.

Meanings are crucial in coping with a loss. Losses have different meanings from person to person and culture to culture (Lofland, 1982). A spouse may or may not be a person on whom one depends economically or with whom one shares considerable information about experiences and feelings. Depending on the personal connections with a spouse, their death may mean a wide range of major losses or a narrow range of not-so-major losses. Moreover, it may be easier in some cultures than in others to replace what one loses when a person dies (Lofland, 1982). Losses may well hurt less if they are understood to be desirable or appropriate. What is desirable or appropriate varies enormously from culture to culture, and how much cognitive work is used and makes a difference also varies enormously from culture to culture.

Among Americans there are people who believe that death ends a relationship and others who believe that it does not (Rosenblatt & Elde, 1990). Among the latter are those who think that there will be a reunion in heaven and those who feel that they continue to have a living spiritual connection with the deceased. Some people are grieving the permanent end of the relationship, while others are grieving the end of one form of the relationship and of those aspects of the relationship that involve concrete actions. There may also be those who have become doubters and who grieve not only the end of the relationship but the loss of the consolation that a belief in eternal life once gave (Garland, 1987). All of these differences in interpretations of events may well lead to differences in grieving.

CONCLUSION

Across cultures, people may differ in what they believe and understand about life and death, what they feel, what elicits those feelings, the perceived implications of those feelings, the ways they express those feelings, the appropriateness of certain feelings, and the techniques for dealing with feelings that cannot be directly expressed. Grief is expressed so differently from culture to culture that it is absurd to use notions of pathology derived from one culture to evaluate people from another. In some cultures, for example, self-mutilation is common in grief, and in others the anger of bereavement is expressed in the suspicion that some person was responsible for the death. An Egyptian mother who for seven years after the death of a child remains withdrawn, mute, inactive, and self-absorbed is behaving normally by the standards of her own culture, as is the Balinese mother who in the same situation remains calm and cheerful, even though the behavior of both would be judged pathological by U.S. standards (Wikan, 1988).

The cross-cultural variations in the behavior of bereaved people are not random but arise out of societal ways of understanding the world. The context for cultural differences in patterns of behavior and of social support includes each culture's sense of what is sane and healthy, as opposed to life- and health-threatening (Wikan, 1988). Thus, what people do protects the bereaved and in some sense everyone around the bereaved from, for example, the contagion of inappropriate feelings or the responsibility for some new disaster arising from inappropriate grieving. The smiling Balinese and the mute Egyptian are equally understood to be sane, healthy, and appropriate by the standards of their own societies.

Differences are present even in American culture. We should not assume that somebody who speaks our own language and comes from the same part of the world has the same beliefs and understandings and will express feelings in a familiar way. It pays to treat everyone as though he or she were from a different culture. The cross-cultural emphasis, in fact, is a kind of metaphor. To help effectively, we must overcome our presuppositions and struggle to understand people on their own terms.

REFERENCES

Garland, M. M. (1987). *Victorian unbelief and bereavement: A study in the utility of religion.* Unpublished manuscript, Ohio State University, Department of History. Columbus, OH.

Good, B. J., Good, M. D., & Moradi, R. (1985). The interpretation of Iranian depressive illness and dysphoric affect. In A. Kleinman & B. J. Good (Eds.), *Culture and depression* (pp. 369–428). Berkeley: University of California Press.

Kleinman, A. (1986). *Social origins of distress and disease: Depression, neurasthenia, and pain in modern China.* New Haven: Yale University Press.

Lepowsky, M. (1985). Gender, aging, and dying in an egalitarian society. In D. Ayers Counts & D. R. Counts (Eds.), *Aging and its transformations: Moving toward death in Pacific societies* (pp. 157–178). Lanham, MD: University Press of America.

Lofland, L. H. (1982). Loss and human connection: An exploration into the nature of the social bond. In W. Ickes & E. S. Knowles (Eds.), *Personality, roles, and social behaviors* (pp. 219–242). New York: Springer-Verlag.

Lutz, C. (1985). Depression and the translation of emotional worlds. In A. Kleinman & B. J. Good (Eds.), *Culture and depression* (pp. 63–100). Berkeley: University of California Press.

Rosenblatt, P. C. (1983). *Bitter, bitter tears: Nineteenth-century diarists and twentieth-century grief theories,* Chapter 10, pp. 122–155. Minneapolis: University of Minnesota Press.

Rosenblatt, P. C. (1988). Grief: The social context of private feelings. *Journal of Social Issues, 44*(3), 67–78.

Rosenblatt, P. C., & Elde, C. (1990). Shared reminiscence about a deceased parent: Implications for grief education and grief counseling. *Family Relations, 39*(2), 206–210.

Rosenblatt, P. C., Walsh, R. P., & Jackson, D. A. (1976). *Grief and mourning in cross-cultural perspective,* Chapter 3. New Haven, CT: Human Relations Area Files Press.

Scheper-Hughes, N. (1985). Culture, scarcity, and maternal thinking: Maternal detachment and infant survival in a Brazilian shantytown. *Ethos, 13,* 291–317.

Schiefflin, E. L. (1985). The cultural analysis of depressive affect: An example from New Guinea. In A. Kleinman & B. J. Good (Eds.), *Culture and depression* (pp. 101–133). Berkeley: University of California Press.

Wikan, U. (1988). Bereavement and loss in two Muslim communities: Egypt and Bali compared. *Social Science and Medicine, 27,* 451–460.

Chapter Two

One Woman's Interracial Journey

Vivian Jenkins Nelsen

THE ASSASSINATION OF A YOUNG PRESIDENT

The Zapruder film of a young man in a convertible, his head rocked by the shock of a bullet, his life energy spraying on a Texas wind, the young woman crawling across the car's back, played endlessly on television in the weeks that followed President Kennedy's assassination. I remember the disgust of my favorite college professor at the public's fascination with the Zapruder clip. He quoted the Greek classic describing the death of a king, "Give me a cloth to cover his face."

This public death caused a national outpouring of grief that we shared as a people and that allowed us to talk about death as a shared reality. Death had been something that happened to "other people," the old, the poor, or the sick. Death did not touch the beautiful, the rich, or the chosen. If and when death intruded, we expected those other people, "the bereaved," not to burden us with their grief, but rather to accept their loss with stoicism and quickly return to normal. The young Jackie Kennedy, and later Coretta King, somber in their veiled widow's weeds, saved us from cohabiting their private hells; and for that we were grateful.

We all remember where we were when Jack Kennedy was killed. That day I knew that whites and blacks view death across a great cultural chasm. I was in Kearney, Nebraska, with two other music majors and a professor from our little Lutheran college. We were at the state college, observing a high school music contest in preparation for our careers as teachers. In a small-town grill, we were surprised when the counter clerk shushed us and turned up the radio, which was blasting out the dread-filled news. Our elderly professor, a former military man, retreated to some inner space and left me frightened and uneasy.

My throat constricted and hot tears rose into my eyes. They were unshed, however, as my colleagues calmly went about ordering their food. What was happening? Was it shock? People sometimes go on walking when mortally wounded. What was to happen to us blacks if the shooting of a president means that life goes on as usual?

Black people had suffered many deaths in the civil rights movement. Each new bombing or lynching seemed more savage than the last. This president seemed to be cognizant of our suffering. His standing up to the governor of my home state, Alabama's George Wallace, was a sign that "the times, they are a'changing." Nebraska was the most Republican state in the last election, but surely the shooting of a president merited more than a short pause. My family was Republican, having come out of the South where Dixiecrats were racists and Republicans freed the slaves, but I was deeply disturbed by this turn of events.

I was aware of being observed by white people in the café. I was the only black woman in our college, so I was used to being watched. Living among whites for the first time was a continuing series of revelations. We finished our lunch; the others ate heartily—I picked at my food. When we arrived at the campus auditorium for the choral competitions, a moment of silence was observed as the president's death was announced. I remember looking at the writing above the stage. It was the same as the biblical passage on the front of our Lutheran grade school: "The truth shall make ye free." I wandered blindly from event to event until we left for our campus.

There, events and people moved as if the world were normal. No one but I seemed to be grieving. Was I over-reacting? I arrived home by bus, a short 17 miles from campus. My parents and I sat at the dining-room table talking about the amazing responses to this death. Tears shimmered in both their eyes. Mom talked about the kids jumping rope outside her classroom to the disgraceful words, "Kennedy's been shot in his big old head." We watched the unraveling saga on television and mourned together with our all-black community. It was a community calamity. We whispered, "Please God, don't let his murderer be black!"

CHILDHOOD LEARNINGS ABOUT DEATH

Although we black folks understood this death in the same way, our ways of grieving were often different, varying from urban to rural, Baptist to Lutheran. As the assistant organist at my father's church, I began playing for funerals when I was 11. Our black Missouri Synod Lutheran Church had occupied the old Danish Lutheran Evangelical Kirke for many decades. As the Danes became more prosperous, they moved to the western suburbs of Omaha, leaving behind them the trappings of a former era. Modern, affluent church-goers had no need of a hand-carved baptismal font or an altar with oil paintings that changed with the church seasons.

We always knew outsiders, black or white, when they attended funerals. They were the people who screamed or cried loudly and were quickly ushered downstairs. My mother used to say that the people who fainted and screamed were the guilty ones. They were guilty of neglecting their loved ones, and the funeral was the place where the mourners would see their guilt masquerading as love. My parents viewed extravagant funerals with great asperity. They understood that poor families who had been coaxed into ordering these lavish displays would soon be hungry and shoeless.

The view of death in our religious community was as an experience to be borne with dignity, solemnity, and something called grace. (For a long time, I thought that this grace had something to do with my Aunt Grace.) Extravagance in emotion, dress, or grieving was merely self-indulgent. I was irritated not only by the funeral practices of our black community but also by the language of dying. "Doesn't he look wonderful? Just like he's sleeping." No, he looks dead. "Mr. Roberts passed last week." Passed from one grade to another? Passed from death to life? Why not, "He died?" Why this shrinking from the truth? Why such care for language? What seemed to me to be a throwback to Victorian civility offered a fascinating view of minority life.

For the person of color in this society, life is full of threats, ever-present and ever-real. Such threats make psychological and physical dents in one's facade that are reminders of everyday ugliness and frailty. The presence of beauty and delicacy in life's most stressful moments can help restore both our human and divine qualities. This need is shown in the careful attention given to dressing the deceased. My mother told us about preparing bodies in Southern rural parishes where morticians were not accessible or affordable. It was the work of churchwomen to bathe, oil, and scent with herbs the loved ones who were kept in the local ice house until the scattered relatives could arrive for the burial. Black people always called each other sister or brother. So "Sister Kizzy," or whoever was the most gifted hairdresser, performed the final ritual. This last, loving toilet seemed wonderful yet remote to me, viewed through a modern lens.

I remember the family discussion following my questions about the children's prayer, "Now I lay me down to sleep, I pray the Lord my soul to keep. If I should die before I wake, I pray the Lord my soul to take." It was abundantly clear to me that if you didn't want to die during the night, you just didn't fall asleep. My mother's idea was even better: to simply nix the prayer. Regular sleep times were quickly resumed in the parsonage.

DEATHS EXPERIENCED IN YOUTH

One funeral of an elderly man who was a faithful parishioner was particularly annoying to me as a young teenager. Why was he buried wearing his glasses? "What is he going to see?" I asked Dad. I don't remember his gentle answer, but I do remember the seemingly endless discussions about how white undertakers never seemed to get a black person's hair or makeup quite right. I resolved then to be cremated and have none of that indecent peeping and chatter. Those practices were for the living, not the dead, I decided, and they should be promptly abolished. I was to discover, years after, that this decision caused my family great upset. The old Africans in our family believed that all parts of one's body must be present at death to enter heaven. This belief had become part of our religious fabric.

Perhaps the most important learnings about death and dying came during summers at my grandmother's home in rural South Carolina. Being black in the South meant that you were connected to everyone else black, in a palpable way. Being a minority had a special meaning—you belonged. Like Alex Haley's return to Africa, when I arrived as a very small girl, every black adult in that town looked at me and said, "She's a Sims. That must be Francis Sims' grandbaby." My grandmother, Francis Sims, was a very tall, lanky woman whose Indian and African ancestry were evident in both her features and bearing. With quiet solemnity, I was introduced to her friends and neighbors as "Bea's girl."

Two of my mother's siblings still lived at home: a teacher sister, Aunt Thel, and Uncle James, who owned several small businesses. My young uncles were handsome and always attentive and respectful to me, even as a talkative and opinionated five-year-old. My Uncle Troy was the local black mortician and school principal. Troy was married to a teacher. Since they were childless, I enjoyed an inordinate amount of attention. From these uncles I learned about the physical aspects of dying, clinical descriptions of embalming, postmortems, and lynchings. The white coroner seemingly couldn't face the broken bodies. He sent his assistant, Troy Sims, to retrieve them. I demanded and received detailed, forthright answers to my questions.

I also witnessed this community's response to death as part of the Sacred Hoop. That was the term our Indian relatives used in reference to the life and death cycle. Murders were a disjoining, a forced breaking of the cycle. Death was accepted with a calmness that, to me, bordered on coldness. There were many stories about my African great-grandfather and his Indian wife, known as the "old ones."

Some of the stories are quite funny. They related to my mother and her siblings going to grandpoppa's house every Sunday. My Indian great-grandmother never quite got the hang of cooking food black-style, and she made a white lumpy gravy that everyone ate and nobody dared criticize. The old ones lived several miles from my grandmother's house and the smoke from their chimney was the daily signal that all was well. My grandmother and her mother still used their wood cook stoves even in blistering summer heat. Although my grandmother had a gas stove, she refused to use it. She also disdained the indoor toilet and used the outside privy. She felt that indoor plumbing was a nasty habit.

One Sunday morning, no plume of smoke rose from the old ones' chimney. Troy went to investigate. Grandpoppa had died in his sleep, but great-grandmother steadfastly refused to come into town with her husband's body. When other relatives went to the homestead to comfort her, they discovered that she had turned her face to the wall and died. She was not ill; she had simply willed herself to die. This was explained as "the Indian way." The old ones were so strong and so attached both to each other and the earth that they could choose to live and die together.

While I was on one of these idyllic childhood visits to the South, the news of the death of a young black boy, Emmett Till, sent a chill through every black community, North and South. Thirteen-year-old Emmett had disappeared while visiting his grandmother in Arkansas. By the time I returned North, Emmett was still missing. I remember opening my mother's drawer in her kitchen and finding a *Jet Magazine*. I gazed in wonder at the photo of his crushed face.

This was the era in which the white establishment discouraged the publication of photos of lynching victims for fear that the black community would rise up in riots. Braving the disapproval of the powerful, Johnson publications published the image of Till's battered face. I was mesmerized by his broken face; I was drawn to it day after day. His eyes looked like flowers—like daisies. Till's body was found in a barrel that had been sunk in a river for several weeks. The horrifying story of the torture, mutilation, and murder of this manchild was whispered among us children. Our friends added gory details.

I was afraid of being alone with whites and being spirited off to a terrible death. Even white elevator operators were suspect. The fear changed to rage. I share the rage of the children of Soweto and the West Bank because I, too, raged at the inability of black adults to exact revenge for the death of a child. Perhaps the most important moment in resolving this distressing death came when Emmett Till's mother, a retiring, pretty schoolteacher from some northern city, came to talk at a local church.

The heat was stifling that Sunday afternoon. The only sound was the whisper of paper fans from the local mortuary. Mrs. Till did not weep. She showed no rage, but a deep sadness, strength, and determination. Emmett was an only child. Allegedly, his crime was whistling at a white woman. Mrs. Till told a quiet tale of perfidy, of lies and deception by state, local, and federal authorities. By its very flatness, her voice held us riveted, convinced that things must change—that justice could no longer be blind to the murder of black people, black children.

These monumental public deaths are shapers of private grieving. For many years, we survivors hoped to look and sound as calm as Jackie Kennedy and Coretta King. We had no idea that we would grieve messily for years, in predictable stages. This cross-cultural journey of mine took several unexpected twists in high school when friends my own age died. Frail Rozzie was on the periphery of my circle of friends—a kind, gentle, intelligent girl. When she died of cancer, I asked for and got a full description of an orthodox Jewish funeral from my history teacher. He told me about his mother being wrapped in funeral linens and buried on a rainy day in a European ghetto the day after her death. I was relieved that it didn't rain the week Rozzie died. It seemed at once merciful that her body be buried quickly and unique that professional mourners were there. But I accepted this way of burial as consistent with that of my African and Indian ancestors. I viewed it as different but normal, understandable.

Later that year, the counselor came into the art room and beckoned to me. I knew, instantly, that one of my best friends, Sara, had "made good" on her suicide threats. A beautiful, brilliant, artistic student, Sara had been seriously depressed. This event nearly repeated itself in college with another friend, Betty, whom we managed to get to the hospital in time.

EXPERIENCING DEATHS AS AN ADULT

Following college, a young friend and art teacher, Kathy, committed suicide at a boyfriend's house. This time, it was my responsibility to make funeral arrangements, pick the casket, notify the family, deal with the insurance company and employers, manage three minor siblings, and buy the burial plot. I was a young black social worker dealing with an impoverished white rural Catholic family. The family fought at the church over whether Kathy should be buried with a rosary in her hands, although she had converted to Lutheranism many years earlier and the service was taking place at her Lutheran church. The disagreement spilled into the parking lot with various family members making obscene hand gestures at each other from the mortuary limousine. Suddenly, the rigid Victorian code of funeral etiquette practiced by Southern blacks made elegant sense. It enforced civility at this most stressful time.

Not long after this funeral, I attended a Sunday-morning lecture on "Preparing Your Own Funeral." Then I took a seminar on suicide. What an enlightenment it was to discover that anger as well as the sadness of depression can play a role in the decision to end one's life. Not long afterward, I became a founding member of the suicide hotline known as Y.E.S.–N.E.O.N. After hearing a radio lecture on the stages of grief by a then-unknown Swiss physician, Elisabeth Kübler-Ross, I enrolled in a course on death and dying at the university. I was alarmed to hear the professor criticize suicide hotlines as a waste of money. She then said that the surviving family of a suicide should be made to walk behind a cart carrying the body through the streets, as had been the custom in medieval times. The public ridicule and curiosity, she said, would surely curb suicides. I found it necessary to give the professor a taste of that ridicule in class.

The most useful thing I learned from that class was to identify the stages of grief. Knowing them helped me understand my own reactions to the death of my younger brother, James. What they did not prepare me for was the depth and length of feelings. What I also discovered is that different cultural traditions value the stages of grief very differently. For example, the anger and denial stages seemed to come more easily and to stay longer in our family than did the acceptance stage. Part of that has to do with what I consider to be an inadequate theology of death. Our conservative faith has answers for everything, most of them punishing. But I was to find that the rawness of grieving was salved by the old, familiar language. not a brutal rendering of the obvious. I was to perform the age-old last toilet for my brother, a gift to me from all the women in my family. It was a linking of our tradition. This toilet, albeit abbreviated, consisted of restyling James's hair at the white mortuary.

The most painful event surrounding James's death was receiving racial hate-mail with his newspaper obituary notice taped inside. My husband and I resolved not to tell the rest of our family at the time. The letter marked 13 years of harassment from job to job, and house to house, by bigots. Bearing a load of hate for interracial families and adopted children, and invective against Asians, Indians, blacks, Jews, Catholics, this letter, coming when it did, weighed more heavily than the combined effect of all the others. I knew, then, the meaning of the scripture passage that describes the Spirit of God as "groaning in travail" for our world "in sighs too deep for words."

We determined to keep this most destructive of letters and prayed that we could find and stop these deviants. I called a mortician friend who told me that other families had been tortured in the same way. They had been receiving this mail at funeral homes. I knew that I could not come to terms with either my anger or my grief until this group had been found and punished. It took more than three years to find the wealthy individual who had singled me out for this special punishment and to bring him to trial.

And so I continue on my pilgrim way. The hymn writer says, "Let the fiery, cloudy pillar lead me all my journey through."

Chapter Three

Personal Reflections on Death, Grief, and Cultural Diversity

Kathleen F. Lundquist
in association with Vivian Jenkins Nelsen

This chapter is a tool for gaining personal insight. The author intends that it provide you with honest and candid assessments of your attitudes toward and understanding of issues related to death, grief, and multi-cultural diversity. The rationale for the inclusion of this interactive chapter is that self-knowledge is the "bottom line" of inner peace, personal understanding, and social change. Self-knowledge engenders individual growth, understanding, and respect.

As you approach the activities in this chapter, it is important to do so in a relaxed, receptive state of mind. In fact, you may want to complete them in a setting that is conducive to introspection and reflection. Before you begin to write, for example, you might choose to assume a comfortable position in order to encourage your mind and body to relax. Deep abdominal breathing, visualization, or listening to music are means you might employ to prepare yourself for the completion of this chapter. One of the activities requests that you draw your responses and analyze them. *Do not be concerned about your artistic ability.* No special talent, training, or time frame is required to complete this chapter. Drawing encourages respondents to call upon inner resources such as visual and spatial perception as well as emotional and intuitive expression.

The purpose of this chapter is twofold: (a) to help identify both the conscious and unconscious perceptions you hold about death, grief, and cultural diversity; and (b) to explore your understanding of those issues. Thus, the author suggests that you complete this portion of the book prior to reading subsequent chapters. You will find that this chapter is divided into three subsections: *Death Awareness*; *Grief Awareness*; and *Multi-Cultural Awareness*. There is no recommended sequence for the completion of the subsections. After you finish each one, you are encouraged to think about your overall responses and synthesize them on a journal page entitled *Self-Reflections*.

After you complete this personalized, interactive chapter, the author hopes that you will find yourself approaching the subsequent chapters with a deeper sense of self-awareness.

DEATH AWARENESS

Activity 1: Words Associated with "Death"

Frequently, attitudes that you might hold toward persons, places, objects, or concepts become clearer through words that you might associate with them. Look below at the word "death." Quickly, without much thought, write down all of the words that come into your mind in response to that key word.

DEATH

Look over the list of words that *death* evoked in you. Identify each word you wrote down as carrying a positive (+), negative (−), or neutral (0) connotation by placing a (+), (−), or (0) next to each word. What is your total for each type of connotation?

$$(+) \underline{\qquad} \qquad (−) \underline{\qquad} \qquad (0) \underline{\qquad}$$

• What, if anything, does that information tell you about the attitudes you hold toward death?
• Because mainstream North American culture has been one that denies death, what are some euphemisms or circumlocutions that people use when referring to dying or death?
• Do members of your immediate family tend to talk about death euphemistically?
• If they do, what are some words or phrases they use?

Activity 2: My First Recollection of Death

Because death is a natural part of the life cycle, it is highly probable that you have experienced the death of someone or something you cherish. This activity invites you to think about your first encounter with the death of a family member, friend, neighbor, or pet. It will be important for you to recapture some of the feelings that you associated with that event. Therefore, before you begin to describe your memory, breathe deeply several times, become relaxed, and give yourself permission to float back in time. When you come upon that initial encounter with death, place the event in a context that incorporates people, places, feelings, and behaviors. The following questions may stimulate your memory. Make notes of dates and feelings as they occur. Take the time to sketch a picture drawn from your recollections:

- How old were you?
- What/who died?
- How did you feel?
- How did you act?
- Who else was there?
- How did they act?

Study your picture. Invite it to speak to you about death. Does it give you insight into attitudes that you currently hold toward death? NO _____; YES _____. If yes, explain.

Do you think that your first encounter with death might influence the way in which you interact with dying or grieving people from ethnic, racial, or religious backgrounds different from your own? NO _____; YES _____. If yes, explain.

Activity 3: My Life History of Death: A Timeline

This activity can be a tool for further exploration of the personal attitudes you hold toward death. It might also be useful in (a) identifying your personal issues surrounding unresolved grief, and (b) examining your own pattern of grieving. Take a moment to recall Activity 2, My First Recollection of Death. Next, look at the timeline that appears in this activity. At either end of the timeline, fill in your date of birth and the current date. Then make a series of vertical lines across it for each death that affected you and write the name of who or what died in chronological order. Ask yourself the list of questions in turn for each death and write down your answers on a separate piece of paper.

Date of   Current
birth   date

- How did you feel?
- How did you act?
- How did other people seem to feel?
- How did others act?
- How did members of your family react to the death?

Look at your timeline. Think about your personal pattern of feeling and acting in response to significant deaths in your life. Do you feel that your pattern was a healthy one? NO _____; YES _____. If no, explain.

Did the pattern of feeling and acting change over time? NO _____; YES _____. If yes, explain.

Considering the deaths you identified on your timeline, do you experience any unresolved grief reactions to them at the current time? NO _____; YES _____. If yes, explain.

Activity 4: Death Anxiety Scale (DAS)*

Death, especially in our dominant culture, is frequently treated as a taboo topic in conversation. To some extent, this tendency reflects both our public and personal anxiety about it. The purpose of this activity is to provide you with insights into your feelings about death. Read each of the 13 statements in the scale. Respond to each item by circling the appropriate letter.

True	False	
T	F	1. I am very much afraid to die.
T	F	2. The thought of death seldom enters my mind.
T	F	3. It does not make me nervous when people talk about death.
T	F	4. I dread thinking about having to have an operation.
T	F	5. I am not at all afraid to die.
T	F	6. I am not particularly afraid of getting cancer.
T	F	7. I am often distressed by the way time flies so very rapidly.
T	F	8. I fear dying a painful death.
T	F	9. The subject of life after death troubles me greatly.
T	F	10. I am really scared of having a heart attack.
T	F	11. I often think about how short life really is.
T	F	12. I shudder when I hear people talking about World War III.
T	F	13. The sight of a dead body is horrifying to me.

*Designed by Donald Templar, Ph.D., 1970. Adapted by permission.

Score 1 point for each item answered in the direction of high death anxiety (see the key below). A DAS score of 0 is equivalent to very low anxiety, a score of 13 to very high anxiety.

Key: 1–T; 2–F; 3–F; 4–T; 5–F; 6–F; 7–T; 8–T; 9–T; 10–T; 11–T; 12–T; 13–T.

What is your score: _____

Activity 5: Death Awareness Questionnaire*

Read each item in this questionnaire and answer it by circling the response(s) of your choice.

1. How many people whom you knew personally have died in the past two years?

   None   1–3   4–7   8 +

2. How many of those people died as a result of _____?

Chronic Illness	None	1–3	4–7	8 +
Accident	None	1–3	4–7	8 +
Suicide	None	1–3	4–7	8 +
Homicide	None	1–3	4–7	8 +
War	None	1–3	4–7	8 +
Other	None	1–3	4–7	8 +

3. How many funerals have you attended in the past two years?

   None   1–3   4–7   8 +

4. How often have you visited someone's grave, other than during a burial service, during the past two years?

   Never   1–3 times   4–7 times   8 + times

5. How often do you think about your own death?

   Never   Hardly ever   Monthly   Weekly   Daily

*Adapted by permission from R. A. Kalish and D. K. Reynolds, *Perspectives of Death and Dying*, Vol. 4 of *Death and Ethnicity: A Psychocultural Study*, 2nd ed. (pp. 200–221), 1981, New York: Baywood. Copyright © Baywood Publishing Company, Inc.

6. Have you ever felt that you were close to dying?

    No   Yes

7. Have you taken out life insurance for yourself?

    No   Yes

8. Have you made arrangements to donate your body or organs after your death?

    No   Yes

9. Which seems more tragic, a sudden death or slow death?

    Sudden   Slow   Equal   Depends

10. Which two deaths seem to be the most tragic?

    Infant   Child   Young person   Middle-aged person   Elderly person   Depends

11. Which two deaths seem to be the least tragic?

    Infant   Child   Young person   Middle-aged person   Elderly person   Depends

12. Which seems more tragic, the death of a man or woman?

    Man   Woman   Equal   Depends

13. Which kind of death seems most tragic?

    Natural causes   Chronic illness   Accident   Suicide   War   Depends

14. Have you taken out a will for yourself?

    No   Yes

15. Have you joined a memorial society or other pre-death plan?

    No   Yes

16. Have you arranged for someone to handle your affairs following your death?

    No   Yes

17. Do you want a funeral/memorial service?

    No   Yes

18. Do you want a member of the clergy to officiate at your funeral/memorial service?

No   Yes   Not applicable

19. Would you object to having an autopsy performed on your body?

No   Yes

20. Where would you want to die?

At home   In hospital   In a hospice   At work   Depends

21. What disposition would you choose for your body?

Burial   Cremation   Donation   Depends

22. Where would you choose to have your funeral/memorial service held?

At home   In a religious site   Funeral home   Other   Depends   Not applicable

23. Do *you* want to select the clergy person who would officiate at your funeral/memorial service?

No   Yes   Depends   Not applicable

24. Do you want an elaborate funeral/memorial service?

No   Yes   Depends   Not applicable

25. Regarding viewing of your body, would you want to have the casket open?

No   Yes   Depends   No viewing

26. How many people who were dying have you visited or talked with during the past two years?

None   1–2   3–4   5+

27. Have you witnessed someone die?

No   Yes

28. Have you touched a dead body?

No   Yes

29. What identifies a person as being dead?

No heartbeat   No brainwaves   Other

30. If you were dying, would you want to be aware of your condition?

No   Yes   Depends

31. With only six months left to live, how would you spend your time?

Withdrawing into myself   Living in the present
Focusing on people   Arranging my affairs
Denying my prognosis   Fulfilling dreams
Completing projects   Focusing on my faith
Other

32. How might you react to a terminal prognosis?

Deny it   Accept it   Fight it   Depends

33. If you were to have a chronic, terminal illness, how do you think you would endure the pain?

In silence   Talk about it   Medicate it   Depends

34. If you were dying, would you want young children under 10 to visit you?

No   Yes   Depends

35. Do you discern that your responses, in some degree, reflect your class/racial/religious/ethnic background?

No   Yes   If yes, in what manner?

36. Have you prepared a Living Will for yourself?

No   Yes   Intend to do so

Journal Page: Self-Reflection on Death Awareness

Having completed some or all of the activities in this subsection, summarize your understanding of and attitudes toward death on a separate piece of paper.

GRIEF AWARENESS

Activity 1: The Word Chain

Ask yourself this question: What do I feel about grief and what do I know about the grief process?

Write the key word, *grief,* then list the words that pop into your mind in response to it. Do not think a long time about your associative responses, but rather let them flow spontaneously, one word triggering another.

Peruse the list of words that you associated with the word *grief.* Identify each word you wrote down as having a positive (+), negative (−), or neutral (0) connotation by placing a (+), (−), or (0) next to each word. What is your total for each type of connotation?

$$(+) \underline{\hspace{1cm}} \qquad (-) \underline{\hspace{1cm}} \qquad (0) \underline{\hspace{1cm}}$$

What, if anything, does that information tell you about the attitudes you hold toward grief?

Activity 2: Loss Awareness List

Loss, like beauty, is in the eye of the beholder. Furthermore, its ubiquitous nature acknowledges no boundaries of age, sex, ethnic background, or religious preference. Loss has been a part of your life since early childhood. The purpose of this activity is to bring to your personal level of awareness the large number of events that you may have experienced and responded to as a loss in your life. It is important to note that when an event occurs, individual members of a family may or may not describe that event as a loss.

Read each item in the various categories of loss on the Loss Awareness List. Place a check in front of each kind of loss you have experienced personally. As you complete this activity, be aware of the thoughts that cross your mind and the feelings you may experience.

Concrete Losses
___ Personal possessions
___ Money
___ Pet
___ Job
___ Stocks, bonds
___ Residence

Abstract Losses
___ Loss of dreams
___ Loss of faith
___ Loss of childhood
___ Loss of humor
___ Loss of femininity/virility

Developmental Losses
___ Loss of fertility
___ Loss of mobility
___ Loss of vision
___ Loss of hearing
___ Loss of natural hair color
___ Loss of hair
___ Loss of skin tone

Losses of Other People
___ Death of parent(s)
___ Death of spouse/partner
___ Death of sibling
___ Death of child
___ Death of grandchild
___ Death of grandparent(s)
___ Death of friend
___ Death of relative
___ Through separation
___ Through divorce
___ Through geographic move
___ Through job loss
___ Through retirement

Loss of Self
___ Through physical illness
___ Through divorce
___ Through spouse's death
___ Through job loss

___ Through retirement   ___ Through miscarriage
___ Through substance abuse   ___ Through drug abuse
___ Through mental illness
___ Through abortion
___ Through surgery
___ Through physical/emotional abuse
___ Through sexual abuse

Look over the losses that you have identified in your life. Have you experienced any loss that does not appear on the list? NO _____; YES _____. If yes, explain.

Activity 3: Grief Awareness Scale

In dominant North American culture, grief is minimized and often misunderstood. Complete the Grief Awareness Scale to provide you with insights about your personal attitudes toward grief and the grieving process. Read each of the 17 statements. Decide whether you find it to be true or false. Indicate your answer by circling either (T) or (F).

True	False	
T	F	1. Children under 12 years old do not grieve.
T	F	2. Family members grieve the same way.
T	F	3. Grief is a universal response to loss.
T	F	4. Family members tend to perceive loss individually.
T	F	5. Death is the sole cause of grief.
T	F	6. The grief process lasts about one year.
T	F	7. Mainstream America understands the grief process.
T	F	8. Grieving people need to stay busy in order to heal.
T	F	9. Religious beliefs influence grief reactions.
T	F	10. Unresolved grief can accumulate over time.
T	F	11. People grieve for many different things.
T	F	12. Ethnic background has an impact on grief reactions.
T	F	13. How a person dies has an impact upon the grief that survivors experience.

T	F	14. Grief reactions are learned through modeling.

| T | F | 15. Following the funeral, most mainstream North Americans lack rituals that might facilitate healing. |

| T | F | 16. Unresolved losses in early childhood can resurface in adolescence and adulthood. |

| T | F | 17. Children are naturally resilient to losses. |

Score 1 point for each answer that is agreement with the key: 1–F; 2–F; 3–T; 4–T; 5–F; 6–F; 7–F; 8–F; 9–T; 10–T; 11–T; 12–T; 13–T; 14–T; 15–T; 16–T; 17–F.

What is your score? _____

Do any of the answers surprise you? NO _____; YES _____. If yes, explain.

Does your performance on this activity provide you with any insight regarding your attitudes toward and understanding of grief? NO _____; YES _____. If yes, explain.

Activity 4: Invisible Scars: Unresolved Losses in Childhood

When traumatic loss is experienced, but not dealt with, in early childhood it can effect a person's reactions to subsequent losses in either adolescence or adulthood. Feelings that surround an early loss may remain unexpressed over decades for a variety of reasons: (a) family beliefs about the expression of feelings; (b) family attitudes that trivialize children's feelings; or (c) the fact that the event was not perceived as a loss by adult family members.

Go back and peruse your Loss Awareness List, Activity 2. Draw a circle and inside the circle write the earliest loss you can recall, using your *nondominant hand*. The rationale for using that hand is that, by doing so, you may "tap into" feelings of grief that you experienced as a child. Some of these might include awkwardness, shame, fear, and lack of control.

Next, draw a few spokes extending outward from the circle. On each spoke, identify any additional losses in your life that you feel you have not grieved for fully, that is, losses that you may have packed away in your "grief-case."

Your ability to grieve for your losses as an adult may correspond to the way in which you grieved for your losses as a child. Your personal healing may resemble the process of peeling an onion—one layer of loss at a time. Having identified unresolved losses in your life, are you able to draw any conclusions about your personal pattern of grieving? NO _____; YES _____. If yes, explain.

Activity 5: Grief Awareness Questionnaire*

Read each item in this questionnaire and answer it by circling the response(s) of your choice.

---

1. Following the death of a beloved family member, how long would you expect the survivor(s) to grieve:

    0–3 months   3–6 months   6 months–1 year

    1–2 years   2 + years

2. How long would "society" expect the survivor(s) to grieve?

    0–3 months   3–6 months   6 months–1 year

    1–2 years   2 + years

3. Would you encourage or allow a child under 10 years to attend a funeral service?

    No   Yes   Depends

4. Would you express intense personal feelings of grief publicly?

    No   Yes   Depends

5. Would you be likely to touch the body at a funeral service?

    No   Yes   Depends

6. Would you try to carry out your family member's last wishes if you had promised to do so, even if they seemed senseless?

    No   Yes   Depends

7. In your own grief, to whom would you turn for support?

    Family   Clergy   God   Friend   No one   Other
    member   person

*Adapted by permission from R. A. Kalish and D. K. Reynolds, *Perspectives of Death and Dying,* Vol. 4 of *Death and Ethnicity: A Psychocultural Study,* 2nd ed. (pp. 200–221), 1981, New York: Baywood. Copyright © Baywood Publishing Company, Inc.

8. How long a period after a death would you allow to elapse before beginning to worry that someone is grieving abnormally?

8 weeks   3–6 months   6 months–1 year

1-2 years   2 + years

9. Which survivor is at greatest emotional risk during grief?

Older	Older	Young	Young	Young	Older
male	female	male	female	child	child

10. After what period of time would you consider it acceptable for a surviving adult to _____ ?

A. Remarry	1–3 months	6 months–1 year	1-2 years	2 + years
B. Return to work	1–3 months	6 months–1 year	1-2 years	2 + years
C. Date	1–3 months	6 months–1 year	1-2 years	2 + years
D. Stop grieving	1–3 months	6 months–1 year	1-2 years	2 + years

11. What is the first task a survivor must complete in order to heal?

Accept	Detach	Keep	Experience	Set new	Don't
reality	from past	busy	the pain	goals	know

12. What is the minimum number of times a widowed person should visit the spouse's grave during the *first* year of bereavement?

1–2 times   3–5 times   6 + times   Unimportant

13. What is the minimum number of times a widowed person should visit the spouse's grave during the *fifth* year after death?

1–2 times   3–5 times   6 + times   Unimportant

14. Which cause of death do you think would involve a longer time to work through in bereavement?

Old age   Illness   Accident   Suicide   Homicide   War

15. Which factor(s) most affect working through the bereavement process?

Cause	Age of	Support	Religious	Ethnic
of death	deceased	system	beliefs	background

16. Do family members grieve in the same way?

     No   Yes   Depends

17. Do normal grief reactions become abnormal if they persist over a long period of time?

     No   Yes   Depends

18. Would an infant grieve over the death of a sibling?

     No   Yes   Depends

19. Which pregnancy-related death would generate the most complicated grief reaction?

     Miscarriage   Abortion   Stillbirth   Crib death   Depends

20. Which experience(s) in childhood might have an impact upon an adult's response to the death of a spouse?

Adoption	Parental death	Parental divorce	Physical abuse	Emigration

21. After a parent dies, what changes might a child experience at home?

Different bedtime	Different meals	Different discipline	Different caregiver	Different spending habits

22. In what way(s) might a teenager grieve over a traumatic loss?

Become aggressive	Dress like deceased	Become a perfectionist	Become a "caretaker"

Journal Page: Self-Reflection on Grief Awareness

Having completed some or all of the activities in this subsection, review your responses and summarize your understanding of and attitudes toward grief.

MULTI-CULTURAL AWARENESS

Activity 1: Personal Identity

The purpose of this activity is to help you identify parameters you use to define yourself. On the line below, write your full name. Next to your name, identify any personal associations you consider significant, such as religious affiliation, ethnic background, and so on.

_____ : _____
Name   Associations

How important are those associations to your sense of identity? Circle your answer.

Very   Unimportant   Neutral   Important   Very
unimportant   important

Activity 2: A Fly on the Wall

Frequently, people from various professions interact with multi-cultural populations. The purpose of this activity is to assess your current understanding of death, dying, and grief within a culturally diverse framework.

Imagine that you are a fly on the wall of the hospital room described in the scenario below, then think how you might answer a series of questions for each of the ethnic, racial, and religious groups specified.

Mike, age 26, is in a suburban hospital in a large metropolitan area. He is dying of a gunshot wound inflicted by a neighbor following a violent argument. Mike's family is present just prior to and at the moment of his death.

Try to answer each of the following questions as they pertain to each of the specific American cultural groups in turn.

African   Arab   Buddhist   European
Hispanic   Hmong   Jewish   Native American

1. Who would constitute Mike's family?
2. What spiritual caregiver(s) might be summoned?
3. What grief reactions might you observe?
4. What grief reactions might you hear?
5. What ritual(s) might occur just prior to death?
6. What ritual(s) might occur immediately following death?
7. What might occur that would make you feel uncomfortable?
8. What might occur to cause miscommunication between parties?

Activity 3: Multi-Cultural Comfort Scale

Each of us has experienced the feeling of being either comfortable or uncomfortable when communicating with another person. The purpose of this activity is to help you identify your personal comfort level in relating to culturally diverse persons in different situations. Read each item that appears below. Circle the number that describes your level of comfort.

How comfortable would you feel? 1—Very uncomfortable; 2—Uncomfortable; 3—Neutral; 4—Comfortable; 5—Very comfortable

1. Caring for a dying person who is _____?

A. African American-Baptist	1	2	3	4	5
B. Arab American-Muslim	1	2	3	4	5
C. Asian American-Buddhist	1	2	3	4	5
D. Hispanic American-Catholic	1	2	3	4	5
E. Jewish American-Orthodox	1	2	3	4	5
F. Native American-Traditional	1	2	3	4	5
G. Swedish American-Lutheran	1	2	3	4	5

[Refer back to each of the seven ethnic groups and insert codes: (A) #; (B) #; (C) #; (D) #; (E) #; (F) #; (G) #]

2. Attending the funeral of a person who was _____?

3. Working as a colleague in the same profession with a person who is _____?

4. Vacationing with a person/family that is _____?

5. Living next door to a person/family that is _____?

6. Socializing with a person/family that is _____?

7. Working as a subordinate to a person who is _____?

8. Visiting a person's home who is _____?

When you have completed this activity, total each response type.

1—Very uncomfortable _____   4—Comfortable   _____

2—Uncomfortable   _____   5—Very comfortable _____

3—Neutral   _____

Activity 4: A Multi-Cultural Checklist

The purpose of this activity is to assess the degree to which you have been proactive in your attitudes and activities toward diversity. Read each of the following statements. Indicate both whether you have or have not engaged in that action to date and whether you intend to take such action in the future.

1. I have actively sought out information to enhance my own awareness and understanding of multi-cultural diversity.

   No   Yes   Intend to   Do not intend to

2. I have consciously pondered my own attitudes and behaviors as they either enhance or hinder harmonious multi-cultural relationships.

   No   Yes   Intend to   Do not intend to

3. I have evaluated my use of terms or phrases that may be perceived by others as degrading or hurtful.

   No   Yes   Intend to   Do not intend to

4. I have suggested or initiated workshops or discussions with friends, co-workers, social clubs, or church groups about multi-cultural diversity.

   No   Yes   Intend to   Do not intend to

5. I have openly disagreed with racial, cultural, or religious jokes, comments, or slurs.

   No   Yes   Intend to   Do not intend to

6. In my work setting, I have utilized appropriate occasions to discuss the multi-cultural climate in the organization with my colleagues and with institutional administration.

   No   Yes   Intend to   Do not intend to

7. When I see a broadcast, advertisement, or newspaper article that is racially, culturally, or religiously biased, I have complained to the author or sponsor responsible for it.

   No   Yes   Intend to   Do not intend to

Activity 5: Multi-Cultural Awareness Questionnaire

Read each item in this questionnaire and answer it by circling the response(s) of your choice.

1. How many people from cultural, racial, or religious backgrounds very different from your own have you known personally who have died within the past two years?

   None   1–3   4–7   8 +

2. How many funerals of people from cultural, racial, or religious backgrounds very different from your own have you attended in the past two years?

   None   1–3   4–7   8+

3. As a professional, how many people from cultural, racial, or religious backgrounds very different from your own have you served?

   None   1–3   4–7   8+

4. As a professional, how many people from cultural, racial, or religious backgrounds very different from your own have you interacted with who were dying?

   None   1–3   4–7   8+

Answer items 5–13 in regard to the following groups.

African American	Buddhist American	Muslim American
European American	Hispanic American	Native American
Jewish American	Hmong American	

5. In which community(ies) do you believe the dying, death, and grief practices to be most different from your own?
6. Which community(ies) might consider an autopsy to be taboo?
7. Which community(ies) might follow specific procedures for burial that are very different from your own?
8. Which community(ies) might consider embalming to be taboo?
9. Which community(ies) might grieve in ways most different from your own?
10. Which community(ies) might profess a belief in life after death?
11. Which community(ies) might encourage the public expression of intense feelings of grief?
12. Which community(ies) might discourage the participation of children in death and grief practices?
13. Which community(ies) might incorporate death education into everyday life?
14. In the past two years, how many personal holiday greetings or other written communications have you conveyed to individuals or families whose cultural, racial, or religious backgrounds were very different from your own?

   None   1–3   4–7   8+

15. In the past two years, how many events (such as conferences, concerts, exhibits) have you attended that *highlighted* multi-cultural diversity?

   None   1–3   4–7   8+

16. In your personal address file, how many entries represent individuals with cultural, racial, or religious backgrounds different from your own?

   None   1–3   4–7   8+

17. In the past two years, in your professional work environment, how frequently have you encountered patients or clients from cultures, races, or religions very different from your own?

   Never   1–3 times   4–7 times   8+ times

18. In the immediate neighborhood in which you live, how many families are from cultures, races, or religions very different from your own?

   None   1–3   4–7   8+

19. If there are some culturally diverse families living in your neighborhood, how well do you know some of them?

   Not   By sight   By name   Well   Very well   There
   at all   are none

Journal Page: Self-Reflection on Cultural Awareness

Having completed some or all of the activities in this subsection, review your responses and summarize your understanding of, experiences with, and attitudes toward cultural diversity.

Part Two

Dying, Death, and Grief among Selected Ethnic Communities

Chapter Four

Mourning and Funeral Customs of African Americans

Hosea L. Perry

Illustrative Episode

Late one hot summer night, in a major metropolitan midwestern city, two young men attending a party had an argument and shots were fired. When the confrontation cleared, an African American teenager, Bob (not his real name), lay mortally wounded on the ground.

Police were called to the scene and the officers realized that the young man was dying. As yet, the partygoers were unaware of the severity of Bob's wounds. Police officers saw several rival gang members in the crowd and, fearing that the situation would escalate if the group knew that Bob was already dead, they ordered the ambulance drivers to take the body to Midland Hospital rather than to a morgue. Located for 80 years on the edge of the city's largest African American community, Midland had an almost all-white staff with a reputation for coolness toward the neighboring inner-city population.

See Appendix C for personal reflections on the African American experience.

Bob's family and most of the partygoers raced to the hospital and gathered, many of them crying loudly and wailing, outside the hospital's front doors as they awaited news of Bob's condition. The hospital administrator told them to go home or they would be removed because they were making too much noise. The hospital security staff then radioed for help from every available police force within the area, and seven separate police agencies responded "to put down a riot." A police canine unit arrived and in the resulting chaos several young African American teenagers were bitten. The hospital staff refused to treat them and told them to go to the inner-city county hospital.

At this point, the news of Bob's death reached his family and friends outside Midland Hospital. The crowd of distressed people was dispersed by the police. The next day brought meetings at which charges of police brutality and racial insensitivity were made by leaders of the African American community. One leader was quoted as saying, "The hospital doesn't understand how black people grieve." Subsequently, demonstrators marched to the hospital and to the city hall.

The city was in turmoil over the incident for weeks. Bob's city council member, a white woman, later lamented that Bob's death had been virtually overlooked in the ensuing controversy over the police actions.

Submitted by Vivian Jenkins Nelsen

POSSIBLE PERCEPTIONS
OF THE PRINCIPALS INVOLVED

The City Police

Called to the scene of the shooting, the city police officers (white) were confronted by an anxious crowd (entirely African American). The presence of rival youth gangs in the African American community heightened police concern about possible crowd reactions to Bob's death. Thus, although Bob was already dead, they ordered the ambulance drivers to take the body to the nearest private suburban hospital instead of to a morgue.

Hospital Administrators, Security Personnel, and "Outside Police"

The Midland Hospital staff received the body. Very soon thereafter an emotional crowd of the victim's relatives and friends had gathered outside the hospital's front doors. Some people were expressing their grief in crying and wailing; others were manifesting anger at the authorities for their handling of this latest "racial incident" involving the death of a member of the African American community. Concerned about what they termed "excessive noise," the hospital security staff radioed for help from "any and all police units" within radio range. Some units came with dogs, expecting the need to control a riot.

Family, Friends, and Neighbors of the Victim

At the party in the community, shots were fired during an argument between youths. Friends called the city police, who came to investigate and found one of the participants mortally wounded. After the ambulance had taken Bob to a nearby hospital, his family, friends, and neighbors went quickly there by whatever means they could manage. They gathered outside the building, hearing rumors of the youth's death, milling around, sobbing and wailing in their grief. The staff requested that they leave the premises. When they did not leave, more police units were called in. Because of earlier experiences, the African American community already had doubts about the hospital's equal treatment. This was the most recent shooting of one of their own. They also were outraged that the hospital refused to treat those who had been bitten by the dogs. They were further aggravated when the police dispersed them forcibly. As a result, the African American community perceived racial inequality and their leaders charged the police with brutality.

There is a list of questions concerning the perceptions outlined here in Appendix B: Questions That Might Be Asked.

Editors

―――――=oɔɔɔ̃ɔɔɔɔ̃c=――――――

INTRODUCTION

Death, often violent death, is a familiar experience to African American people. Yet death has been almost ignored in formal and academic studies of their lives (Kalish & Reynolds, 1981, p. 95). One cannot make definitive statements about how blacks die and mourn because of the diversity that exists across such a wide and varied community. In contrasting Southern Baptists, northern Unitarians, and black Catholics, for example, there are great differences in how death is experienced and how grief is expressed.

Over a number of years I have devoted myself to the study of how blacks confront dying, death, and grief, particularly through review of the scholarly literature and by analyses of newspaper articles, novels, and plays, but chiefly through numerous extensive interviews and attendance at hundreds of funerals. Many individuals have invited me into their homes and places of business to interview them about the dying and death of someone they loved. The 120 subjects were middle- and upper-lower class blacks: 115 in Alabama, Florida, Georgia, Kentucky, Mississippi, and North and South Carolina, and 5 in Arizona, California, and Minnesota. Hundreds of black ministers, priests, and funeral directors were also very helpful and supportive. In addition to their interviews, they shared with me copies of funeral programs, which are unique sources of data. I was also fortunate in having access to the extensive collection of materials related to blacks at the Atlanta University Center.

Several scholarly publications have been most useful. In 1963, Mitford's *The American Way of Death* put forward the hypothesis that funeral customs of black Americans have become similar to those of the white majority. The classic by Genovese (1976), *Roll, Jordan, Roll,* provides excellent insights into funeral customs that blend together European and African features dating back to the period of slavery and earlier. *Community in a Black Pentecostal Church* (Williams, 1974) includes realistic accounts of Pentecostal funerals. In *The Myth of the Negro Past,* Herskovits (1958) documents the importance of funerals in the survival of African customs among black slaves in America. White's *The Psychology of Blacks* (1984) contributes fine insight:

> Death in the black community is perceived as a celebration of life, a testament to the fact that a life has been lived, that the earthly journey is completed. Those who serve as witnesses in the presence of death, extended family, friends, and church members, to affirm the essence of the person's existence, are ready to testify to the fact that the deceased has fought the battle, borne the burden, and finished the course; they are ready to understand and say well done. (p. 46)

VESTIGES OF AFRICA AND SLAVERY

An old proverb, "To weep too much for the dead is an affront to the living," suggests the affective response that has come to be expected within the white American culture. This tendency to "weep not too much for the dead" is illustrated in this scene at a country funeral in the 1800s:

> Everyone as he entered, took off his hat with his left hand, smoothed down his hair with his right hand, walked up to the coffin, gazed down upon the corpse, made a crooked face, passed up to the table, took a glass of his favorite liquor, went forth upon the plat before the house, and talked politics, or the new road, or compared

crops, or swapped heifers or horses, until it was time to lift. (Coffin, 1976, pp. 95, 195)

Although there is no one pattern of mourning behavior in any one culture, in general one thinks of funerals in the white culture as more formal and less emotional than within black death rituals. Pentecostal and Southern Baptist funerals, with long emotional sermons and wailing and sobbing in response from the mourners, have become stereotypes for all black funerals. Have black funeral customs become similar to those of the white majority or do black funeral customs represent a unique blend of African and European customs dating back to the period of slavery and earlier?

The work of Genovese (1976) supports the latter hypothesis. The importance of the funeral among the slaves, according to Genovese, was highlighted during the early 1800s after the 1800 insurrectionary plot associated with Gabriel Prosser in Virginia, which was organized among slaves at a child's funeral, and especially following the Nat Turner revolt of 1831. Genovese refers to decisions to bar black preachers and to forbid public funerals that were not presided over by white men. Genovese then stresses the salient role of such funerals:

> Never did the white reaction succeed in suppressing big slave funerals. Too many planters considered the repressive regulations inhuman, and others noted that they either could not be enforced or would so embitter the slaves as to increase, rather than decrease, the threat of violent resistance. . . . The significance of proper funerals for the slaves lay not in the peripheral if real danger of conspiracy, but in the extent to which they allowed the participants to feel themselves a human community unto themselves. (pp. 194–195)

The importance of slave funerals as a means of building up this sense of community among the slaves was intensified by any attempt on the part of the slaveholders to repress them. Such attempts to restrict slave funerals stem back to the very early years of slavery, for example, in 1687 in the northern neck of Virginia. In 1772 a New York City law restricted slave funerals to daylight hours and limited the number of persons in attendance to no more than 12 (Genovese, 1976, p. 194). The slaves often preferred night funerals, and this desire "existed throughout the South but especially in areas of high black density and cultural continuity with Africa, and it strongly suggests African patterns" (Genovese, p. 197). There were, however, several reasons why blacks preferred night funerals. They allowed friends from neighboring farms and plantations to attend and also did not interfere with their required hours of work. This preference for night funerals remained long after the Civil War (Genovese, p. 197).

Among the slaves, it was particularly important to bury their dead as soon as possible; then a more elaborate ceremony could be held later. This practice was also true among whites in the period before embalming was practiced. But it was even more the pattern among slaves because the slave cabins had no glass windows, and the shutters had to be left open during most of the year. In order to protect their dead from animals, immediate burial was necessary (Genovese, p. 197).

Genovese describes the burial processions that were organized to and from the cemetery, "complete with chanting and singing and 'shouts' at the grave":

> The processions moved slowly, led by six or more pallbearers, their way through the dark woods lit by pine torches. The slaves sang their mournful dirges going to, at, and returning from a grave that had earlier been prepared for the body. The sermon would usually be brief. . . . The most common slave funeral had a black man [presiding]. The solemnity dissolved afterwards in a convivial dinner. . . . It was the combination of more vigorous moments in the procession, especially the use of those drums which were so reminiscent of Africa and so threatening to white ears, and the sometimes boisterous dinners that provided the occasion for many whites to consider these funerals "pagan festivals" and to interpret them in one or another self-serving racist way. (pp. 199–200)

Other practices that Genovese traces back to Africa includes throwing dirt into the grave. While not exclusively African, the custom seems to have been brought to the American continent by African slaves. Also, the practice of decorating graves with broken earthenware, still seen in certain areas of the South (Mississippi, Georgia, and South Carolina), has been traced to Angola. The significance of the broken pottery, according to Genovese and others, is the traditional West African belief in "a sense of death as a broken body and to the need to compensate the spirit." (Genovese, p. 201)

AFRICAN AMERICAN FUNERAL PATTERNS
IN TRANSITION

The following account of an actual Pentecostal funeral highlights what Genovese wrote about the significance of community building as a primary function of black funerals. Williams (1974) depicts the funeral director's assistants escorting the near relatives to the casket to say their words of farewell to the deceased:

> After many admonitions to "sinners" and much praise of Sister Backler, the pastor ended his sermon, the last soloist sang, and the church prepared to see Sister Backler for the last time. Two assistants to the funeral director went to the casket, arranged the interior lace in its appropriate place. Then they stood on either end of the casket while two other assistants accompanied by a church nurse, took each member of the immediate family to view the body. . . . After all the family had viewed the body, leaving the members of the church distraught by their emotional

outbursts, all the rest of the congregation stood and formed a line and marched around to view Sister Backler. They touched her, kissed her, embraced her, and frequently had to be restrained in their emotions. (p. 100)

However, the emotionalism of this Pentecostal rite would not be found at every black funeral. In an interview with Sarah Dobbins, she indicated that the wishes of a dead person to have only a simple ceremony at the graveside were respected by his survivors:

HP: Did you have a church service?

SD: We had a graveside rite for him.

HP: What did the other members of the family think about having grave-side rites rather than the traditional church funeral?

SD: The other members of my family, I think, thought very well of it. We are Episcopalian and we don't have all those long funeral sermons anyway. But since that time my father has died and we had one [a graveside rite] for him. (Personal interview with Sarah Dobbins, Albany, GA, July 26, 1982)

In many of the interviews with black mourners in the South, there were differences in the amount of emotionalism manifested at funerals and that shown during the period of grieving, perhaps related to the personality and temperament of the mourners. This statement made in an interview with Ann James provides several insights:

So far as the family is concerned, I guess there it goes back to the environment the funeral has had. Sometimes it's expected that the family should just give in to wailing. That shows how much they care. And if you don't do that . . . [they say] "That was quite a funeral wasn't it? . . . they certainly didn't care for 'em." . . . But then if you go to another church it can be just the opposite. People contain themselves. More and more people are not showing that much emotion. My mother was speaking about this . . . she said, "I know that if anybody in that family die, they turn the church over, turn it out—that loudness, and that weeping and that hollering and all." But she said, "Even they don't do it anymore". . . . I think the shorter the funeral is, the less display of emotion you have. (Personal interview with Ann James, Donalsonville, GA, January 4, 1982)

Some interviewees spoke about the positive effects of being emotional at funerals. They contended that the trend to less emotional funerals, shorter sermons, and less "wailing" is evidence that the black funeral customs are becoming more like those in the white community. W. F. Pugh, a person who had been in charge of funeral music for more than 30 years, was convinced that the role models of famous American survivors have influenced behaviors at funerals:

WP: You take Kennedy's wife, she walked around in a daze and viewed that body. You never see her break down. Now that was a real shock. He fell over in her lap. When Robert Kennedy got killed . . . Hubert Humphrey . . .

they had the funerals on TV. You never see any of them break down . . . they were able to control their emotions.

HP: What about Martin Luther King?

WP: She did the same thing—I mean, Mrs. King. She controlled her emotions. And old Dr. King, his wife got shot in the pulpit, playing the piano.

HP: What do you think is the right way to act at funerals?

WP: I think they should try to control their emotions. . . . I think at a funeral if they could control their emotions it could be a more proper way to act. Try to keep themselves under control. The least little thing will stimulate and start everybody hollering. (Personal interview with Willie F. Pugh, Donalsonville, GA, December 29, 1981)

Hylan Lewis (1964) has presented a summary of typical black funerals held in churches of the Piedmont South. He describes the pattern in a community comprised of "old aristocrats," an up-and-coming middle class, textile mill villages, and a sizable black population:

> An essential feature of religion and church membership is the expectation of a church funeral; indeed, it is one of the motives for maintaining church membership. Among the first questions asked after death are: "To which church did the deceased belong?" and "Whom do you want to preach the funeral?" . . . As in the case of other practices, there tends to be a basic pattern within which variations occur. The basic pattern combines these essential steps: return of the corpse to the home the evening before the funeral; on the day of the funeral, body and funeral party are driven to the church. (For all exits and entrances, the corpse is borne between parallel rows of women "flower girls" who are usually dressed in white). The corpse is borne into the church while the church bell tolls and the choir sings or the minister utters an incantation; a song is sung by the choir and audience; a Scripture reading and/or prayer is delivered by assisting minister or prominent church member; obituary, acknowledgment of flowers, messages, and testimonies by friends and neighbors are delivered; a eulogy is rendered by the pastor; final view of the remains is taken by the audience; interment follows, with male volunteers filling the grave after final rites.
>
> The quality and length of each of the above steps depend upon such factors as the importance of the deceased, community reputation, family wishes, and his relation to the church. . . .
>
> The chances are high at the Baptist and rural churches, particularly if the relatives of the deceased are persons of limited means, that a collection will be taken as the mourners file by the corpse. . . . This practice probably had its beginning as a form of mutual aid. (Lewis, pp. 140–141)

No matter how much the customs among mourners have changed, either through the influences of the white culture or as a result of the increased urbanization and education of blacks, the pervasive quality of black mourning customs is their use as a builder of community. One rarely sees clearer evidence of black community than that of a small-town Southern funeral.

SOME PSYCHOLOGICAL INSIGHTS

Gorer's contention that mourning develops in three stages also has a universal quality: ". . . an initial period of shock, a stage of violent grief and disorganization, and a usually longer period of reorganization" (Gorer, 1967, p. 152).

Descriptions of African American mourning practices exemplify some of the most organized and elaborate efforts to aid mourners during their various stages of grief. From the moment news is out about a death in a black community, help arrives in the home of the mourner or mourners. Rituals are in place—from the church "sisters" who come to bring and prepare meals and do "what their hands can find to do," to the members of the church who say "their words" about the dead, to the church "nurses" who accompany family members to view the body individually. These people, along with the pastor and the funeral director and assistants, all assist the mourners to work through their distress.

There are, of course, infinite ways that blacks give expression to their grief—some similar to and others different from the ways more commonly used by white people. There are wide variations within the white culture also. Georgian Dorothy Crumbley spoke of such differences between whites and blacks in their expressions of grief and also about the differences within her own family:

> I really hadn't cried at the funeral and I didn't really cry, and really didn't go through any period of grief until I got back here [from Mississippi]—I lost weight— I dreamed about her. . . . I'm convinced that if I had been able to just scream and yell as Richard Pryor said . . . Mr. Pryor said, "White people deal with death in a funny sort of way . . . they don't cry over their dearly departed . . . what they usually do is say something like, oh, she was nice old soul (sniff, sniff) and they go on about their business. But black folks they Ahhhhh, and they just holler . . . say things and carry on," and he said that he thinks that's an appropriate way to deal with this, just scream and just get it all out.
>
> Well, I think he has a lot of good; and I think Richard Pryor did that when his grandmother died. They showed him in *Jet* magazine. He was all distraught. He was carrying on just awful. He was acting the way he felt he should act in order to help him get through that grief. I really feel if I had been able to just do that at the moment that I felt the need to, in Mississippi, I probably wouldn't have gone through losing weight over here, having an upset stomach . . . for about six months because I just don't deal with my grief that way. Other members of my family like my sister Nancy . . . seems to be making it better than I did.
>
> But I remember one thing: Nancy cried a lot; Nancy cried all the time [at the funeral in Mississippi]. Every time somebody came to the house . . . she'd start crying. She just cried every minute she got a chance, it seemed, and we started looking at her funny, you know, like what in the devil is wrong with you, girl? Why

are you crying when all of these folks come up here? Well, anyway . . . I just assume that Nancy got her crying out in Mississippi, whereas I didn't and Joyce (another sister) didn't either. (Personal interview with Dorothy Crumbley, Ft. Valley, GA, 1982)

INSIGHTS FROM AFRICAN AMERICAN LITERATURE, DRAMA, POETRY, MUSIC

The rich body of African American literature proves to be an excellent source for understanding how black people express their grief, the importance of funerals, and how these affect black family and societal relationships.

Baldwin's 1964 drama, *Blues for Mr. Charlie,* based loosely on the racist murder of Emmet Till in 1955, centers around relationships in "Blacktown" and "Whitetown." Just as the murder of Emmet Till became a pivotal episode in the burgeoning civil rights movement, the murder of Richard in *Blues for Mr. Charlie* serves as the critical moment in the play. Answers are not given, but the audience is left with many questions and emotions. Meridian Henry, Richard's father, a pastor in a black Southern church, is moved to question his very Christianity:

My son's dead, but he's not gone to join his ancestors. He was a sinner, so he must have gone to hell—if we're going to believe what the Bible says. Is that such an improvement, such a mighty advance over B.C.? I've been thinking. I've had to think—would I have *been* such a Christian if I hadn't been born black? Maybe I *had* to become a Christian in order to have any dignity at all. Since I wasn't a man in men's eyes, then I could be a man in the eyes of God. But that didn't protect my wife. She's dead, too soon; we don't really know how. That didn't protect my son—he's dead, we know how too well. (Baldwin, p. 56)

Other novelists, playwrights, and poets who have brought insights into how blacks mourn include Maya Angelou, Gwendolyn Brooks, Countee Cullen, Ralph Ellison, James Weldon Johnson, Paule Marshall, Claude McKay, and Richard Wright. Brooks (1963), in her poem "The Rites for Cousin Vit," illustrates a familiarity with death. She is comfortable with the subject and through her description we can see Brooks's appreciation for Cousin Vit without judging her past life:

Carried her unprotesting out the door.
Kicked back the casket-stand. But it can't hold her,
That stuff and satin aiming to enfold her,
The lid's contrition nor the bolts before.
Oh oh. Too much. Too much. Even now, surmise,
She rises in the sunshine. There she goes,
Back to the bars she knew and the repose

In love-rooms and the things in people's eyes.
Too vital and too squeaking. Must emerge.
Even now she does the snake-hips with a hiss,
Slops the bad wine across her shantung, talks
Of pregnancy, guitars and bridgework, walks
In parks or alleys, comes haply on the verge
Of happiness, haply hysterics, Is.
(p. 58)

The uniquely African American art forms—jazz, blues, and gospel music—provide distinctly black expressions of grief and mourning. Black music makes manifest the moods and essences of how blacks feel and how they express their feelings when faced with the death of a friend, a loved one, a family member.

Spirituals, dating back to slave times, present some of the best-known forms of black funeral music. The words of the spirituals may be interpreted in different ways as expressions of grief and views of death. One author, Roy Lester Clark (1979), believes that many spirituals express a final wish, a death wish. In his analysis of "Deep River," Clark contends that the song signifies a wish to die, to "cross the River Jordan and go home to Jesus."

Deep river,
My home is over Jordan,
Deep river, Lord,
I want to cross over into camp ground.

According to Clark, "Deep River," as well as words in the following spirituals, had a double meaning for slaves. They expressed their wish to be transported out of slavery, across the river to the North as well as to their final home with Jesus. The words remind us of the current usage that speaks of "homecoming:"

Roll, Jordan, roll,
Roll, Jordan, roll,
I want to go to heaven when I die,
Just to hear ol' Jordan roll.

Until I reach-a my home,
Until I reach-a my home,
I never intend to give the journey over
Until I reach-a my home.

Going home, going home,
I am going home.

Sometimes I feel like a motherless child,
Sometimes I feel like a motherless child,
Sometimes I feel like a motherless child,
A long way from home, a long way from home.

The musical traditions of the contemporary black church and funeral rituals can be traced back earlier than the period of slavery. The music is rooted in the African origins of black Americans as well as in the biblical traditions, especially those found in the Old Testament. Thus, the present-day musical responses to death are derived from a combination of ancient Hebrew and African laments and dirges. Both the Hebrews and ancient African tribes based their dirges and laments on oral traditions.

In his study connecting oral traditions to the celebration of death in the black church, Craggett (1980, p. 11) examines several different types of dirges and laments. The following example is from Jeremiah (9:20–22):

> Hear, O women, the word of the Lord,
> and let your ear receive the word of his mouth;
> teach your daughters a lament,
> and each of his neighbors a dirge,
> For death has come into our windows,
> it has entered our palaces,
> cutting off the children from the streets
> and the young men from the squares.
> Speak, "Thus says the Lord:
> The dead bodies of men shall fall
> like dung upon the open field,
> like sheaves after the reaper,
> and none shall gather them."

An example of a black American poem-dirge is James Weldon Johnson's "Go Down Death (A Funeral Sermon)." This classic, first published in 1941, has influenced the style of funeral sermons and songs as well as black spirituals. Some excerpts follow:

> And God said: Go down, Death, go down.
> Go down to Savannah, Georgia,
> Down in Yamacraw,
> And find Sister Caroline.
> She's borne the burden and the heat of the day,
> She's labored long in my vineyard,
> And she's tired—
> She is weary—
> Go down, Death, and bring her to me. . . .
>
> And Death took her up like a baby,
> And she lay in his icy arms,
> But she didn't feel no chill.
> And Death began to ride again—
> Up beyond the evening star,
> Into the glittering light of glory,

On to the Great White Throne.
And there he laid Sister Caroline
On the loving breast of Jesus.

And Jesus took his own hand and wiped away her tears,
And he smoothed the furrows from her face,
And the angels sang a little song,
And Jesus rocked her in his arms,
And kept a-saying: Take your rest,
Take your rest.
Weep not—weep not,
She is not dead;
She's resting in the bosom of Jesus.
(Johnson, pp. 535–537)

CONCLUSION

In the universal language of mourning, the external expression is the funeral ceremony. When there is a death in the African American community there will customarily be an all-out ceremony attended by family members and friends from all parts of the country. A description of a "standard" black funeral is not possible because of divergences by religious denomination, geographical region, educational background, and the economic levels of the families and communities involved. However, some aspects have been virtually universal among blacks in America in recent times. Everyone—family members, close friends, even acquaintances—will endeavor to attend. There is felt to be an absolute obligation to be present, regardless of the familial relationship. If one dies, the others are duty bound to attend the funeral, which may be delayed several days to enable all to come. There is much family and social pressure to conform to this expectation.

There are shared expectations, also, regarding the appropriate events and "proper" behavior during the funeral. People from discrete segments of the community may participate in the rituals. Generally, however, a prescribed normative pattern is followed. Most blacks today either have passed through a hospital or die in a hospital. Indeed "going to the hospital" has come to signify dying for many middle- and lower-class blacks. For the religious, illness, recovery, or death are all viewed as reflections of God's plans.

Traditionally, especially in the South, a number of customs remain as features of African American funerals. "Flower girls"—the female counterparts of pallbearers—give special attention to the closest family members. "Nurses" in white dresses care for those who may be overcome by emotion. The reader of the obituary generally is chosen from within the same "social class" or as a member of the school class of the deceased adult, adolescent, or child. Solos, choir renditions, or other musical offerings are important. Flowers add significantly to the ambience. The reception line may be arranged from the oldest to the youngest mourners.

In sum, "historical" black funerals in America have numerous vestigial elements based on traditions from West Africa. Such rituals are more common among those in the rural South, among the more evangelical religious groups (e.g., Church of God, Missionary Baptist, Pentecostal), and within population segments having less educational and fewer economic resources. "Modern" nontraditional black funerals are more prevalent in urban areas, in the North, within the upper economic and social classes with more education, and among Roman Catholic and mainline Protestant congregations. Thus, the funeral customs of many African Americans have come to be similar to those of the dominant majority, although they may remain distinctive in some particulars. The customs of others have remained both culturally and ethnically distinct from those of the dominant white society.

REFERENCES

Baldwin, J. (1964). *Blues for Mr. Charlie.* New York: Dell Publishing Company.

Brooks, G. (1963). The rites for cousin Vit. In *Selected Poems* (p. 58). New York: Harper & Row.

Clark, R. L. (1979). *A fantasy theme analysis of Negro spirituals.* Carbondale: Southern Illinois University Press.

Coffin, M. M. (1976). *Death in early America: The history and folklore of customs and superstitions of early medicine, funerals, burials, and mourning.* Nashville: Thomas Nelson.

Craggett, F. T. (1980). *A form critical approach to the oral traditions of the black church as they relate to the celebration of death.* Claremont, CA: Unpublished doctoral dissertation, Doctor of Ministry paper, Claremont School of Theology.

Genovese, E. D. (1976). *Roll, Jordan, roll: The world the slaves made.* New York: Vintage Books.

Gorer, G. (1967). *Death, grief and mourning.* Garden City, NY: Doubleday.

Herskovits, M. J. (1958). *The myth of the Negro past.* Boston: Beacon Press.

Johnson, J. W. (1941). Go down death: A funeral sermon. In A. Kreymborg (Ed.), *An anthology of American poetry: Lyric America, 1630–1941* (pp. 535–537). New York: Tudor.

Kalish, R. A., & Reynolds, D. K. (1981). *Death and ethnicity: A psychocultural study.* Farmingdale, NY: Baywood.

Lewis, H. (1955, 1964). *Blackways of Kent.* Chapel Hill: University of North Carolina Press.

Mitford, J. (1963). *The American way of death.* New York: Simon & Schuster.

White, J. L. (1984). *The psychology of Blacks: An Afro-American perspective.* Englewood Cliffs, NJ: Prentice-Hall.

Williams, M. D. (1974). *Community in a black Pentecostal church: An anthropological study.* Prospect Heights, IL: Waveland Press.

ACKNOWLEDGMENTS

The author acknowledges the assistance of Hamline University student Paulette Susens in preparing the bibliography for this chapter.

BIBLIOGRAPHY

Abrahams, R. D. (1982). Storytelling events: Wake amusement and the structure of nonsense on St. Vincent. *Journal of American Folklore, 95,* 378:39–413.

Crocker, C. (1971). The Southern way of death. In J. K. Morland (Ed.), *The not so solid South: Anthropological studies in a regional subculture* (pp. 114–129). Athens: University of Georgia Press.

Gorer, G. (1962). *Africa dances.* New York: W. W. Norton.

Jackson, M. (1972). The Black experience with death: A brief analysis through Black writings. *Omega, 3*(3), 203–209.

Kearns, F. E. (1970). *The Black experience: An anthology of American literature for the 1970s.* New York: Viking Press.

Masamba, J., & Kalish, R. (1976). Death and bereavement: The role of the black church. *Omega, 7,* 23–24.

McGee, C. L., & Scoby, P. P. (1981). *A comparative study of current practices of secular mortuary chapel funeral services of black and white families.* Unpublished master's thesis, California State University, Dominguez Hills.

Nelsen, H. M., & Nelsen, A. K. (1975). *Black churches in the sixties.* Lexington: University of Kentucky Press.

Pollard, L. J. (1980). Black beneficial societies and the home of aged and infirm colored persons: A research note. *Phylon, 41*(3), 230–239.

Richardson, B. C. (1981, Spring/Summer). Migration and death ceremonies on St. Kitts and Nevis. *Journal of Cultural Geography, 1*(2), 1–11.

Roediger, D. R. (1981, Spring). And die in Dixie: Funerals, death and heaven in the slave community, 1700–1865. *The Massachusetts Review, 22*(1), 163–175.

Sisk, G. N. (1959). Funeral customs in the Alabama black belt, 1870–1910. *Southern Folklore Quarterly, 23*(3), 169–171.

Wilkerson, M. (1976, April). The funeral drama. *Black World, 25:*6.

Chapter Five

Mexican American Perspectives Related to Death

Barbara Younoszai

Illustrative Episode: Puerto Rican

Ramona (not her real name) was a black Puerto Rican woman in her mid-to-late 30s, a single mother of seven children, when she arrived in New York City in 1971. She was from our home town in Puerto Rico and was one of my mother's intimate friends. My mother encouraged her to come and planned to assist her in finding a better life for the family in the United States.

With help from my mother, Ramona enrolled her children in school and secured social and medical assistance. Slum life in Spanish Harlem was dangerous, and Ramona always feared for her life and for the lives of her children. When she later began to have nightmares and precognitions of her family being hurt, she naturally turned to a san-tero, who provided advice, herbs, and prayers. (Santería, or es-piritismo, is a religious syncretism consisting of African, Indian, and Catholic rituals in which the santero, or espiritista, *known as a "me-*

See Appendix D for personal reflections on the Hispanic American experience.

dium," contacts dead spirits for advice. It is widespread in Puerto Rico and the Caribbean countries.) Ramona would spend long hours studying santería. Once she used precious funds to visit Haiti, and later, Santo Domingo, where she hoped to secure additional training. Many of the ancient rituals are preserved and practiced there unobstructed by official religious sanctions. Known by now as a santera, Ramona made herself available to assist the sick and dying.

Her practices did not sit well with either her Irish American priest or the white social worker, who thought they constituted witchcraft and who then considered Ramona to be a demented person.

The priest had strong reservations about what he perceived to be the evil nature and intent of santería. He was also concerned about the increase in santería sites of worship (called centros in the Puerto Rican/Cuban/Dominican communities), which competed for members with the Catholic church. The social worker viewed Ramona's household conditions as "unacceptable": a deviant family style and child-rearing practices; use of welfare funds for herbs; many visitors; the presence of santería altars, and so on. Not long after, the Social Services Department challenged her parenting skills and removed the children from her care. She was subsequently examined by an Anglo psychiatrist who ordered her placed in a sanatorium, where she remained for six years. Her conversion to santería was diagnosed by the doctors as a psychological-psychotic problem.

After her release from the mental hospital, Ramona went back to santería and was initiated as a santera mayor (a high priest of santería). Her conversion to santería was diagnosed by the doctors as a psychological-psychotic problem. Today, she is an elder santera who heals the sick and comforts the dying. She also trains would-be santeros from as far away as Africa and Haiti.

Submitted by Jorge L. Chinea

POSSIBLE PERCEPTIONS
OF THE PRINCIPALS INVOLVED

The Physician and the Social Worker

The social worker initially, and subsequently the New York City Social Services Department, deemed Ramona's nightmares, precognitions, and related behaviors to be very abnormal and sufficient cause to consider her mentally ill. Being so defined made her an "inadequate mother," one unable to make a proper home for her children. Thus, they acted to remove the children from her care. After the removal of the children, the psychiatrist who examined her found her sufficiently disturbed to consign her to an institution for the mentally ill.

The Priest

The Catholic priest presumably was disturbed by Ramona's belief in and practice of *santería*. Such aberrant behaviors in an unfamiliar faith that was contrary to his religious orthodoxy enabled the priest also to consider Ramona not fully sane.

Ramona and Others Committed to *Santería*

Herbs have been known to be useful in treating some diseases. Prayers have seemingly led to the recovery of ill people and to give comfort to the dying. A belief in the presence and power of the spirits of the dead, who can be contacted for advice, enables *santeros* to use such guidance as they receive in relation to those in need. The syncretism of beliefs in the Caribbean area provides cultural support in maintaining the practices. Ramona, following her release from confinement in the institution, was able to gain greater knowledge of *santería,* attain a respected role within her community, and develop a practice in curing and comforting.

There is a list of questions concerning the perceptions outlined here in Appendix B: Questions That Might Be Asked.

Editors

Death is different in Mexico. Not biologically different, and not emotionally less stressful, but different in a way that Kübler-Ross would understand (Kübler-Ross, 1969). Elisabeth Kübler-Ross has delineated four categories of individuals who probably accept death more easily than others (Kübler-Ross, 1975). These people do not celebrate death joyfully, nor with less pain or suffering, but with more acceptance and more understanding.

FOUR FACTORS AFFECTING EXPERIENCE WITH DEATH

First are rural populations who come in contact with death daily and understand nature's way of "clearing" in order to replenish the earth with new life and opportunities. A country with a large rural population would also have that same understanding of coming and going, of replenishment that can only come after death has cleared the way. Mexico is by many standards still a rural country, and its population certainly understands the ritual cycle of birth and death.

The second category of people who seem to accept death with more equanimity consists of the very young who are innocent and who do not yet know what life is all about. In their gentle and trusting way they accept what happens to them, often not knowing the price to be paid. Mexico is a country of the very young, with a large percentage of its population under the age of 15 (Todaro, 1989, p. 196). It is a nation in which the exuberance of youth is evident everywhere. The loss of young lives is equally evident. We have taken groups of students to the small villages in Tlaxcala, where they have seen young children and infants die. We know that those deaths have not been the only deaths in a family, but often represent the third, fourth, or fifth victim. We realize this when we go to the gravesite with a family and see the names of children aged one year, six months, and three years old—all young children from the same family lying in small graves side by side.

The third category includes the very poor. Poor people constantly come into contact with death because their poverty puts them in continual jeopardy. They suffer from malnutrition and poor health care—if, indeed, they receive any care at all. The poor are also more likely to be involved in work that is dangerous and that often leads to tragic, accidental death. The very poor are exposed to death almost daily. They feel all the pain and the agony of death, but they are more accepting of it because death is a common occurrence in the poor urban ghettos or in extremely impoverished rural communities. The constancy of this contact with death does not lessen the sorrow surrounding loss; it simply makes it more familiar. When we are more familiar with something, we are more accepting of it.

The fourth category is one that may be more familiar to people in the First World: those who are religious. Whether a very religious person believes in one of the world's great religions or another, less widely known faith, some studies suggest that he or she may be prepared to accept death with more equanimity. To a genuinely religious person, death is all in the scheme of things. God, or the gods, or nature, or whatever life and death forces are believed in, exist for a purpose. Their existence is necessary to achieve the continual destruction and replenishment of the earth. Many religious people believe in an afterlife. They believe that life is transient, a mere stage in one's existence. Sometimes it is a happy and fruitful stage, sometimes a stage of suffering, humiliation, or degradation to be endured. To such people, it is what comes after life that is important. Therefore, there is an easier acceptance of death and the need for death along with the concept of a transition that brings one to a greater or more exalted state of being.

These four categories delineated by Kübler-Ross—the very poor, the rural, the very young, and the religious—coexist in Mexico. Poverty is no stranger there, nor has it been in the past. Mexico has been and is still a rural country, although it is developing very rapidly and becoming increasingly urbanized. It is also a country populated mainly by the young. Catholicism is extremely important in Mexico, especially among poor, rural, and very young people. These four categories, then, provide us one of several frameworks within which to examine Mexico.

DEATH CONSIDERED AGAINST A HISTORICAL BACKGROUND

It is important to examine the historical reality, both before and after the Spanish Conquest. A visit to the Anthropological Museum in Mexico City brings the visitor face-to-face with statues of death squatting or standing, in murals or in bas-reliefs, in the rooms that house pre-Columbian art. (Just one example of the statues of death to be found at the museum is the *totonaco,* dated between A.D. 600 and 900.) Obviously, death was a very familiar figure for the Aztecs, the Mayas, and other pre-Columbian groups.

Any student of Mexican history knows that the Aztecs practiced ritual human sacrifice. Aztec pyramids have at their apex a place where priests would cut out a live victim's heart and sacrifice it to the god of the sun. Other body parts would then be thrown down off the pyramid. There are ruins in Mexico where lines of skulls appear in bas-relief along buildings and on murals. The Aztecs were a warlike people and they made a ritual out of death. Shedding blood in the act of killing, and then smearing it on the hair and on the faces of the priests who performed these rites, were part of the bizarre aftermath of the wars the Aztecs waged against their neighbors. There were knights of these Wars of the Flowers, as they were called, and ritual human sacrifices always followed the fighting. Some say the reclining Chocmol figures were meant to be the recipients of these recently beating, torn-out hearts.

While the Aztecs made a cult of death, they also believed that a dog would transport the souls of the dead to the afterlife. Interestingly, in Greek mythology, the dog Cerberus guarded the gates of Hades, while continents away, the Aztecs, too, associated dogs with death. The Buñuel film, *Los Olvidados,* for example, ends with a barking dog and the death of the young protagonist.

In pre-Columbian times, a little yellow flower (not unlike our marigold) had also been associated with death. One would not want to give a Mexican person marigolds (they call them the *zempasuchitl*), because the belief still persists that yellow flowers are associated with death. The Aztecs used this little yellow-orange flower to decorate graves, often in very elaborate designs. The Mexicans still use the *zempasuchitl* to adorn graves by drawing figures and writing names out of flowers. These flowers traditionally are also strewn all over the house of a family that has suffered a death during the past year. They can be used to make a pathway from the home to the cemetery where the dead one is buried (Toor, 1947). "After the grave is filled, it is covered with *zempasuchitl,* the yellow flowers of the dead since before the Conquest." (Toor, p. 164).

Thus, death rituals that included the symbol of the dog, use of the *zempasuchitl* flower, the presence of skulls, the exhibition of dead victims' bodies, making of sacrificial offerings, and displays of blood all were involved in the elaborate ceremonies of killing thousands of people at one time, many of whom were captives in war. The people of this region of the New World were very familiar with the concept of death and faced it in a dramatic and visually violent way. Many in our culture would pale at the very sight of blood, especially smeared over a priest's head and hair. They certainly would be faint of heart were they to view the opening of the chest and the extraction of the still-beating heart from a victim. Without doubt, a considerable amount of stamina, acceptance, and tolerance of pain, violence, and death, would be required for a person to be able to confront, or participate in, those Aztec rituals.

When the Spaniards arrived, they were shocked by what they saw. However, they, too, brought with them their own religious attitudes and rituals. Although the Spaniards were scandalized by Aztec practices, as orthodox Catholics they regularly paraded statues of Christ through the streets with blood flowing freely from the thorn wounds on his head, the sword thrust into his side, and the nails pounded into his hands and feet upon the cross. Surely the Aztecs who beheld these figures of Christ and other martyrs on public display must have felt that they were seeing elements in the new religion that were familiar to them. We need only turn to the letters of Cortez written during the Conquest to find his analysis of the bloody Aztec rituals, and to Bernal Diaz del Castillo's account of the Conquest (1986), in order to realize how Catholicism blended with the Aztec and other local religions. This blending was facilitated by certain common denominators. One of these that cannot be overlooked was the idea of martyrdom—whether it was the martyrdom of Catholic saints or the martyrdom of victims of the Aztec Wars of the Flowers. (It is important to realize that death was the *reward* for the *winning* team playing *pelota* or ball games on sacred occasions.) Here is a historical perspective that must not be disregarded, one that involves the pre-Columbian Aztec rituals just as completely as the Catholic rituals that came to the New World from the Old.

SOME CONTEMPORARY EXPERIENTIAL CONTACTS WITH DEATH

In Mexico City's El Prado Hotel the beautiful mural by Diego Rivera used to be on display. (It has since been moved to a building across the Alameda because of an earthquake.) In that mural, which depicts the history of Mexico, Death stands in the middle, wearing a feather shawl (which is in the form of a snake) and a stylish hat. Death in this particular case is a woman, and she is "all decked out," taking a walk through the Alameda Park across from the Prado. Death is definitely the center of attention. That always disturbed our North American students who sat in front of the fresco and could not understand why the figure had such a prominent position. Furthermore, Death was on the arm of Diego Rivera, the artist himself, who was certainly not rejecting her. In fact, he was courting her, walking through the park with her, celebrating her, giving her center stage.

How can we explain this to a North American who is not used to seeing skeletons walking through the park on the arm of a very attentive admirer? It is due to the Mexicans' cultural familiarity with death, a familiarity that may come from poverty, religious faith, rural life, historical experience, or from all of the above. Indeed, it *must* be from all of the above.

DAY OF THE DEAD

A second experience that faces North Americans going to Mexico are the many paper designs that have been cut out of very thin tissue paper and hung in the middle of the streets. Travelers to Mexico during October and November will also see an abundance of skeletons, tiny coffins, death masks, and especially the candy *calaveras* or skulls. This is the season for the celebration of death, which again represents a wedding of two historical realities: the pre-Columbian Day of the Dead and All Souls' Day on the Catholic calendar. (October 31st is All Hallows' Eve, or Halloween; November 1st is All Saints' Day; and November 2nd is All Souls' Day.) One sees these paper designs of Death dancing, Death playing the guitar, Death doing anything that the living do. The paper cutouts in many different sizes are everywhere, making it impossible for visitors to escape a confrontation with Death in any shop or on any street corner.

The third experience that brings one face-to-face with death is more startling: the disinterred bodies that are on public view in Guanajuato, Mexico. It is believed that the ground in the cemetery there contains specific chemicals that preserve bodies. There are also very few opportunities in Guanajuato to bury people in the ground, and so they build cubicles or niches in which to place the coffins of the dead. These niches are rented, but only for a certain number of years. When those years are up, the dead one is removed to make room for a new corpse. Survivors hope that the body will have "disappeared," that is, disintegrated, or that, at most, only the bones will be there. However, because of the unusual conditions, these dead ones are often well-preserved and mummified. The bodies, dressed, or in winding sheets, are propped up against both sides of a narrow hallway. Visitors from other cultures often find this a grotesque, existential experience.

DEATH CONCEPT IN MEXICAN LITERATURE

There is a wonderful book called *La Vida Inútil de Pito Pérez*, or *The Useless Life of Pito Pérez* (Romero, 1970). In this book, a kind of modern picaresque novel, the protagonist, Pito Pérez, does not have much luck with women. One woman whom he falls in love with marries someone else, another cheats on him, and so on. Finally, Pérez decides that the only true love of his life is the skeleton of a female that has been hanging in the doctor's office for years. One night, he slips in unseen and takes her out and woos her. He takes the skeleton home with him and sleeps with her, telling us that she is the best woman he has ever had. After he decides that he must go on a trip with her, they board a train and travel together. He can not understand why other people look at him strangely. It is a delightfully funny and bittersweet relationship which Pérez finally has to abandon because too many people protest—although there are some people who accept it. And the very fact that it occurred to the author to include among the protagonists in his book a willowy skeleton wooed, seduced, and stolen by Pito Pérez for his pleasure and consolation is significant in itself, as is the book's great popularity.

DEATH AND THE *MACHO*

Octavio Paz is a writer who has tried to examine the Mexican reality from a more sociological perspective in his book *The Labyrinth of Solitude: Life and Thought in Mexico* (Paz, 1961). Death for Paz is an omnipresent reality. He talks about the need to confront death, the need not to be afraid, the need to always be ready to die, and the need to never give in, but rather to welcome death whenever it comes, whatever its form, and whatever the reason.

Paz tells us about the *macho*, the person who above all must be brave. The *macho* may be wearing a mask behind which fear lurks, but that mask, that exterior, is what is supposed to be real for the *macho*. (Although *macho* simply means male in Spanish, the connotation is more complex.) A *macho* is quite different from a Don Juan, who merely seduces. The *macho* must violate. He must intrude. He must bring one close to death, if not introduce one to death itself. The macho must be violent, and violence that is not afraid of death is violence that can kill. The Mexican male is angry. Paz would say he is angry because of the Conquest, angry because an Aztec woman named La Malinche was a traitor who caused the defeat of the native civilizations. It was she who gave Mexico up to be violated by Cortez. That violation, that willingness of the woman to capitulate, surrender, and aid the conqueror must be revenged and punished violently. For Paz this partly explains the need men feel for violence against women as well as against other men who are perceived as conquerors. Both must be confronted over and over again, always fearlessly and with a readiness for death.

Many stories are told in which Mexican males confront death courageously, albeit violently. The *macho* would pillage and rape, would defile and desecrate, would destroy, would always give death its due. The Mexican male would not be afraid to drink, offer a drink, drink, offer another drink, until the one who could not sustain the invitation would be weakened and humiliated. Then the knives come out, or the guns, or whatever other form of confrontation is available. In the aftermath, in a Tlaxcalan case known to us, a man was found in a barranca with his throat slit and his body covered with wounds. Death could have come at the end of a drinking bout, a fight, or a confrontation over a woman. But death would always come.

DEATH AND POVERTY

B. Traven was not a Mexican, but he wrote many books in Spanish while he lived in Mexico. One of those books, *Macario* (Traven, 1960), is the story of a poor man living in a rural area. He gains his livelihood by picking up twigs and wood to sell for firewood. He is very poor and has many children to feed. He prefers to starve himself and spend what little money he earns on food for his family, however meager that food might be. As he grows thinner and thinner, and hungrier and hungrier, he has an overwhelming wish to eat an entire turkey, and talks about that wish constantly with his wife. Finally, she steals a turkey and prepares it for him because she loves her husband so much that she wants to give him what his obsession demands.

Macario takes the turkey into the fields to eat by himself, and there he is visited by the Devil, who tries to tempt him, and then by God, who tries to get him to share the turkey with Him, and finally by Death. Macario is able to turn the Devil and God away, but he does invite Death to eat with him, saying that at least he knows that while Death and he are eating, Death will be too occupied to take him away. Death is again a protagonist, a friend, one with whom a meal can be shared, even though it may be one's last. Macario and Death talk and eat and talk some more. It isn't until the end of the book that the reader learns that actually half of the turkey was never touched. Death, not needing nourishment, had not eaten his half. Macario ate his half of the turkey and died at the moment that Death came to sit with him. Even a non-Mexican like Traven understood the cultural importance of death.

Our group of students was twice involved in the process of making bread for the Day of the Dead in the pueblo Zumpango, Tlaxcala. The shapes are different; each village has a characteristic *pan de los muertos*. The bread is one of the important items on the menu when one prepares the meal to be taken to the cemetery. This meal is left on the grave of the loved ones. Their spirits are expected to come out and eat the food. After the spirits have satisfied their hunger, the family either takes home what is left behind, or eats it there in the cemetery. This practice varies from village to village. Often there is a big picnic in the cemetery with candles and flowers. The *zempasuchitl* flower is featured prominently. Thus, the family, which includes both the living and the dead, dines and communes together.

DEATH EXPRESSED IN FAMILY, RELIGION, AND SOCIETY

Death, then, is present everywhere in Mexico. It is in the literature, on murals, in cutout paper figures, and on the streets. It is a historical reality one is aware of when visiting the pyramids or the museums. It is an everyday occurrence in poor and rural areas. Death is seen as a companion, or sometimes as a lover. Death is omnipresent and a part of life. Sometimes death is viewed as a woman, and sometimes it is a man. There is no gender preference. Death is death. And it must always be included as a part of the Mexican reality.

Death and bereavement in Mexico today and among Mexican Americans, whether in a rural or an urban setting, generally follow the pattern of the orthodox Catholic service. Everything possible is done to bring a priest to the bedside of the dying person in order to administer the last rites. Funeral arrangements are made as quickly as possible, because a prompt burial is desirable. The Catholic church does not encourage cremation. Friends and relatives in rural areas will come to the home of the deceased where the body lies in state. The casket will be set atop a table or on a stand, underneath which herbs and candles will burn, creating an aroma not unlike incense.

If the wake is held in an urban setting, it is more likely that the body will be on view in a mortuary. The ceremony in the church follows the usual ritual pattern. The priest will say kind words for the deceased. Family members will be there to mourn. All the friends, the extended family, and the extended community make every effort to be there for the funeral ceremony. An openly emotional response to death is expected. No one is ashamed to cry and to freely express their grief. Children are socialized early to accept death in a very informal way. They are trained and expected to be part of the wake and of the church service. They also go with their parents to the burial site for yet another ceremony. When the body is lowered into the grave, relatives will often take a handful of earth and throw it on top of the casket before the men from the cemetery come to fill in the grave. Novenas are said during the nine-day period following the death. People take candles to church to light at the altar. Prayers for the departed person are said, and every effort is made to console the grieving family.

Mexicans and Mexican Americans give great importance to family and family life, especially when a death occurs. The extended family is united, often in a way that it may not have been united for years before the death happened. In rural areas, where the body is viewed inside the family home, drinks are served, and people talk and chat. Not much ado is made over the body itself; the body is simply present. People may occasionally go and look at the deceased, but for the most part they are talking and socializing, with the children running about. It is not unusual to remember the dead one and talk about his or her activities and interactions with family and friends. It is very much like a wake in most other parts of the world: an occasion to bring the family together in sorrow, to foster informal socializing, and to renew friendships and family ties.

The emotional response in Mexico is perhaps more open and demonstrative than it is in the United States. The casket is always accompanied to the gravesite at the *camposanto,* or cemetery. People may stay there longer than they do in the United States. They will walk about the cemetery and look at other graves, reminisce, and remember who died and when and from what cause. Then all the family and friends will walk back to the village, if it is a rural area, or will drive back to the home of the family in the town or city.

Increasingly, the Mexican treatment of death is becoming more like the traditional orthodox service that is performed in Catholic churches worldwide.

REFERENCES

Del Castillo, B. D. (1986 reprint). *The discovery and conquest of Mexico, 1517–1521* (A. P. Maudslay, Trans.). Cutchogue, NY: Buccaneer Books.

Kübler-Ross, E. (1969). *On death and dying.* New York: Macmillan.

Kübler-Ross, E. (1975, March 13). Putnam Lecture in Social Ethics, "Ethical approaches to the acceptance of death." Hamline University, St. Paul, MN.

Paz, O. (1961). *The Labyrinth of solitude: Life and thought in Mexico.* New York: Grove.

Romero, J. R. (1970). *La vida inútil de Pito Pérez.* Mexico City: Editorial Porrua.

Todaro, M. P. (1989). *Economic development in the third world* (4th ed., p. 196). New York: Longmans.

Toor, F. (1947). *A treasury of Mexican folkways* (p. 164). New York: Crown.

Traven, B. (1960). *Macario.* S. R. Wilson (Ed.). Boston: Houghton-Mifflin.

BIBLIOGRAPHY

Beimler, R. R., & Greenleigh, J. (1991). *The days of the dead (Los Días de los Muertos).* San Francisco: Collins.

Brodman, B. (1976). *The Mexican culture of death in myth and literature.* Gainesville, Florida: University of Florida Press.

Dancigers, O. (Producer), & Buñuel, L. (Director). (1984). *Los Olvidados* [Film]. Clasa Films Mundiales. Macmillan Films, Inc. [Video, English subtitles].

Eames, Charles and Ray (Producers and Directors). (1957). *Day of the Dead* [Film]. Waltham, MA: Film & Art Programs.

El Dia de los Muertos "The Day of the Dead" [Audiotape]. Baltimore: American Public Radio—WJHU.

Fuentes, C. (1964). *The death of Artemio Cruz.* New York: Farrar, Straus & Giroux.

Green, J. S. (1972). The days of the dead in Oaxaca, Mexico: An historical inquiry. *Omega, 3,* 245–261.

Hellbrom, A. B. (1971). The All Saints' cult in Mexico. *Tememos, 7,* 58–63.

Jordan, T. G. (1980). *Texas graveyards: A cultural legacy.* Austin: University of Texas Press.

Kalish, R., & Reynolds, D. K. (1981). *Death and ethnicity: A psychocultural study,* pp. 155–184. New York: Baywood.

Kelly, I. T. (1965). *Folk practices in northern Mexico: Birth customs, folk medicine, and spiritualism in the Laguna Zone.* Austin: University of Texas Press.

Kelly, P. F. (1975). Death in Mexican folk culture. In D. Stannard (Ed.), *Death in America.* Philadelphia: University of Pennsylvania Press.

Lewis, O. (1969). *A death in the Sánchez family.* New York: Random House.

Gavaldor, R. (Director). (1984). *Macario* [Film]. Madera, CA: Madera Cinevideo. Clasa Films Mundiales. (Spanish edition.)

Menget, P. (1968, January). Death in Chamulo. *Natural History, 77,* 48–57.

Moore, J. A. (1970). The death culture of Mexicans and Mexican Americans. *Omega, 1,* 271–291.

Moore, J. A., & Pachon, Harry. (1985). *Hispanics in the United States.* Englewood Cliffs, NJ: Prentice-Hall.

Nash, J. (1967). Death as a way of life: The increasing resort to homicide in a Maya Indian community. *American Anthropologist, 69,* 455–470.

Osuna, P., & Reynolds, D. K. (1970). A funeral in Mexico: A description and analysis. *Omega, 1,* 240–269.

Otero, G. G., & Harris, Z. (1980). *Death: A part of life [Day of the dead].* Denver: University of Denver, Center for Teaching International Relations.

Padilla, E. (1958). *Up from Puerto Rico,* pp. 275–300. New York: Columbia University Press.

Puentes, T. (1991, October). El día de los muertos. *Hispanic,* 28–29.

Rogler, L. H., & Hollingshead, A. B. (1961, July). The Puerto Rican spiritualist as a psychiatrist. *American Journal of Sociology, 67,* 17–21.

Saunders, L. (1954). *Cultural difference and medical care: The case of the Spanish-speaking people of the Southwest.* New York: Russell Sage.

Chapter Six

Hmong Death Customs: Traditional and Acculturated

Bruce Thowpaou Bliatout

Illustrative Episode

A much-beloved Head Start teacher developed pneumonia and succumbed to a stroke. During her December illness she received from the school a get-well card shaped like a Christmas tree. Ornaments made from photographs of her 36 Head Start pupils—more than 20 of whom were Hmong—hung from the branches. Her family, aware of the affection the teacher felt for the children, decided to place the card in the casket before the teacher was buried in a local cemetery.

However, Hmong parents demanded that the pictures of their children be removed and returned, believing that their children would otherwise be susceptible to later misfortunes and an early death because the pictures separated them from their spirits. Further, they indicated that their children would not return to participate in Head Start until the photographs were recovered. The Lao Family Community executive stated, "If you are alive but your picture or hair or some other thing from the body is buried, it causes your spirit to leave your body."

Thus, about three weeks later, the woman's body was exhumed so that the photographs could be recovered. A "spirit calling ceremony" was then performed, using an egg, rice, and incense to lure the spirits out of the grave along with the pictures. Later, two further ceremonies were conducted. The spirits were called individually to each of the children's homes in a ritual using an egg and a live chicken. Finally, the chicken was killed and both the egg and the chicken were boiled and placed on a plate alongside the photo of the child from that home. A shaman then signaled the spirit to call it back.

Based on an article in the Minneapolis Star Tribune,
January 24, 1990.

POSSIBLE PERCEPTIONS
OF THE PRINCIPALS INVOLVED

Teacher's Family, Euro-American Friends, and Professional Staff

The Head Start teacher's occupation involved her daily in the nurture of those young children. The youngsters were beloved by her, and they developed affection for her as well. Thus, it seemed natural and appropriate for her family to place in her casket a class photograph of the children whom she had so recently taught and cared for. Sentimental items are often buried with deceased persons in the dominant American culture. Seemingly, this action was taken without either the family involved, the school administration, or professionals aiding with the funeral arrangements giving any thought to possible cultural differences.

Parents of the Children and the Hmong Community

For the Hmong, the inclusion of the pictures of their children in a class photograph buried with the teacher brought much anxiety. That act was genuinely believed by them to bring disgrace and dishonor to the children whose likenesses were involved. The parents felt that their children's future fortunes and good health would be affected undesirably. There is no evidence that the Hmong families had been consulted in advance and given an opportunity to express their concerns prior to the burial decision. Thus, after the fact, they felt they had no recourse but to request that the threat they felt to themselves and their children be removed, employing the leverage of nonparticipation in the Head Start program meanwhile.

There is a list of questions concerning the perceptions outlined here in Appendix B: Questions That Might Be Asked.

Editors

INTRODUCTION

The Hmong are an ethnic minority found throughout southern China, Vietnam, Laos, Thailand, and Burma. The earliest known reference to the Hmong is from the legendary Emperor U-Wang around 2700 B.C. (Quincy, 1988). Other references are in the Chinese Book of Documents from 2255 B.C. (Wilcox, 1986), and the Shu Ching or Chinese Classic of History during the time period of Yii the Great circa 2205–2198 B.C. (Chindarsi, 1976). There are other Chinese references to them, between the 12th and 17th centuries A.D. In the 18th century some Hmong migrated out of China into Vietnam, Laos, Thailand, and Burma, where Hmong communities remain today (Bliatout et al., 1988).

During the 1960s and 1970s, the Hmong of Laos became involved in political upheaval. Known for being resourceful, sturdy, and good fighters, many Hmong were recruited into the Royal Lao government's army, backed by the United States. In 1975, when the government of Laos changed hands, many Hmong were forced to flee that country for fear of their lives. Most Hmong fled first to Thailand. After a stay in Thai refugee camps, they were placed in a third country for resettlement. The United States has by far the largest number of Hmong refugees outside Asia.

There are an estimated 120,000 Hmong refugees now living in the United States, scattered throughout the country. Fairly large communities exist in the Central Valley of California as well as in the Twin Cities of Minnesota and in Wisconsin. There are smaller Hmong communities in many other cities.

Hmong have often been divided into several subgroups. The Chinese have referred to different groups: Flowery, Black, Red, and Blue Hmong (Quincy, 1988). Often these designations refer to some aspect of a group's attire. The Hmong of Laos, those in the United States, have two recognized subgroups: Green and White Hmong. While both are well able to understand each other, there are variations in speaking patterns as well as in dress. There are also variations in culture, related to the region of Laos they came from. Still, there is a strong feeling of being Hmong, compared to being non-Hmong, and inter-marriages are common between the subgroups.

HMONG TRADITIONAL RELIGION

The Hmong beliefs about death and afterlife are so closely entwined with the traditional Hmong religion that it is impossible to speak about them separately. The Hmong religious beliefs are a mixture of ancestor worship and animism. Traditionally, Hmong religious practices and rituals were handed down from father to son orally and by observation. Over time, regional, clan, and family variations developed. Though it is difficult to present a cogent theology of Hmong religion or clan rituals, broad outlines have some consistencies among most Hmong clans within the various regions.

The Hmong believe that a spiritual world coexists with the physical world. The spiritual world is inhabited by a wide variety of spirits, many of which can influence human life. Spirit types include ancestor spirits, house spirits, nature spirits, and evil spirits. Ancestor spirits include any deceased member of the family, and most Hmong believe that ancestors on the father's side of the family (either male or female ancestor spirits) can most influence the lives of their descendants.

House spirits are believed to inhabit the house of each Hmong. There are several varieties: four corner spirits (one for each corner of the house); two door spirits (one for each door of the house); two stove spirits (one for the small and one for the large fireplace usually found in a traditional Hmong house); a spirit that resides in the altar that most Hmong families have at the center of the house's back wall; and many others. It is also thought that ancestor spirits return to reside in the main pillar of the Hmong house.

There is a wide variety of nature spirits, ranging from powerful deities to lesser spirits that inhabit localized areas. The Hmong believe that all things in nature are inhabited by a spirit: mountains, trees, streams, valleys, caves, ponds, even wind currents. Evil spirits are also thought to live in nature, usually in uninhabited areas. However, they have malevolent feelings toward humans and may attack passersby or even come to attack a village for no apparent reason.

Supernatural beings are involved in almost every aspect of traditional Hmong life. A person is thought to be allotted time on earth by the Chief of Gods. It is believed that people receive a "visa" or "papers" to come to earth into a certain clan or family. There are many ritual activities, particularly during the season of the new year, that are performed to ascertain the will of the ancestors and to please the ancestors as well as nature spirits. It is thought that if the ancestors are pleased, they will protect their descendants from sickness, poverty, and bad luck. If nature spirits are pleased, they will protect against natural disasters such as drought, fire, earthquakes, landslides, or floods. The Hmong raise pigs, chickens, and some cows and buffaloes, many of which are used as ritual sacrifices to please the ancestors, as well as in birth, marriage, death, and other ceremonies. They are also sacrificed ritually during healing ceremonies because it is thought that most illnesses are caused by a variety of spirits.

GENERAL BELIEFS ABOUT DEATH

The Hmong strongly believe that proper burial and worship of ancestors directly influence the health, safety, and prosperity of the family. Thus, considerable effort goes into the funeral process. The general process itself is similar for all Hmong groups, but the way in which the gravesite is prepared and the specific rituals and ceremonies that take place after the funeral are individualized for each family line. Each extended family has a set of postfuneral ceremonies and rituals that must be performed strictly in accordance with the family rules. A wide variation exists between families and clans. In fact, Hmong families of the same clan differentiate the closeness of relationship by how similar their death rituals are. Those following exactly the same death rituals are considered closer than others, and are therefore entitled to more assistance and support.

Despite wide variation in some rituals, general customs and many beliefs about life and death are consistent among most traditional Hmong. They believe that when someone is born, she or he is taken from the spirit parents and inducted through ritual into the world of the living. When a person dies, she or he must be sent back to the spirit world to be with the ancestors. Souls of the recent dead can cause harm to the living if they are not sent back appropriately. Moreover, most Hmong believe that the remembered dead retain an interest in the living and can bring sickness if they want a sacrifice. It is crucial to give generous and appropriate sacrifices at the time of death as well as at the new year and other periodic times to ensure that the ancestors have plenty.

The Hmong believe that each person has several souls. There is regional variation in the number of souls each is thought to have, ranging from three to 32. A common belief is that each person has three major souls. Each of these souls has three shadow souls, which means nine shadow souls in all. Each person would then have 12 souls: three major souls and nine shadow souls. It is believed that at death, one major soul first returns to heaven and then comes back to watch over and guard the family. Some say it is this soul that returns to live in the main spiritual pillar of the home. The second major soul is thought to return to heaven later and eventually be reassigned to earth either as another human or as some other entity, depending on one's past actions and chance. The third major soul (some say this is only a shadow soul) is thought to remain at the gravesite (Bliatout, 1982).

In the perception of many Hmong people, life in human form is very desirable. It is thought that if one lives in an ethical and moral way, rebirth as a human will come sooner. If one does not live in a good way, she or he will accumulate karmic debts that will have to be paid. As a punishment, the person may be reassigned to earth as an animal or even a plant. Being reassigned as a rock is considered especially terrible because a rock never dies, and the soul may never be able to re-enter the world as a person.

Hmong infants are usually named and inducted into the world of humans on the third day of life. For any person who has died who has already been named, a funeral ceremony is held. The size of the funeral depends on the age and sex of the deceased and the status of the family. The older the person (for those who are male) and the wealthier the family, the more elaborate the funeral.

A person is not allowed to die in someone else's house, especially the house of someone who is not spiritually and blood-related. Should it happen that the person nearing death is in a distant relative's or a different clan's house, those in that household will wait until almost the last moment and then bring the person out into a hut in the yard to die. If a person from a different clan dies within someone's house, it angers the house spirits and they may withdraw their protection from the family and cause illness and/or misfortune. That is why most Hmong people insist on living with their family or at least with those of the same clan.

PREFUNERAL CUSTOMS

Some families with elders prearrange funeral activities for these respected family members. Others feel it is bad luck to preplan a funeral because this may somehow precipitate a death in the family. However, for those families who feel it is wise to prepare for a possible funeral, a major activity before a funeral is to pick an auspicious gravesite. This may take several months or years.

To pick a funeral site, some Hmong may consult a geomancer, one who has studied the art of divination by means of signs derived from the earth. Certain places on earth are considered more auspicious than others. Also, the direction in which the coffin is placed is thought to have an influence upon the future of the deceased's clan. All edifices should be arranged to be in harmony with nature in order to bring luck, health, wealth, prosperity, stability, and nobility to those remaining in the living world.

For families of greater wealth and status, the coffin may be purchased ahead of time. According to Hmong legend, there were originally only 12 Hmong clans. Each one buried their dead in a coffin made from a certain type of wood designated for their clan. If this was not done, the person would be reborn into the clan corresponding to the wood of the coffin the individual had been buried in. As Hmong clans increased in number, each clan chose a different wood for itself, through a specific ceremony and rituals.

The Hmong provide sets of clothes and animal sacrifices for the deceased to take with them to the spirit world. Wealthier families put aside specific sets of clothes and assign certain sons to be in charge of procuring appropriate animal sacrifices for elders in the family. A man must have at least a complete suit of Hmong clothes including a shirt, pants, and a special type of shoes made out of hemp. A woman must have at least one Hmong shirt and one Hmong skirt, turban, and set of leggings as well as shoes. The wealthier the family, the greater the number of complete sets of clothing that are put on the deceased person in the coffin and the greater the number of animal sacrifices that are provided. At least one chicken and a pig must be sacrificed, although oxen and buffaloes are preferred.

Lastly, some Hmong families will select some of those who will officiate. There are three key officials at any traditional Hmong funeral, as well as several other important participants. The three key officials include the guide to the spirit world (*tus qhuab ke*), the reed pipe player (*txib qeej*), and the descendant counselor (*tus txib xaiv*). These funeral officials may be selected from either inside or outside the clan. Most officials are males, who have learned their arts from elder males or through long experience in dealing with funerals.

The guide to the spirit world is the person who must come immediately after death and, through ritual and the recitation of various texts, guide the deceased's spirit from the world of humans to the world of spirits. The reed pipe player plays the Hmong reed instrument called the *qeej*. Various musical patterns are played through the *qeej,* and this ritual is considered necessary for the spirit to find its way and have a safe journey to the world of spirits. The descendant counselor, toward the end of the funeral, sings various songs and texts to the family that encourage them to accept the death, give guidance to the family in resuming their lives, and instruct each of them how to live a better and more healthy life.

As the time of death grows nearer, family members gather around the sickbed. They give comfort and tend to the needs of the dying family member and gain mutual support from each other. Later they will share the many duties a Hmong funeral entails. Family members and members of the community make great efforts to visit a person prior to the person's death. One of the important reasons for this is the belief that part of a dying elder's skills, abilities, and goodness will be imparted to those who are there at the time of death. Another reason family members come is that dying elders who are able to talk often pass on parts of the family oral tradition at this time. Others come to support the family of the dying, because the exchange of labor during funerals is one of the major reasons Hmong communities form and stay together.

HMONG FUNERAL RITUALS AND CUSTOMS

Immediately after a death, family members will wail and cry for some time. Soon after the death, a member of the family or of the village fires a gun three times. This announces to the village that there has been a death. Members of the family then bathe the deceased and dress the body in the funeral clothes already set aside. After the body is dressed, it is placed on the floor with the head perpendicular to and touching the main spiritual pillar of the house. The feet of the deceased must be pointing to the wall of the house that is nearest to the mountainside. If the deceased is a woman, four more gunshots are fired; if it is a man, six are fired.

If a decision has not already been made, the head of household and/or the elders of the family briefly discuss who they will ask to help perform the funeral. After the decision has been taken, members of the family are sent off to ask these persons for assistance. Males of the family are usually assigned this duty, and they must kowtow when asking for assistance.

The Funeral Helpers

The helpers mentioned below are all needed and are usually selected in the following order.

Guide to the Spirit World (*Tus Qhuab Ke*)   The guide to the spirit world can be a man of any clan who has studied and memorized the *Qhuab Ke* text, which is a series of verses. The Hmong believe that if the *Qhuab Ke* is not recited, the deceased will not know that he or she has died. The purpose of the *Qhuab Ke* is to help start the person's first major soul on its trip to the spirit world; it also itemizes those things that the family must provide the deceased's souls for making a successful trip and explains to the souls how to make the trip.

The guide must include mention of every place the deceased has lived. This information is provided by a family member and incorporated into the guide's recitation. This is to direct the deceased's souls step by step back to his or her birthplace, symbolically to obtain the individual's maternal shirt, meaning their placenta. A boy's placenta is buried next to the main spiritual pillar, while that of a girl is buried under the parents' bed in the house in which the child was born. Without symbolically obtaining the placenta, the deceased person's souls will not be able to return to the spirit world.

Reed Pipe Player and Drummer   The reed pipe player may be preselected. However, usually two persons able to play the reed pipes are necessary because they take turns playing the reed pipes and beating the funeral drum. When Hmong people hear the reed pipes and drum together, they can be certain a death has occurred. The reed pipes are vital to a successful Hmong funeral. Through the music of reed pipes, the souls of the deceased are guided through the whole journey from the world of the living to the world of the spirits. The reed pipe is the communication point between the living, the deceased, and the spirit world.

Funeral drums are passed down within families from father to son and are thought to have a special spirit residing within them. The funeral drum is very sacred and is used only at the time of a death. There is usually only one in a village, and families must ask to borrow it for the funeral. If there has been more than one death in the village at the same time, a drum from a nearby village must be borrowed or a temporary drum made for one-time use only, which is destroyed immediately afterward. The reed pipes and funeral drum are played almost continuously throughout the whole funeral process. Playing is a long and strenuous job, and sometimes others who know how to play the reed pipes and beat the drum may help.

Descendant Counselor   An elder who has memorized certain texts is selected and will sing these texts to the family during the evening on the day before the funeral. This function provides comfort and counseling for the living. A descendant counselor only recites his text at the funeral of an elder. Younger persons have less elaborate funerals and this activity does not take place. This helper is the only one to receive monetary payment from the family for the services.

Many other helpers may be appointed, depending on the occasion and the amount of resources the family of the deceased has.

1. A funeral director and an assistant are usually chosen quickly. They are coordinators who make sure that all the funeral tasks assigned to others are completed in a timely manner.

2. The stretcher and shoe makers are responsible for constructing a stretcher on which the deceased will lie from three to 10 days within the family home, depending on which auspicious day for burial is chosen. The stretcher is made from two long wooden poles with bamboo thatch forming the pallet. The stretcher symbolizes a horse for the deceased's souls to ride on the journey to the spirit world. Usually the same people make shoes for the deceased out of woven hemp, if these have not already been prepared. These special shoes turn up at the toe; without them, the souls will be unable to cross the big river, walk on treacherous paths, step over valleys of snakes and other living forms, and arrive at the spirit world.

3. The food server to the dead is a person trained in the recitation of certain verses that call the souls of the deceased to come and eat the family's food by using two small split bamboo sticks. The Hmong believe that the souls of the deceased still need to eat three times daily. When it is mealtime, the food server speaks to the deceased and tosses the sticks onto a piece of board next to the body's head. The souls must agree to accept the food. If the two sticks land either with both sides up or both down, there are no agreements; the deceased accepts the food only if one stick lands facing up and the other down. This ritual is performed three times daily until burial.

4. The warrior is charged with assisting the deceased's spirit on its trip to the spirit world. The trip is believed to be perilous, and the deceased will often have to struggle to make it through. The reed pipe player is the communication point between the deceased, the spirit world, and the family. The warrior will shoot arrows or fire his gun into the air and run around the house either seven or nine times, depending on the sex of the deceased. This action provides strength and support to the souls, enabling them to fight better.

5. Meat and vegetable chefs are needed to prepare food constantly and sufficiently for the family, friends, many helpers, and villagers who are there to attend the funeral.

6. Rice chefs are in charge of cooking only the rice needed for the family and guests during the funeral process.

7. Food servers serve the meals to all and clean up afterward.

8. Firewood gatherers procure firewood for the cooking stove and fireplace. In traditional villages there was little or no electricity.

9. Water carriers must ensure that water is available for the cooks and all others for drinking and washing. Water would have had to be carried from the nearest stream or well; so the task was time-consuming.

10. Rice pounders and corn grinders are needed to supply the cooks with enough corn and rice to feed everyone.

11. A light supplier makes sure that there are enough candles and/or oil to keep the home lighted. He remains up each night until the funeral is over.

12. The presider is a man not usually a member of the deceased's clan. He is selected to preside over any financial matters that have to be settled: debts the deceased may have incurred or debts owed him or her by others. If the former are not paid, the deceased will be poor in the next world. Or if a Hmong individual does not pay back a debt to someone deceased, that obligation continues into the next world, to be paid back there, or in the next life on earth.

13. Coffin makers must look for the right clan's tree to cut down and make planks for constructing the coffin, if one has not already been prepared. All Hmong coffins must be devoid of any metal; they must be made completely of the appropriate wood.

14. Sacrificial ox slayers, relatives of the deceased, will be chosen to kill an ox or oxen to be sacrificed. If an adult male has died, his sisters' husbands or his daughters' husbands will be asked to do the task. If an adult female has died, the deceased's brothers or the deceased's daughters' husbands will serve in this capacity.

A Hmong funeral may last from three to 10 days or more. By custom, the body of the deceased must lie in the family home for at least three days before burial. A funeral may last more than 10 days because the elders of the family must select an auspicious day for the actual burial. Usually a proper day can be selected within a two-week period. If the deceased is buried on an auspicious day, it is believed, the dead person will be prosperous in the spirit world, and descendants of the deceased will also be prosperous. Delaying the burial also gives time to send messages to faraway relatives to come and attend the funeral. By Hmong custom, it is considered absolutely necessary to inform the deceased's relatives of the death. Failure to let in-laws know of a death can cause rifts in family ties, because an in-law family that was not informed of a death has the right to fine the deceased's family should any future marriages occur between the two families. Among the Hmong in Asia, there were no telephones or cars, so communication and travel were very slow. Unfortunately, corpses often would begin to rot and become malodorous prior to burial. Sometimes the first auspicious day after the death will be passed by because the coffin is not yet made or the appropriate sacrificial animals have not yet been procured.

During the time the body lies in the home, there is much work for the family and helpers to do. After the deceased has been bathed, dressed, and laid by the main pillar, a chicken egg and some rice are boiled and cooked. The food server to the dead is summoned and he offers the chicken egg and rice to the deceased. Then the guide to the spirit world is summoned and he recites his text to help the first major soul start its trip to the spirit world. A chicken is then sacrificed and offered. The chicken is laid above the head of the dead person and it is thought that this chicken will accompany the soul to the other world. The liver of the chicken is specially cooked for the deceased and put into a food container that is laid on the floor next to the person's head and later hung on the wall nearby.

While the guide to the spirit world recites his text, the assigned family members and helpers hurry to make a stretcher and a pair of hemp shoes. When the shoes are completed, they are put on the deceased's feet.

After the guide's text is completed, the reed pipe player and the drummer come to provide the first song, which is a song of parting. Then a pig is sacrificed for the deceased. The family members and helpers prepare and eat the pork. This symbolizes the parting between the deceased and the living family members.

After the meal, the reed pipe player and drummer continue playing. The body is placed on the stretcher that symbolizes a horse, which the first major soul will use to ride to the spirit world. The stretcher is hung by strings to the back wall of the home, about chest high. An umbrella, a crossbow, a sword, and three balls of thread are also given to the deceased, to be used along the way to the spirit world. The journey to the spirit world is fraught with peril for the newly deceased. The umbrella is for use by the soul in case of rain or too much sun in the other world. The crossbow and sword will help the deceased to fight a way through; and the balls of thread are to throw into the mouths of man-eating stones to trick them into closing, which will permit the deceased to pass through certain dangerous paths on the way to the next world. The reed pipe player and the drummer are thought to guide the first major soul through all these hazards. The reed pipes and drums play continuously, no matter how long the wait is until the burial.

All other work ceases during the funeral process so that the various funeral tasks can be completed. While the reed pipes play, the funeral drum beats, the coffin is made, and the sacrificial animals are found and prepared, relatives may stand beside the corpse and cry. They may praise the deceased for the person's virtues, say how lonely they are, and how they worry that misfortune will fall upon them now that the deceased is no longer there.

Funerals provide long-separated families with opportunities for reunions to share news of each others' lives and villages. While friends and relatives arrive to help with the many chores, it is still the family's responsibility to make sure that enough resources are available to feed and house the many visitors. All visitors must be greeted and thanked by family members kowtowing two times. After greeting, everyone has something to eat.

DAY OF SACRIFICES

During the waiting period prior to burial, some animals may be sacrificed to feed the guests and family members. These animals are also offered to the deceased for spiritual consumption. However, the day before the actual burial special animal sacrifices are made specifically for the deceased to take to the spirit world. While the number and type of animal sacrifices vary according to the wealth and status of the family, in general there are certain expectations held by most Hmong. For example, a spouse usually provides an ox for a sacrifice. Every grown son should each provide an ox for his parent's funeral. Daughters are not expected to provide an ox, but occasionally they may pool their money and jointly provide an ox for their parent.

Only oxen or male buffaloes are used for sacrifices. Those with horns are preferred; cows are not used. Very poor families may substitute a pig for an ox, but this is frowned upon. For a person with many sons and daughters, many oxen may be sacrificed.

The day of sacrifices is the appropriate day for those selected to kill the oxen or other sacrificial animals to arrive at the home of the deceased. It is customary for them to provide gifts for the deceased and the deceased's family. These gifts include one or two cooked chickens and some alcoholic beverage which, after due ritual, will be consumed by the family and guests, some incense and paper money, which will later be burned for the deceased, and a length of white cloth which is tied to the stretcher where the corpse lies. There is an appropriate protocol for the presentation of these gifts. When the family bearing gifts approaches the borders of the village or the yard of the deceased's home, they shoot a gun into the air twice to announce their arrival. The family of the deceased, upon hearing the two shots, respond with another two shots into the air. The visitors are then greeted and escorted into the house. Their gifts are given to the funeral director, who passes them on to the appropriate elders of the family.

The funeral directors coordinate the activities surrounding the sacrifice of the oxen. Large wooden stakes placed in a cross position are made for each ox. The oxen are lined up in the front yard of the deceased's home. White strings are tied from the oxen and connected to the body of the deceased. After appropriate ritual, the designated persons kill each ox with an ax. Helpers come to divide and prepare the meat for distribution.

It is appropriate for the family of the deceased to divide the meat of the sacrificial oxen among family members and helpers. In general, chest meat and the left front leg of the ox, as well as three ribs, go to the killer of the oxen. Three ribs of every ox killed, plus a strip of meat cut from the chest, are given to the reed pipe player, drummer, and the owner of the drum. Remaining portions are consumed during the funeral process.

In the evening of the day of sacrifices, the descendant counselor will be called upon to recite his text to the immediate and extended family members. Visitors may also participate. This can be a time-consuming process and sometimes takes the whole night. Family members and visitors gather and listen to the counselor as he takes on the role of an elder or father of the family, giving guidance to the living. The content ranges from advice on how to work and study hard, how to live a moral and ethical life, and how to bring luck, prosperity, wealth, stability, nobility, and long life to the descendant family.

BURIAL DAY

It is not uncommon for the descendant counselor to sing all night until the morning of the burial day. After he completes his song, it is the appropriate time for the monetary affairs of the deceased to be settled. The presider coordinates the discussion of any claims that other clans may have regarding debts of the deceased and hears from those who owe the deceased money.

If a funeral site has not already been selected, the elders of the family will meet and select a site prior to the burial day. On the day of the burial, the male members of the family, along with helpers, carry the planks of the coffin with them and go to dig the gravesite. When the digging is completed, they return home so that they can join in the funeral procession.

All Hmong burials are conducted in the afternoon. It is culturally inappropriate to bury someone in the morning because (a) it is believed that the souls of the dead leave the body at sunset, and if the corpse is buried too early, the souls may return to bother the living; and (b) an auspicious time usually falls sometime in the afternoon. As midafternoon approaches, the funeral director sees to it that everyone needed is present. The reed pipe player, through long experience, knows when to start the funeral procession. He communicates with the family and guests that it is time to start the burial process. Family members cut the stretcher from the wall. Male members of the family are assigned to carry the stretcher with the deceased on it. The reed pipe player leads the procession. The funeral drum is tied onto the back of a man who carries it so that the drum, with its drummer following behind, can accompany the funeral procession. A girl, usually either a daughter or daughter-in-law of the deceased, is asked to carry a torch. She is the third part of the procession. Behind her come those bearing the deceased on the stretcher, the mourners, and the helpers.

As soon as the mourners come out of the house, the drum beating ceases and the drum is returned to its owners. Not far from the house the reed pipe player also stops playing. At this point in time, it is believed that the reed pipe player has concluded his task. The first major soul has already reached the land of ancestor spirits safely. However, there is considerably more ritual to deal with the second major soul. After the reed pipe player stops playing, the girl carrying the torch drops the torch and they both walk under the coffin and return home. This is thought to confuse the soul of the deceased so that it will not return home before appropriate ritual is safely completed.

About a third of the way to the grave, the food server to the dead, or some other elder, announces to the deceased, "Tomorrow morning you come here to get your food." About two-thirds of the way to the grave, the same person announces to the deceased, "Two days from now you come here to get your food." At the gravesite itself he announces, "Three days from now you get up and eat your food here." These statements are addressed to the second major soul.

At the burial site, before placing the body of the deceased in the coffin, the sons and/or close relatives must search the clothing and body of the deceased to make sure that there are no foreign objects. Because being buried with metal is believed to cause illness and bone disease to the descendants, any metal jewelry, pins, or nails must be removed. In addition, it is believed that if a deceased person is buried with either photographs of, or any item belonging to, a living person, this will cause severe illness and death to that person in a very short time. If it is suspected that foreign objects may have been buried with the body, the grave will be exhumed so that these objects can be removed. Exhuming graves is usually forbidden in Hmong culture so the search before burial is quite important.

After the search, the coffin is first lowered into the grave, then the body is placed in the coffin. The stretcher, which symbolizes a striped horse, is cut into two pieces so that the deceased cannot return home to take others back. Mourners gather around and say whatever last words they want to say to the deceased. Many pay their respects by kowtowing. Then helpers cover the coffin with dirt and place the pieces of stretcher over the grave.

The mourners then begin the trip back. At the place where the girl threw down the torch, family members have placed a bucket of water. All members of the funeral procession must wash their hands in this bucket to wash away any illness or misfortune they may have come in contact with by being near the deceased.

Upon returning to the home, guests are free to leave. However, many stay or come back in the evening to continue giving support and assistance to the family. There are some postfuneral events that traditional Hmong families conduct. Many extended family members stay to assist with these.

POSTFUNERAL ACTIVITIES

It is believed that the second soul of the body must remain with the body at least 13 days before being sent to join the first soul in the world of ancestors. This is considered an orientation time period for the deceased's soul, during which some assistance from the family is still needed. For the first three days after the burial, the family must prepare food for the soul of the deceased and bring it to the sites specified during the funeral procession. The food is offered every morning at the appropriate place and consists of whatever is customary for the family.

During these three days while the soul is newly inducted into the spirit world, it is feared that the soul may try to return and cause problems. To prevent this, the family makes three whips. Each whip is made from a peach-tree branch with an attached length of hemp rope. As darkness falls, the head of the household or an elder takes the three whips and waves them around all areas of the house, saying some ritual words. The whips are then taken out the front door in the direction of the funeral procession. They are stuck in the path to act as deterrents for the soul coming from the grave. It is believed that souls are afraid of peach-wood whips.

The third day after the burial is the day on which it is necessary to decorate the grave according to the rules of each family. Some families prefer to make a cairn by placing stones in certain patterns over the grave. Some families prefer to build a bamboo fence around the grave. It is very important to follow the rules of each family in doing this. The way in which Hmong families decorate their graves defines how closely related they are to each other. Families of the same clan who decorate their graves in exactly the same manner are considered very close both "bloodwise" and spiritually.

From the fourth to the 13th day, the soul is believed to be in an orientation period. In case the spirit does not yet know how to find food in the spirit world, an extra place is set at the dining table whenever the family eats, and the soul is invited to join the family for meals.

The 13th day marks the end of the orientation period and a ritual called The 13th Day End is performed. Early in the morning, a family elder visits the gravesite and ritually invites the soul of the deceased to return home. When the elder has returned home, a chicken is killed and offered to the soul of the deceased.

Following this ceremony, most families hold a soul releasing ceremony. That day is the earliest the soul releasing ceremony can be performed after the burial, but if the family so desires it can be delayed. However, it is believed that until this ceremony is performed, the second major soul cannot make its way to the world of ancestors to be rejoined with the first major soul. And until that happens, the deceased cannot receive a reassignment to earth.

If it is decided to conduct the soul releasing ceremony, most, if not all, of the earlier mentioned funeral officials and helpers must reassemble at the home of the deceased. This ceremony offers those family members who were unable to sacrifice an ox on the Day of Sacrifices a second opportunity to do so. If necessary, the soul releasing ceremony will last an extra day.

For the soul releasing ceremony a large mannequin (upper half only) is fashioned and clothed with traditional Hmong clothes. If the ceremony is for a man, a hat is placed on the head; if it is a woman, a turban is used. The mannequin is placed on a large plate woven of bamboo. An elder invites the soul of the deceased to return to the home, and it is thought that the soul comes to reside in the mannequin. A chicken is killed and portions offered to the mannequin. Pieces of the chicken and rice are offered to the mannequin three times during the course of the day.

The reed pipes and funeral drum again play for the whole day. Now the musical pattern of the reed pipes is to help free the soul of any worldly concerns in preparation for leaving and rejoining the first soul in the world of ancestors. Towards the late afternoon, when the hour is auspicious, the reed pipes player and the funeral drum again lead the mourners out of the house. This time the destination is towards the nearest small hill or slope in the road. The mannequin is removed and the plate carried to the hill and bowled down it. The plate must roll at least three complete rolls and fall face down or must be done again. The complete rolls with the plate falling face down symbolizes the soul's acceptance of leaving for the spirit world. This ends of funeral process.

APPROPRIATE BEHAVIOR AFTER A DEATH

Immediately after a death, all work in the family ceases until the burial. During the 13-day period following the burial, it is acceptable to return to the fields to work. However, women should not do women's work such as embroidery and cutting cloth in the house. This type of work symbolizes rough and slippery roads for the deceased's soul. At the end of the 13-day period, normal work in the family can resume and it is no longer necessary to invite the soul of the deceased to share meals with the family.

In general, it is considered best if those who have lost a spouse or a parent refrain from getting married for at least six months, although a year is preferred. The longer a widow or widower stays unmarried, the more highly she or he is respected. In Hmong communities where polygamy was accepted, the exception to this was when a widow planned to be remarried to a younger brother or younger cousin from the same clan of her late husband. In Hmong culture this often was done to keep the woman and children within the clan.

After the death in the family, descendants may occasionally offer incense and burn paper money for the deceased. At the new year there is much ritual involving the ancestors and some sacrifices may be made then for the deceased. When facing a situation of danger, family members may call upon an ancestor for assistance and offer a sacrifice—usually a chicken, pig, or ox—if this assistance is received. When illness strikes the family, it may be thought to represent an ancestor needing something in the spirit world, and a shaman may be called to negotiate a sacrifice to the ancestor.

DEATH EDUCATION

Funerals are a part of normal village life and children participate in all aspects of funeral activities to the extent that their age and abilities allow. In general, Hmong society, being patriarchal in nature, puts more emphasis on male youths learning how to conduct and perform the many funeral ceremonies and rituals. Each extended family encourages younger generation males with the aptitude to study some aspect of the funeral rites. Some are encouraged to learn the text of the guide to the spirit world; some learn how to be a descendant counselor; others to be a funeral director; yet others learn to play the *geej* and the drum. The *geej* can take several years to master, and there are different levels for the apprentice to learn. A few special individuals may learn all aspects of the Hmong funeral, but this is rare. Some may serve as apprentices under others who have mastered a particular text. In most cases, the older generation teaches the younger at no cost. However, it is customary to pay a fee to a descendant counselor for him to teach the text to another. Often, if a teenager or child shows aptitude in learning a particular funeral text, he is sent to observe another funeral rite to gain knowledge and experience.

All males are taught how to find the appropriate trees to provide the coffin wood for their clan. Each male child also learns the special way to decorate and prepare the grave. This aspect of funerals is very important because conforming to the family rules for a gravesite defines membership in the Hmong extended family. Most males are also taught which areas are considered auspicious to have as gravesites, and which hours and days are auspicious as well.

Most other aspects of the funeral activities are learned by observation and participation in village funerals. There are set protocols for almost every aspect of what happens at a funeral, including how to greet guests, how to appropriately thank funeral attendees and those who bring gifts, how to announce that food is ready to be served, and so on. Girls and women learn how to behave and help in funeral activities through watching and helping their mothers and aunts. Much of the cleaning, cooking, and caring for the family and guests falls upon the women, under the direction of the funeral director and the family elders. Through constant exposure from childhood to adulthood, the Hmong funeral customs become ingrained in Hmong youth, which is how they have been transmitted from generation to generation.

HMONG ACCULTURATION

The Hmong in the United States at the present time have had no choice but to adapt their funeral process. In general, it has been drastically shortened because they have been forced to utilize the services and time frames of funeral homes rather than hold the funeral in their own homes as they did in Laos or other countries in Asia. There are some issues that cause concern to many Hmong who follow their traditional religion.

Most Hmong in the United States now die in hospitals. Many are subjected to autopsy as required by law. This is considered one of the most horrible things that can happen to a Hmong person, as it is believed that the person will be born mutilated in the next life. Also, the souls of the person may become unhappy and come back to cause illness to the remaining family members and their descendants. Hmong also dislike embalming, which alters the natural state of the body and may also cause future misfortune.

When death occurs in a hospital, the Hmong can no longer have access to the body. They cannot wash and dress it, nor can they hang the body on a stretcher. Without a stretcher, it is believed that there will be no horse in the next world. The sacrifices of the egg, chicken, and pig are delayed or deleted. The recitation of the text of the guide to the spirit world is delayed until the body of the deceased is transferred to the funeral home. Most of the time the guide to the spirit world's text, which normally lasts three hours or more, is shortened to an hour or so. This is considered incomplete.

In many cases the reed pipes and funeral drum are not allowed to be used for fear that they will disturb the neighbors. The sacrifice of oxen cannot be carried out appropriately. If it is done, it is in secret at home or at a farm, for it is feared that neighbors or public health officials may not approve. In several instances, when landlords or neighbors have seen Hmong families using live animals for spiritual or religious sacrifices, they have called the police. In one case, the police officer and public health officer confiscated a sacrificial pig from a Hmong family and never returned it. Another time, a landlord became very angry at his Hmong tenants because they had stained the carpet during an animal sacrifice. He ripped the carpet out and forced the tenants to pay for a new carpet. Shortly after that he evicted them. And, of course, firing guns must also be given up.

Because of fire codes, paper money and incense may not be burned at most funeral homes. This is a big concern, for Hmong believe that if this is not done the deceased's soul may be poor in the next world and will come back to ask for money from the family, thus causing illness to family members.

Most Hmong feel that the amount of time a funeral home normally allows for a funeral is not nearly enough time for them to complete the many ceremonies that are needed. Most funeral homes allow about three hours, and the Hmong must squeeze up to 10 or more days of ritual into that time. Although it is sometimes possible to rent the funeral home for longer hours, it is not possible to do so for several days at a time. Funeral homes do not permit all-night services, so both these and early-morning rituals cease.

The coffins that are available in the United States also cause distress for many Hmong traditionalists. First, the specific types of wood for each clan are not readily available, and the types of wood normally used for coffins in the United States are unknown to the Hmong. In addition, the Hmong strongly believe that coffins must be entirely made of wood, because the bodies buried with metal, even nails and needles, will be reborn with diseased bones. American-made coffins have many nails and screws. To the Hmong, these would not only have negative effects upon the deceased's soul but also upon the family's descendants.

As time passes, more and more Hmong have learned how to preselect a gravesite. However, in the United States, geomancy is not taken into consideration, and the selection of available cemeteries is not always in areas appropriate for the Hmong to use.

One major concern for many Hmong is the time of day at which the burial occurs. It is bad enough that it is difficult to choose an auspicious day for the funeral—that is usually decided for them by the schedule of the mortuary. It is also very important for the burial to occur at an auspicious hour in the afternoon. Even if the auspicious hour is not possible, the burial should at least be after the sun has reached its zenith. At times, Hmong funerals have been scheduled in the mornings and this has caused much distress.

To avoid illnesses and misfortunes for family members, including future descendants, a cairn must be built or the grave must be decorated according to family line specifications. U.S. cemetery rules and regulations also prevent the Hmong from carrying out this tradition.

The rituals normally conducted during the 13 days after burial can still be done in the privacy of their homes, including the soul releasing ceremony. However, the rolling of the woven bamboo plate is also difficult to accomplish. When it is not done, many Hmong are concerned, as they are unsure whether or not the deceased's soul has actually agreed to return to the spirit world. It is only this last final act of seeing the plate fall face downward that assures the family that the soul is returning to the ancestors' world and that the funeral process is truly over.

In summary, the major adaptation that the Hmong in the United States have made in regard to their funerals is to give up or shorten many of the rituals normally performed prior to burial and a few of the rituals following the burial.

HMONG CHRISTIANS

There is currently a sizable percentage of Hmong refugees who have converted to some form of Christianity, undergoing a great deal of acculturation in religious and funeral practices. Hmong Christians have more readily adapted to the dominant American funeral customs.

However, Hmong Christians still retain many aspects of the traditional funeral customs. There is still the obligation of informing all of the deceased's family of the death. Relatives and friends still gather at the home of the deceased to give moral and physical support. Often, instead of the traditional recitation of texts, they will sing religious hymns and pray together. The family still assigns individuals to coordinate aspects of the funeral. Chefs are still selected and guests are still served food and drink after being greeted and thanked by the relatives. There is no kowtowing, however.

In many cases, the family of the deceased may decide to slaughter an animal for consumption during the funeral process. However, this action is taken not for sacrificial purposes but only for practicality. Many Hmong families feel this is a more economical way to feed the many friends and relatives who come to visit. If the relatives are non-Christians, they may offer whatever oxen or other animals the family may want to contribute. But out of respect for the religion of the deceased, most Hmong choose not to do this. Yet it is not uncommon for Christian Hmong families to accept some small financial contribution or gift of food from friends and guests.

While there is no need to offer the deceased food, many Hmong families still dress the deceased for burial in traditional Hmong clothes, including the special shoes used for this occasion. After the funeral they will return to the family home to give whatever assistance is needed. While the Hmong Christians no longer require special wood for their coffins, they still prefer that there be no nails or other metal in them. They often still like to consult with a geomancer in selecting a gravesite and to decorate their graves as their families have done in the past—but with the addition of a cross to denote that the person was a Christian.

Hmong Christians feel that they can die in another family's or clan's house, for they all believe and practice the same religion. Currently, the numbers of Hmong Christians are small and there are no major subdivisions in the group. Hmong Christians throughout the United States feel a bond with each other and are usually willing to help other Hmong Christians to the best of their ability.

Other adaptations of traditional Hmong beliefs regarding deaths and funerals include the belief that the person has only one soul and that this soul will go to heaven to be with God rather than being reborn. This being the case, the rituals of the guide to the spirit world, the descendant counselor, and the soul releasing ceremony are no longer needed, nor is it necessary for the reed pipes nor the funeral drum to play. Thus, Hmong Christians generally have a simpler service and funeral process than those who follow more traditional ways.

Hmong Christians and non-Christians still aid each other with funerals, however. They help in almost all aspects of the funeral except those specifically related to rituals and sacrifices (most Hmong Christians prefer not to eat the meat from sacrificial animals).

CONCLUSION

Acculturation of the Hmong regarding traditional funeral customs has been one of the more difficult aspects of Hmong resettlement in the United States. Having to give up so many religious and funeral rituals has caused a high level of stress, emotional difficulties, and mental health problems among the Hmong. Abandoning such rituals not only causes short-term discomfort but long-term anxiety. Many continue to worry about the future well-being of their family members and all descendants to come.

Although it may seem easier to conform to American funeral practices, Hmong who desire to continue traditional practices should be encouraged to maintain and pass on their culture. The traditional funeral process is a very culturally appropriate way for the Hmong to express their grief. As an unintended but beneficial secondary process, the funeral also provides the Hmong community with an opportunity to meet, regroup, and come together to help each other. Thus, ways to assist the Hmong in retaining their traditional funeral ceremonies and rituals should be actively sought.

ACKNOWLEDGMENTS

The editors gratefully acknowledge assistance with Hmong materials from Charles R. Johnson, Associate Professor of French, Emeritus, Macalester College, St. Paul, MN, and from Ava Dale Plummer, his wife.

REFERENCES

Bliatout, B. T. (1982). *Hmong sudden unexpected nocturnal death syndrome.* Portland, OR: Sparkle Publishing Enterprises.

Bliatout, B. T., et al. (1988). *Handbook for teaching Hmong-speaking students.* Folsom, CA: Folsom Cordova Unified School District, Southeast Asia Community Resource Center.

Chindarsi, N. (1976). *The religion of the Hmong Njua.* Bangkok, Thailand: Siam Society.

Quincy, K. (1988). *Hmong: History of a people.* Cheney, WA: Eastern Washington University Press.

Wilcox, D. (1986). *Hmong folklife.* Penland, NC: Hmong Natural Association of North Carolina.

BIBLIOGRAPHY

Bliatout, B. T. (1980, August). *Causes and treatment of Hmong mental health problems.* Paper presented to the National Refugee Conference, Irvine, CA.

Bliatout, B. T. (1980, December). *Mental health problems of the Hmong refugees in the United States.* Paper presented to the Pan-Asian Conference at the University of Southern California, Los Angeles.

Bliatout, B. T. (1982). Prevention of mental health problems. In *Refugee mental health: Paths to understanding and helping* (pp. 29–32). Kansas City, MO: Department of Health and Human Services—Region VII.

Bliatout, B. T. (1982). Understanding the differences between Asian and Western concepts of mental health and illness: Hmong and Lao. In *Refugee mental health: Paths to understanding and helping* (pp. 17–28). Kansas City, MO: Department of Health and Human Services—Region VII.

Bliatout, B. T. (1986). Guidelines for mental health professionals to help Hmong clients seek traditional health treatment. In G. L. Hendricks et al. (Eds.), *The Hmong in transition* (pp. 349–363). Staten Island, NY: The Center for Migration Studies.

Bliatout, B. T. (1988). Hmong attitudes toward surgeries: How it affects prognosis. *Migration World Magazine, 16*(1), 25–28.

Bliatout, B. T. (1990). Hmong beliefs about health and illness. In S. Young (Ed.), *Hmong Forum,* Volume 1 (pp. 40–45). Minneapolis: Haiv Hmoob.

Hayes, C., & Kalish, R. (1987–1988). Death-related experiences and funerary practices of the Hmong refugees in the United States. *Omega, 18*(1), 63–70.

Lartéguy, J., & Yang, D. (1979). *La fabuleuse aventure du peuple de l'opium* [The fabulous adventure of the opium people], Chapter 8. Paris: Presses de la Cité.

Lemoine, J. (1986). Shamanism in the context of Hmong resettlement. In G. L. Hendricks et al. (Eds.), *The Hmong in transition* (pp. 337–348). Staten Island, NY: The Center for Migration Studies.

Lemoine, J. (1983). *L'initiation du mort chez les Hmong* [The initiation of the dead among the Hmong]. Bangkok, Thailand: Pandora Press.

Lewis, P., & Lewis, E. (1984). Hmong (Meo). In *People of the golden triangle* (pp. 100–133). New York: Thames & Hudson.

Savina, F. M. (1930). *Histoire des Miao* [History of the Hmong]. Hong Kong: Paris Society of Foreign Missions. [His findings are reported in Bernatzik, H. A. (1970). *Akha and Miao: Problems of Applied Ethnography in Farther India* (pp. 32–36). New Haven: Human Relations Area Files.]

Siegel, T., & Conquergood, D. (Producers). (1985). *Between two worlds: The Hmong shaman in America* [Video]. Chicago, IL: Siegel Productions.

Thao, X. (1986). Hmong perception of illness and traditional ways of healing. In G. L. Hendricks et al. (Eds.), *The Hmong in transition* (pp. 365–378). Staten Island, NY: The Center for Migration Studies.

Trueba, J. T., Jacobs, L., & Kirton, E. (1990). *Cultural conflict and adaptation: The case of Hmong children in American society.* Bristol, PA: Falmer Press.

Chapter Seven

Native Americans: Adapting, Yet Retaining

Martin Brokenleg and David Middleton

Illustrative Episode

Tom Bear, a Native American veteran, recently retired from the local paper plant where he was a supervisor. Mr. Bear lived in a suburb in a large metropolitan area. One Sunday afternoon, he experienced severe chest pains. His wife, Alice, called 911 and an ambulance took the Bears to a neighboring suburban hospital.

Alice, a retired nurse, had a conversation with the emergency-room physician and was alarmed when he told her that he had prescribed for her husband a medication used to treat chronic alcoholism. When she protested that her husband had never had an alcohol problem, the doctor walked away from her.

Tom remained in the hospital for two weeks and then died. The Bears' two sons, Bill and Tom, Jr., were present at his death and sang funeral chants at their father's bedside. A nurse entered the room, heard the chants, and called hospital security to remove "those drunken Indians" from the hospital. Shortly after, the security guards hustled Tom and Bill from the room. Tom's doctor arrived to announce that an autopsy should be performed and to convince Alice to sign a form agreeing to this. Tom's tribe was firmly opposed to autopsies.

Submitted by Vivian Jenkins Nelsen

POSSIBLE PERCEPTIONS OF THE PRINCIPALS INVOLVED

An Administrative View of Regulations

An ambulance properly and promptly took Tom Bear and his wife to a nearby suburban hospital after 911 was called on a Sunday afternoon. After the patient's death in the hospital two weeks later, a physician indicated that an autopsy should be performed and "the next-of-kin (wife) should be asked to sign the authorization." Two sons were present at their father's death and sang funeral chants at his bedside. A situation perceived to be disturbing to other patients and staff developed, and security guards were called to remove those responsible.

Attitudes of Individual Hospital Staff Personnel

An emergency-room physician with seeming haste had prescribed a medication used to treat chronic alcoholism for incoming patient Tom Bear. When the wife questioned him, he walked away. Later, at the time of death, a nurse heard the sons singing funeral chants and called hospital security personnel to "remove those drunken Indians" from the hospital. Finally, a physician indicated that an autopsy should be performed, although it came to be revealed that Tom Bear's tribe was firmly opposed to autopsies.

Tom Bear's Wife

Alice, Tom's wife, was a retired nurse. She became alarmed upon learning that the emergency-room physician had prescribed medication for alcoholism when her husband was admitted to the hospital; she insisted that he had never had an alcohol problem. After two weeks of presumed misdiagnosis and/or mistreatment, her husband died. When her sons then sang chants at the bedside of her deceased husband, the hospital staff was unable to accept the singing and responded to them as if they were "drunken Indians." Finally, she was asked to sign an autopsy form; but his tribe was opposed to the conducting of autopsies.

There is a list of questions concerning the perceptions outlined here in Appendix B: Questions That Might Be Asked.

Editors

═══════••••••••═══════

DEFINITION OF NATIVE AMERICAN

Native American identity is better defined in terms of culture than race. Genetically, Native American people are similar to the Chinese and the Koreans. Culturally, however, Native Americans exhibit values and behaviors consistent with at least one of the many tribes. Because of the prevalence of intermarriage, people may, for example, have only 1/64th Cherokee ancestry and still identify themselves as Cherokee. On the other hand, persons with Native American ancestry may choose to identify themselves as white, but their behaviors may or may not exclusively reflect that culture.

Under federal law, a person must have at least one fourth verifiable Native American ancestry in order to be identified as a Native American, although there is some variation among tribal regulations. This composition is important in determining legal rights to services from federal and tribal governments, such as health care or burial benefits.

TRIBAL DIVERSITY

There are approximately 350 distinct tribes in the United States, and 596 different bands among the "First Nations" of Canada. The focus of identity is on the tribe, rather than on simply having Native American ancestry. It is crucial that those involved with Native Americans have an understanding of this, because values and beliefs vary from nation to nation. For example, the Apache regard a dead person's body as an empty shell, while the Lakota speak to the body, visit it, and understand it to be sacred. The Navajo do not believe in an afterlife, while most of the other Native American nations do. It must also be understood that while these are traditional beliefs and cultural values, there have been varying degrees of influence by the dominant culture. Thus, an understanding of tribal cultures requires the conscientious practitioner to avoid operating on assumptions.

There may be similarities among nations originating in the same region, but this is a generalization. It may aid in understanding the significance of tribal distinctions to note that the Cherokees, for example, are as culturally different from the Crows as the English are from the Chinese.

Because of the significance of tribal diversity, our discussion will focus on the Lakota (Sioux) customs and rituals surrounding dying, death, and grief. The

Lakota are the second largest nation of Native Americans in the United States and the largest in the Upper Midwest.

THEOLOGY/PHILOSOPHY OF DEATH AND DYING:
SOUL, PERSONALITY, AND AFTERLIFE

Native American religious life has been influenced in its practice by Christianity at various levels for more than 100 years. Thus, most Native American families represent an amalgam of both Christian and tribal elements, the tribal being the basic foundation, at least in terms of practice. For this reason, our focus will be on tribal beliefs, assuming that this element is the lesser known of the two.

The Lakota religious system allows little speculation about the specifics of afterlife, but it offers a specific system of dying and the expression of grief. The idea of a balanced universe pervades Lakota thought. Death, therefore, is understood to be the natural counterpart of birth, and because of this cyclical quality both death and birth are sacred. Any natural stage in life that creates significant change is regarded as sacred. In contrast to traditional Western thought, afterlife is assumed to be automatic and for everyone, rather than a state that must be earned. Religion is a means of living life on earth in a complete and good way.

The afterlife begins at some point after death, when the soul journeys south until it comes to the Ghost Road, also known as the Milky Way. The Ghost Road leads to *Wanagi Makoce,* the Spirit Land. This is the place where all dead go, whether human or animal. Spirituality, then, focuses on how to live here and now, not on a reward in the afterlife.

Death is not feared inordinately; it is understood to be a natural part of human existence. This attitude about the continuity and cyclical nature of human life takes form in many expressions. For example, "Today is a good day to die," can be used at any time when one is experiencing a particular zest for life.

Death is also used as a motivation to treat another person kindly. This is not a threat but rather the realization that this life should be good, and that it is finite. Lakota parents sometimes remind their children, "Be good to your brother, because someday he is going to die." This reminds the children that they have both the opportunity and the obligation to enhance the goodness in life.

For the Lakota, the soul exists before birth. It accompanies the person in life and leaves some kind of presence behind in this world when it goes on to the afterlife. This belief has no elaborate rationale or philosophical foundation because the Lakota system does not require it. Sacred things are explained only up to a point. Excessive curiosity is seen as inappropriate, because it is understood that some things are simply beyond human comprehension. To dwell on such things, therefore, would be seen as arrogance or as an incorrect under-standing of one's place in the natural order of things.

There is an enormous reverence for the body, because it is both the resi-dence and the manifestation of a person's essence. This is true both in life and after death. In life, one respects the body and cares for it. This is supported by the fact that, although hallucinogens such as marijuana were known in earlier times, they were not used. The use of peyote in religious ceremonies by some "traditional" Lakota medicine men does not have a long history: It was intro-duced from Mexico about 100 years ago. We see today, however, that the use of alcohol violates this traditional respect for the body. Because alcohol is not indigenous to North America, the lack of cultural rules about its use may be a contributing factor to the widespread alcohol abuse problems facing modern Native American populations.

Prayer is understood as a medium through which one might accept the outcome of a situation, whatever that result might be. Prayer is not petitionary, and it is inappropriate to ask the question, "Why?" Because of the inappropri-ateness of asking why in the Lakota system, Lakota philosophy differs funda-mentally from Western culture. Likewise, the Lakota grief model differs from current Western models, because denial and anger are minimal. This is a func-tion of the acceptance of the natural order of things as opposed to the cognitive inquiry of Western culture.

DEATH EDUCATION

From the time they are born, Lakota people learn about death and grief through participation in all the functions of the Lakota community. Members of the community learn through observation of rituals and verbal instruction by elders. Because people attend wakes and funerals from early childhood onward, they observe how they are expected to behave. It is understood that by virtue of attending, one will know all one needs to know. When appropriate, people who are respected by virtue of being aged, or those who personally knew the dead person, will be asked to speak to those gathered, either about the dead person's life or about the process of grieving. This formal but indirect style reaffirms the values and beliefs of the community so that all may be mindful of life's purpose and the necessity of grief.

Mourning is considered natural, and the unrestrained expression of grief is appropriate and regarded as a good thing for both sexes. Women will typically wail loudly; men will often sing emotional, mournful songs. This, like every-thing else, is done in the presence of the whole community.

Because of the cohesiveness of the Lakota family, relatives of a dead person will go to any lengths to be present at the wake and funeral. A person's death is understood to be a sacred thing, and during such a time the community gathers to support its members. It is not uncommon for relatives to travel from another continent to be present. It may be well to point out that the Lakota family system includes all those to whom one is related, and that, unlike the Euro-American nuclear family, this includes second and third cousins. This illustrates the value of family cohesiveness in the Lakota system: One is never to be apart from relatives in times of need, and death is a time when all relatives need the support of the family unit.

There are certain taboos that surround social occasions. To conduct oneself in any way less than virtuously is unacceptable at any time, but especially at family-oriented events, because the family depends on each of its members to personify and perpetuate the proper Lakota life-style for the sake of the group as a whole. This is especially important for the development of the youth. To behave inappropriately at a social gathering would reflect unfavorably on the nature of the person who did so. Intoxicants are absolutely forbidden to the mourners from the moment of the death until after the burial. They are not part of the Native American tradition, and the problems that result from their use are known to all. Anyone who ignores this taboo is shamed and asked to leave the gathering.

Peculiar to those taboos surrounding death, there is a fear of the sight or sound of an owl, which signifies that someone close is to die soon. This belief is part of the tradition of many Native American nations and is unquestioned.

There is also an abhorrence of cremation because it is considered disrespectful to the body, which is sacred because it housed the essence of the deceased. Autopsies are also to be avoided. A Lakota family will occasionally consent to an autopsy, but only if the family is uninformed as to what really happens to the body. Authorities who want an autopsy done may say that "tissue samples will be taken"; but the family would not consent if they knew that samples are taken from the brain and other organs and that the remains are usually stuffed into the chest cavity before the body is returned for burial.

RITUALS, ACTIONS, AND EXPRESSIONS PRIOR TO DEATH

Many of the Native American experiences prior to death seem fantastic to people from a Western cultural and philosophical heritage. When studying these occurrences, it is essential that the concept of a paradigm be fully understood. A paradigm is a model for processing information. To illustrate, suppose consecutive images of playing cards were flashed on a screen for 1/30th of a second each. Some of these playing cards would be exactly as they appear in a regular deck, but others would be the same—except that the color would be wrong (i.e., an eight of hearts would appear in black, not red). A person might be able to identify some of the cards, but most likely they would only be the ones that are commonly seen. Even if the speed were slowed to 1/20th of a second, it would be very unlikely that the cards of the "wrong" color would be identifiable. This is because those that are the wrong color do not fall within the paradigm in which playing cards are associated. They are not within common experience. Likewise, in Lakota experience, spiritual events are often manifested physically, but such a manifestation is, for the most part, outside the realm of Western experience.

With this in mind, one may now begin to have some understanding of the reality of Lakota experience. Death is often forecast by unusual spiritual or physical events, which are understood to be natural and in the order of things. For example, at the time of a person's death, another family member will often see the ghost of the person and be told of the death soon afterward. Another relatively common sign that a family member has died is that a blue light will be seen coming from the direction of the dead relative's home or room. An accepted sign that a person will die soon is that she or he will report being visited in dreams by dead relatives.

In the spring of 1990, four children died in a trailer fire on the Rosebud reservation. Earlier that day, the children had seen four eagles circling overhead and had pointed them out to their mother. The importance of this was not understood until after the children had died. The significance of this event is the rarity of four eagles circling together, along with the fact that eagles are messengers from the spirit world.

People close to death will often ask for traditional Lakota foods, even if there has been no medical diagnosis of impending death. These signs are considered neither demonic, evil, nor good, but are simply accepted as part of the natural order of things.

When a Lakota person knows that death is near, valuables and goods will be gathered by that person and distributed to significant family members and friends. This is done to acknowledge the impending death and to show appreciation to the recipient for the relationship.

RITUALS, ACTIONS, AND EXPRESSIONS
IMMEDIATELY UPON DEATH

When someone dies, there is always a substantial gathering of family and friends. It is important for hospital staff to understand the importance of family in the Lakota system, because they will need to adjust rules to accommodate the presence of many people at the time of death. McKennan Hospital in Sioux Falls, South Dakota, has shown respect for this Lakota value and accommodates the wishes of its Lakota patients. In the spring of 1990, for example, a young man was dying in the intensive care unit. There were 23 of his relatives and friends at his bedside when he died. This is an invaluable courtesy that has been shown the Lakota people and a model for any institution concerned with an holistic approach to health care.

Because of the extensive Lakota family unit, the gathering of people who attend the wake and funeral may range from 50 to over 1,000. The ceremonies take place at a school, church, or community hall that can accommodate the large number of people expected. The family of the dead person will feed all who attend.

As each person greets the family mourners, the mourners' expression of grief is renewed in intensity. Cutting the hair, cutting or scratching the forearms and face, tearing clothing, and wearing black are common and appropriate outward displays of grief. These are no empty displays, but rather the ritualized expressions of deep grief.

Typically, medicine men are only minimally involved in death rituals. It is more likely that Christian clergy will be involved, even if the dead person's family follows the historic Pipe and Sundance tradition of the Sioux. Upon entering the wake gathering, each person present will grieve over the body for as long as she or he deems appropriate. Prayers will be interspersed throughout the wake, along with talks, breaks for conversation, and the serving of refreshments.

It is a major concern that mourning and burial take place at the home reservation. Even if the person's family has lived in an urban area for generations, it is considered vitally important that these ceremonies be held at the person's cultural home. Lakota people have an inseparable bond with their land. Even if economic considerations may have forced the family to leave the reservation, they will return for any social occasions—and especially a death.

It is important for the mental health professional to know that no Lakota wants to die alone. This is consistent with the phenomenally strong family bonding in Lakota culture. Consequently, if a person dies alone, the family will suffer a fair amount of guilt as a result.

DISPOSAL OF THE BODY

The body of the deceased will be taken to a mortician, but the family will want access to the body as soon as possible. Because of the number of people who attend, a funeral home is rarely utilized. If the wake is held there, however, access will be assumed around the clock.

The body will lie in state for three days, during which all members of the community remain with the mourners. Friends may assist with gifts of money or food, to help cover the cost of the food served by the family. Information about the death and the location of the gathering is spread by family members and friends. Clergy of all denominations and medicine men are asked to attend. The singing of Christian hymns and/or tribal songs will be interspersed with prayers, condolences, admonitions, and reminiscences about the dead person. Admonitions include instructions pertaining to death and grieving and the meaning and value of living a virtuous life. Admonitions usually begin with a humorous story, most often delivered by elders of the community. Acquaintances and relatives tell anecdotes that are humorous, amplify an admirable quality of the dead person, or indicate the bond that exists between the speaker and the person who has died.

If the death is a result of negligence, the speaker will first acknowledge the state of grief that the community, and especially the family, is experiencing. Then a most stern and direct reprimand will be given publicly to those who have acted negligently; this is endured and accepted without question. Then the speaker will address the people compassionately and urge them to make some resolution as a future preventive measure.

These rounds of prayers and admonitions are followed by a full meal; then the cycle continues. Cigarettes are distributed with the meal, as tobacco use is a centuries-old, semireligious social custom. Because 70 percent of youth and adult Native Americans smoke tobacco, this is well received.

Throughout the wake, it is usual for portions of the same food that will be offered to the mourners to be collected on a plate and brought outside to feed the spirits of dead relatives in attendance. It is also customary to bring the mourners water and tobacco before the meal.

The body of the dead person is viewed, even if there has been considerable damage to it. When the mourners first encounter the body, there is a crescendo of grief and calling to that person. There are no taboos about touching the body; it is often kissed and embraced. Rarely, the body may be almost lifted out of the casket.

Goodbyes are said at the end of the wake or funeral, before the casket is closed for the final time. Objects, significant either to the dead person or to the mourner, will be placed in the casket, such as jewelry, food, or locks of the mourners' hair. Larger objects, such as star quilts, are placed with the casket at burial. Often drums are played. Old Lakota songs are sung. At the wake, people begin to form a line, with the family closest to the casket. Then those at the end of the line will shake the hand or embrace everyone on the way to pay their last respects to the body. When they get to the immediate family, intense mourning may again be expressed. The mourners talk to the body, touch, or embrace it for the last time, and then wait quietly until others have done the same. At last, the family members have their chance to say a final farewell to the body.

At the funeral itself, grief is subdued, with the exception of the last hymn, where wailing may recur. If there are more people than the church can accommodate, people will stand quietly outside close to the entrance. It is customary for members of the older generation to wear black, although this custom seems to be waning. There is little use of floral arrangements during these proceedings. Those who wish to contribute something usually give money to the family to help cover the expenses of feeding all who attend.

At the gravesite, it is customary for relatives and friends to assist in filling in the grave. This is important for funeral directors to know, because the family will not leave until the burial is complete. The burial takes place regardless of weather conditions; bodies never lie in a mausoleum until winter is over. Instead, friends will go to the gravesite ahead of time and dig the grave, even if the ground is frozen. At the conclusion of gravesite rites, mourners will be comforted, and there will be much keening and crying on the part of both men and women.

Before the funeral and burial, all of the personal possessions of the dead person, if the possessions are not burned, are collected at the site of the wake. Then, after the burial, the community gathers once again to have a final meal together. During this time, the family mourners give away all of the dead person's other possessions to those present. The rationale behind this is twofold. First, it is understood that a Lakota person has nothing in life apart from the family. Material possessions are accorded very little importance throughout life, and these are understood to be communally shared. Nothing of value is obtained apart from the community. Therefore, what the community has given the person in life has been returned through the life of the person and that person's involvement in the community. The material possessions also are returned at death so that the cycle is complete.

Secondly, it is understood that when a person dies, the family must start to lead a new life without the physical presence of that person. For this to happen more easily, therefore, all material goods are given away so that they may benefit others and make the family's passage through the grieving process less stressful.

RITUALS, ACTIONS, AND EXPRESSIONS AT LATER STAGES

Sometimes a major religious ceremony, *wanagi yuha* (which means retaining the person's spirit), is held. This involves taking a portion of the dead person's hair and keeping it in a particular place in the home throughout the year of mourning that follows the death. The family will often speak directly to the dead person, who is understood to be present in the hair. Even if family members do not practice this particular ritual, they observe a year of mourning, during which they strive toward exemplary behavior and thought. The family will avoid controversy, jealousy, anger, and licentiousness. Again, this is done because it is understood that the true character of a person emerges in a time of grief. Behavior considered less than virtuous is avoided.

The family will accumulate goods and money during the year of mourning for the purpose of giving them away on the anniversary of the death of the loved one. Those who have been helpful and significant family and friends are invited to this occasion.

If the ritual is observed, the hair and its container will be burned following a church service conducted as a memorial. If the hair is not kept, a modern practice is for the family to substitute a picture of the dead person and show it to each person attending the memorial. The person chosen to show the photograph occupies a position of great honor and is presented with lavish gifts. After the memorial service there is a big meal, with more food than could possibly be eaten. Any food that remains is given to those who have attended.

The mood of the anniversary gathering changes from one of somber acknowledgment to a festive and joyful social gathering once the hair has been burned or the picture has been passed around. At this time, significant people may be asked to speak about the dead person: they may commend the family if they have shown the deceased proper respect and behavior during the past year. Someone will then be asked to speak on behalf of the family and will call forth certain individuals and thank them by presenting gifts that have been saved from the deceased person's belongings especially for them. After these special gifts have been given, gifts of a practical nature, such as clothing, tools, etc., are distributed to everyone present.

It is not uncommon for close relatives to remind others of the dead person for years afterward, on occasions that were special to the dead person. For example, every year for 10 years, on the anniversary of her husband's ordination, one Lakota woman brought a plate of food for every man in the church where her husband had been ordained a priest. She asked the men to pray for her husband as she handed them the plates.

CONCLUSION

The Lakota people have very successfully amalgamated their culture with Christian and modern trends associated with death and grief. Contemporary institutions, especially those involved in the medical and mortuary sciences, need to be aware of cultural customs and values. They should be equipped to accommodate the Lakota extended family so that more people than the immediate nuclear family may be present in an intensive care unit, for example. A funeral director, understanding the importance of immediate access to the body, may provide this service. If these needs are not met, the result is institutionalized racism at a time of deep crisis in the lives of Lakota people. Networking with fellow professionals who have experience in working with Native American families is probably the most effective way to deal in a humane way with this population.

BIBLIOGRAPHY

Attneave, C. (1982). American Indians and Alaska native families: Emigrants in their own homeland. In M. McGoldrick, J. K. Pearce, & J. Gordinano, *Ethnicity and family therapy.* New York: Guilford Press.

Beck, P. V., & Walters, A. L. (1977). *The sacred: Ways of knowledge, sources of life.* Tsaile, AZ: Navajo Community College Press.

Brendtro, L. K., Brokenleg, M., & Van Bockern, S. (1990). *Reclaiming youth at risk: Our hope for the future.* Bloomington, IN: National Education Service.

Coffin, M. T. (1976). *Narrative obituary verse and Native American balladry.* Folcroft, PA: Folcroft Library.

Craven, M. (1973). *I heard the owl call my name.* New York: Dell.

Deloria, E. C. (1979). *Speaking of Indians.* Vermillion, SD: Dakota Press.

Grobsmith, E. S. (1981). *Lakota of the Rosebud: A contemporary ethnography.* New York: Holt, Rinehart & Winston.

Powers, W. K. (1982). *Yuwipi: Vision and experience of Oglala ritual.* Lincoln: University of Nebraska Press.

Stoltzman, W. J. (1986). *The pipe and Christ: A Christian-Sioux dialogue.* Chamberlain, SD: St. Joseph's Indian School.

Chapter Eight

To Honor the Dead and Comfort the Mourners: Traditions in Judaism

Barry D. Cytron

Illustrative Episode

The remodeling of a community hospital in a midwestern city of 50,000 included plans for a new chapel.

Within the large area served by the hospital there is a substantial Native American community. Many of its members practice traditional worship. Those who are Christians have appreciated efforts to recognize their traditions in some local churches. An increasing number of Asian and African refugees and professional people are also moving into the city.

One person who was working with refugees asked if the new chapel could be interfaith. The planners she spoke to concurred with her desire for the new chapel to be interfaith. She started making a collection of designs from chapels and churches, concentrating on symbols that were common to people all over the world, such as water, trees, and sun.

Late in the planning process she was told that there was a fine example of an interfaith chapel at a reform school in the nearby city. She went to see the chapel and was astounded. Although the chapel was simple, it was a typical example of Christian church architecture. On entering, she was surprised to see rows of long wooden pews, a larger-than-life statue of the Virgin Mary on one side of the altar and one of Jesus on the other. On the altar were both a crucifix and a plain cross. She realized then that, for the committee, the concept of inter-faith was Roman Catholic and Lutheran–the two dominant religious groups in the surrounding community.

She went back to the member of the new chapel committee whom she knew best and pled once again for a truly interfaith chapel. There were signs of understanding on the part of the Lutheran minister to whom she spoke; but she was told that the chapel plans were already completed and that he saw no possibility of change.

The hospital remodeling has been completed. Nearing the chapel, on the third floor, the first aspect one sees is a stained-glass window depicting Jesus praying in the Garden of Gethsemane. The chapel is simple, with a few rows of wooden pews. On the altar there is always a movable crucifix or a plain cross. The hospital administration speaks of the chapel as a place of quiet and a space available to all for meditation.

Submitted by Joanne Spears

POSSIBLE PERCEPTIONS
OF THE PRINCIPALS INVOLVED

Lutheran Minister and Members
of Planning Committee

Considerable time, endeavor, and resources were invested in develop-ing this plan for a chapel in the hospital. All members of the adminis-trative staff were consulted and were satisfied. The goal of the admin-istration was to provide a place for meditation and prayer, which they believe was achieved.

Community Person

An interfaith chapel needs to serve the wide variety of constituents in our society. The needs of all need to be considered, without offending those of majority or minority faiths. Being cross-cultural means more than being interdenominational within a Christian tradition. The plans can be altered to permit flexibility. A hospital chapel is not a church, a mosque, nor a synagogue/temple. Symbols that are common to people around the world could be used in its architecture and decoration.

There is a list of questions concerning the perceptions outlined here in Appendix B: Questions That Might Be Asked.

Editors

———————◦◦◦◦◦◦◦◦◦◦◦———————

JEWISH ORIENTATIONS TO DEATH AND MOURNING

In the book of Psalms (13:3), we read: "Open my eyes lest I sleep the sleep of death." This yearning to clasp life close reflects the famous urging of Deuteronomy (11:26): "I call heaven and earth to witness against you this day: I have put before you life and death, blessing and curse—choose life."

Considering the Jewish tradition and its attitude toward death, one must begin with the passionate embrace of life it espouses. Yet, in the words of Steinberg (1954, pp. 272–277), a noted American rabbi who himself died young, the emphasis within Judaism has ever been "to hold close to life, but with open arms, to embrace it, but loosely." Balancing these opposing tendencies—holding life infinitely close, yet accepting the inevitability of death—informs the Jewish tradition. It especially shapes its rites of death and determines the way rabbinic writings approach ultimate questions on matters such as autopsy and suicide.

Looking at the Jewish rituals of death and mourning, I do so as a rabbi of a Conservative congregation, which represents the largest denominational affiliation in this country. The other major movements within American Judaism, Reform and Orthodox, also enjoy substantial membership throughout this country. Though it is always a challenge to speak for the other groups, I will try to reflect the *full* range of religious practice in American Jewish life, well aware that although there are certain constants of mourning rituals among Jews, each denomination approaches these questions differently.

As one surveys the Jewish tradition, one discovers that there are two overriding values at the heart of its orientation to death and mourning. One is *kavod hamet*, the requirement to "honor the dead." The second is *nichum avelim*, the obligation to "comfort the mourners." In each of the specific rites of mourning, one finds present each of these values, as the tradition assists its adherents to show deepest regard for the sanctity of the deceased, while simultaneously helping them bring solace to the mourners.

Kavod hamet, or honoring the dead, requires that the body of the deceased person be treated with respect and dignity, that the body is considered vulnerable and alone. Judaism demands that those who remain alive must shield it, continually watching over the body until it reaches its resting place within the grave.

ATTITUDE TOWARD AUTOPSIES

This requirement of respect has implications, as we shall see, for how the body is readied for burial. It also gives rise to a firm teaching found within the Jewish tradition that there be no autopsies. As in most other legal systems, in Jewish law, too, there are exceptions to accepted norms, frequently based on other, overriding principles and values. Such is the case in the Jewish teachings on autopsies.

Classical Jewish sources spoke of the human body, indeed of all life, as a divine "gift." That status conferred an obligation: Human beings must guard that gift, never treat it lightly. Among other implications, that meant that routine autopsies were prohibited as inappropriate and serious violations of the integrity of the body. Yet, just as it is reported that over the door leading to Oxford University's Department of Pathology there is a sign reading "This is the place where death serves life," when it is *clear* that performing postmortem examinations can serve life, voices within the Jewish tradition permit—even mandate—that such examinations be carried out.

Some Jewish authorities would interpret this exception narrowly; others would do so more broadly. Even the most traditional voices, however, would argue in favor of performing such an examination if it will provide immediate, useful knowledge that will help others live. One example, the most profound in my rabbinic experience on this issue, demonstrates this exception well.

Several years ago a member of the congregation I served in Iowa, a man in his early 50s, had a coronary attack while playing tennis. He was "dead on arrival" at the hospital. The family and many friends gathered around, in both shock and anguish. The deceased was himself a physician, and the family was asked if there should be an autopsy. Their instinctual reaction (perhaps the instinctual reaction of most Jews) was no.

Then, in the course of the conversation, the attending physicians learned that this individual was an identical twin. The doctors pleaded with the family for permission to perform an autopsy, which was granted. It revealed the cause for the coronary—blocked arteries leading to the heart. As soon as the funeral was over, the brother of the deceased had an angiogram, which revealed a blockage in exactly the same place. Soon thereafter, an operation was performed.

Now, when I see the surviving brother, from time to time, I cannot help but think back to the discussion within the family and among his friends that morning, about whether or not an autopsy ought to be performed. Was it right to do? Did that surgery save the life of the surviving brother? We may never know, but there is surely reason to think so. This case demonstrated the meaning of "death serving life."

"SAYING GOODBYE"—FAREWELL RITES

In the case of my congregant who died that early fall day, his family was unable, because of the suddenness of death, to "say goodbye," and engage in any of the final rites that the Jewish tradition has developed as death approaches. In many cases, as death draws near, families may be in attendance. In the Orthodox tradition, there is a rite of "confession," which enables the person near death to ask forgiveness for his or her errors of judgment and action, as well as to express hope for the welfare of those who will survive and ask a blessing upon them. Within the Conservative and Reform communities, some choose to use the traditional language of this "confessional," while others have replaced it with other forms of a "gathering and farewell" rite. Like the classical confessional, this more modern custom allows the family to say their final goodbyes and recite together prayers of affirmation and hope.

ATTENTION TO THE BODY AFTER DEATH

As soon as death has occurred, the ritual of death begins with the removal of the body to a place where it may be prepared properly. Traditionally, the readying of the body for burial was done by a *chevra kadisha*, or holy society. This last communal service was usually performed by lay people. That is still the case today, but some communities lack sufficient volunteers and this procedure is becoming more professionalized. In my current congregation, people who are especially trained volunteers continue to carry out these rites of ritually washing and shrouding the body.

Whether it be handled by lay people or by professionals, this preparation, called *tahara*, entails washing the corpse with water and draping it in a *tachrikin*, a simple linen garment. This rite is performed with the recitation of prayers and in deepest reverence. After its completion, the body is placed in a plain coffin. Initially, that meant the simplest of wooden boxes, reflecting a sense of egalitarianism within Judaism that argued against pretentious display. To be sure, today some families choose more elaborate coffins and much more expensive arrangements. But classically, at least, the teaching was that the final "home" of the dead be as simple as possible, so as not to impede the natural decomposition of the body.

Between the time of death and burial, the body is to be guarded, called by the Hebrew term *shemirah*, "watching." At one time, this might have been because of actual fear of what might happen to an unattended corpse. Now it has been transvalued, so that we might speak of watching over a body that is vulnerable and unable to watch over itself until it has "come home" to its final resting place. *Homecoming* is a term used by many religious faiths when they speak of death and ultimate destiny. It is a term that resonates within the Jewish sources as well, for those sources do speak of the body as being returned home, to the life-giving earth from which all human beings initially sprang. All this is done so as to conform to Scripture's teaching that "from dust we come, to dust we return" (Genesis 3:19).

For that reason, cremation is most unusual within Judaism. There are a few cases of it, which one can likely attribute to the power of acculturation. Yet because it has historically been frowned upon as an unnatural means of treating the human body, and because the Holocaust is so closely associated with cremation, most Jews eschew it and rely on the custom of burial, which the Bible refers to in the earliest narratives that speak of death, such as those of Abraham and Sarah, or Moses and Aaron.

THE FUNERAL: HONORING THE DEAD, COMFORTING THE MOURNERS

Burial is often in a family plot. Today, given the mobility of American society, large family plots, where families were gathered together in death as they were in life, have become increasingly rare. Among the most traditional of Jews, there is a deep yearning to be buried in the land of Israel. Some few actually arrange for their bodies to be transported to Israel and buried on the Mount of Olives outside the ancient walled city of Jerusalem. Many others fulfill this yearning to associate burial with the land of Israel through the custom of bringing some earth from that land, and either placing it within the coffin or mixing it with the earth that covers the coffin.

Along with these rites, reflecting the requirement of showing respect for the deceased, there is need for comforting the mourners. One is deemed an official mourner, upon whom the obligations of mourning devolve, when related to the deceased in one of seven ways: as father, mother, brother, sister, spouse, son, or daughter. The tradition designates these seven relationships as particularly in need of the full range of mourning practices.

Comforting the mourner is enacted in a number of different ways. Before the funeral the family is excused from many other ritual obligations. They need not occupy themselves with regular prayer or most other recurring rituals until the funeral has taken place. This is done so that they may attend to the funeral arrangements. Some within the tradition have supported this "excuse," but suggested that its reason was not only that the survivors were distracted by the necessities of the hour, but that they were also too emotionally distraught to be able to devote themselves properly to the routines of normal religious expression.

The Jewish funeral service begins with the cutting of a garment or a black ribbon. This first rite symbolizes the individual being "cut away" from loved ones. For children, the cut is made above the heart. For all others, it is done on the right side. At the funeral, psalms of comfort are recited, especially the 90th and the 23rd. Those readings, as well as others chosen by the officiant, or perhaps even newly prepared by the rabbi, are then followed by a eulogy that offers personal words about the individual's life, achievements, losses, and loves. One of the striking aspects of my life as a congregational rabbi involves the act of listening to families share their grief and their memories, with the hope that I then try to pass on those memories and emotions in the eulogy.

Following the eulogy, and the chanting of a slow dirge, known as *el molei rachamim*, the family makes its way to the cemetery for the interment. Frequently, the funeral service will have been held at a funeral home, or in some cases, depending on local custom, in a synagogue. At other times, especially if the deceased was advanced in years, or if the family anticipates that an especially small number of people will attend the funeral, the entire service may be conducted at the gravesite. At the burial site itself, some additional brief prayers are usually recited.

Many families choose to participate personally in the act of placing some earth upon the lowered coffin. Doing so is quite traditional, and orthodox Jews have always done so. In recent years, members of the more liberal branches of American Judaism have found renewed meaning in this ancient rite. For many, it symbolizes a powerful way of accepting the finality of the death as well as a means by which those in attendance illustrate their concern for the deceased's vulnerability by seeing to a proper burial.

As the final act of the service, the family rises and recites the "homecoming" prayer called *kaddish*, which affirms life while accepting death. The prayer makes no overt reference to death, but is instead an ancient formula praising God as the author of life and its wondrous ways.

Following the service, the family returns to the home for a special "meal of consolation." This meal is frequently prepared by friends and relatives and often includes some symbolic foods, especially eggs, which are a sign of life, death, and rebirth in many religious traditions.

THE PERIOD OF MOURNING

Then begins the actual period of mourning. The initial period of mourning for one week is called *shiva*, Hebrew for "seven." Some commentators have spoken of this period as one of personal estrangement, because, classically, the survivor would remove himself or herself from regular living patterns and habits. Such deviations from regular living patterns might include, for instance, that a man might not shave, or that men and women might avoid wearing new clothes or engaging in some other personal pleasure for the first seven days. Couples might choose to forego physical intimacy during *shiva*. Each of these changes from normal routines was meant to show grief by acts of self-sacrifice, as well as to enforce awareness of the disruption to all life that death has brought.

In many ways, it seems that the ultimate intention of this *shiva* period is to enable the mourners to engage in the fullest range of grief by bringing the family together so that they may share memories and stories and talk through their normal feelings of loss, anger, or guilt. I can still recall my first personal experience with this period of *shiva*. My father died in his sleep at the age of 69, without warning. My brothers and I gathered together with my mother. It was a very important time for us to have people visit us in our family home, talk about what my father meant to them, which in turn empowered us to speak of what he meant to us. It was a time of deep grief and true healing, a psychological gift that the rabbis in their wisdom, thousands of years ago, continues to help mourners today.

The *shiva* period ends with a remarkable custom. The family members say the final prayers for the week together, then rise from their chairs and go for a short walk outdoors. (In some instances, especially among the Orthodox, mourners are restricted to low stools rather than regular chairs during the *shiva*.) This simple act is meant both to announce that the initial mourning period has come to an end and to serve as a form of internal teaching to the family that deep grief must give way to worldly acts, that the time has arrived for the mourners to turn from preoccupation with their loss to their own responsibilities to the world around them.

LATER REMEMBRANCE

Of course, mourning does not come to an automatic end once *shiva* is over. The tradition recognized that the mourners still had more grieving that they would have to work through. Traditional acknowledgment of this is found in the two other mourning periods that follow each death. One is *sheloshim*, "thirty," which refers to the first month after the funeral; the second is the entire year, until the first anniversary of the death has arrived.

In each successive period, additional customs are observed. Mourners may choose to avoid frivolity or light entertainment and engage instead in more somber reflection and study. They may decide to alter some typical pattern, such as where they sit in the synagogue. Whatever act they choose, it is meant to suggest to them that their lives have been altered by death, that grief has caused them to feel somewhat estranged from themselves and from life itself, and that it takes time and healing to permit one to return to a more normal pattern.

Customarily, no matter what home or personal patterns were observed, the mourners participated throughout the year in regular attendance at daily worship services. They would join not only for the customary service but also recite the *kaddish* that they first said at the funeral.

The anniversary of the death has a special name: *yahrzeit*, the Yiddish word for "year time." For the family, it is a time to gather at a synagogue, to recall the individual, to light a special candle that burns for 24 hours, and in other ways to reflect upon the life and gifts of the deceased. It is also quite customary that on the first anniversary of the death, family members visit the cemetery, where they might dedicate the tombstone with prayers and brief remarks about the deceased. It is usual also to donate to those in need, often in the name of the person whose *yahrzeit* is being observed.

As well as the opportunity to recall the person at the annual *yahrzeit*, the ritual calendar of Judaism also provides five other times when the community engages in common remembrance of family members. Four of these occur at festival services: on the Day of Atonement, and on the three pilgrimage holidays, Passover, Shabuoth or Pentecost, and Sukkoth, the Feast of Tabernacles. During the services on each of these days a significant portion of the worship is devoted to *yizkor*, "remembrance" in Hebrew. Collective prayers, as well as individual meditations, are recited. This is an especially poignant time, as individuals share their grief with one another in the comfort of, and sustained by, their religious community.

The fifth time of communal remembrance occurs immediately before the High Holy Days, which fall in the autumn of the year. It is customary for family members to visit the gravesite and pay respects to their ancestors. Here, too, individuals are able to gain strength and solace as they renew acquaintances with others who have come to pay homage to their relatives in that final resting place.

CHANGES THROUGH ACCULTURATION

This pattern of mourning is somewhat idealized. For a variety of reasons, many American Jews today engage in what might be labeled "fast grief." Rather than observe all seven days of the *shiva*, they might choose to mark only the first two or three with the usual customs. Others might not even do that, feeling that there are no compelling reasons to embrace such feelings of estrangement and grieving as the traditional sources mandate.

Some of these changes result form the increasing secularization of all Americans, including members of the Jewish faith. But some of the alteration has to do with the changes in medical care today, when so many people linger for so long and hover near death for such a long period that many family members feel that they have observed *shiva*, at least on a symbolic level, even before the death occurred. In fact, people in my congregation have spoken very much along these lines, as they seek to justify why they feel unable or unwilling to practice the traditional customs.

There have been other changes, too, in the way American Jews observe the regular mourning customs. It seems that many in my religious community are more emotionally controlled than was once the case. There is less outpouring of emotion after death has occurred. One hesitates to use the word "sterile," but some seem less willing or able to let their emotions show. Perhaps this is due to the increasing age at which so many people now die, so that death in old age is simply less of an occasion for deep grief. When a death is sudden, however, or when the person has died at a particularly young age, there is naturally a flood of emotion, as family and community seek to reconcile themselves to the anguish occasioned by such a sudden and cruel loss.

DEATH EDUCATION

Death education is a customary part of the congregation's education. Children are encouraged to participate in the experiences and rituals, including visiting a funeral home and talking about these ultimate issues. To help younger children think through some of these questions, we have found very useful the books, *The fall of Freddie the leaf: A story of life for all ages,* by Leo Buscaglia (1982), and *Saying goodbye to grandma,* by Jane Resh Thomas (1988).

In the confirmation (10th grade) classes, as well as in many adult forums, our congregation, like many others, studies life-and-death issues. Euthanasia is one of the topics that is regularly explored, as we seek to examine the traditional views, which speak strongly against active euthanasia, as well as those instances when the classical sources would condone passive euthanasia. This is, of course, a complex area, and we try to understand the complexities and the ethical implications of each of our decisions. We have also sponsored congregational meetings where we have spoken about "living wills" and the need for all families to think through the forms of life support that they would wish for themselves.

We have sought to understand changing views in the tradition about how suicide is treated. Traditionally, it was viewed with horror as a reprehensible act, and the person who committed suicide was denied the full range of funeral practices. There was no eulogy, no personal words of reference; and burial was on the side of the cemetery, on the margin. But the sources also recognized that these strictures were not to be applied if there were extenuating circumstances at the time of suicide, such as the person being under great psychological stress. Over time, as we have become more attuned to the emotional issues involved in suicide, religious communities have grown increasingly reluctant to deny the fullest range of mourning customs to the survivors of those who have taken their own lives.

LIFE AFTER DEATH: DIVERSE VIEWS

Recently, there has been increased interest on the part of young Jews as well as adults in seeking to understand what Judaism teaches about afterlife and the world to come. Indeed, this interest seems to parallel a similar concern in popular culture, with many movies having explored these themes, among them, *Ghost, Defending Your Life,* and *Flatliners.* Several new books within the Jewish faith, including Sonsino and Syme's *What Happens After I Die?* (1990), have sought to help contemporary Jews appreciate how Judaism's teaching of "triple hope" might be best understood.

This classical teaching first affirms personal survival in some form after death—though the form of that survival is a matter of considerable debate within the traditional sources. The second hope is for the survival of the people of Israel and their gathering in their historic land. Finally, the tradition speaks of "a new world" and of "eternity," of the rebirth of the cosmos, as envisioned in the messianic aspirations of the great prophets. Each of these great hopes reflects a yearning to survive death, and thereby makes real and everlasting that passionate plea in Psalm 13: "Open my eyes—lest I sleep the sleep of death."

REFERENCES

Buscaglia, L. (1982). *The fall of Freddie the leaf: A story of life for all ages.* New York: Henry Holt.

Holy Bible. Deuteronomy 11:26; Genesis 3:19; Psalms 13:3.

Sonsino, R., & Syme, D. (1990). *What happens after I die? Jewish view of life and death.* New York: UAHC Press.

Steinberg, M. (1954). To hold with open arms. In S. Greenberg (Ed.), *A treasury of comfort* (pp. 272–277). Los Angeles: Wilshire.

Thomas, J. R. (1988). *Saying goodbye to grandma.* New York: Clarion.

Wilets, B. (Producer & Director). (1985). *The fall of Freddie the leaf.* [Film, video, video disc].

BIBLIOGRAPHY

Kresky, C. (Producer), & Stuart, W. (Director). (1977). *A plain pine box* [Videotape]. ABC Media. [or rent from National Academy for Adult Jewish Studies, 155 Fifth Avenue, New York, NY.]

Cytron, B. D., & Schwartz, E. (1986). *When life is in the balance: Life-and-death decisions in light of the Jewish tradition.* New York: Youth Commission, United Synagogue of America.

The day grandpa died. (1970). [Film]. Seattle: King Screen Productions.

Goodman, A. M. (1981). *A plain pine box: A return to simple Jewish funerals and eternal traditions.* New York: KTAV.

Lamm, M. (1969). *The Jewish way in death and mourning.* New York: Jonathan David.

Riemer, J. (Ed.). (1974). *Jewish reflections on death.* New York: Schocken Books.

Chapter Nine

Death and Dying in Buddhism

Ken and Nga Truitner

Illustrative Episode

A viewing was being held for a deceased member of a Southeast Asian Buddhist family at a metropolitan funeral home. As an aspect of the ceremonial occasion, which was attended by numerous other people from that culture, heavy incense was used. The sweet aroma began to permeate the building and enter an adjacent room in which another viewing (non-Buddhist) was being conducted. The second family complained to the mortuary personnel. The use of incense, a custom unfamiliar to them, diffused what they described as an unwelcome, almost "sickeningly sweet" scent within their room, that was disturbing to their guests.

After the staff conferred with the Southeast Asian family, it was found possible to close connecting doors and segregate more completely the two grieving family groups.

Submitted by Nga and Ken Truitner

POSSIBLE PERCEPTIONS
OF THE PRINCIPALS INVOLVED

Southeast Asian Family

The Buddhist family was conducting the viewing for their deceased loved one in a manner appropriate to their traditions, which had already been considerably modified to adjust to the American setting. Thus, they planned the occasion and proceeded to do what was natural for them in their culture. They probably did not realize that incense would be offensive to others, if indeed they were even aware that another viewing would be held on the same floor at the same time.

Euro-American Family

Because the family members were unaccustomed to the use of incense on such an occasion, and had not anticipated such a "problem," the awkward situation arose. Noting that the aroma was disturbing to their guests and family members who had come to the viewing, they conveyed their honest reactions promptly to the mortuary staff.

Mortuary Staff

Having scheduled two viewings for the same evening on the premises, and probably unaware of possible cultural differences that might cause awkwardness, the staff had not anticipated any problems. Once it was brought to their attention, they promptly acted to seal off the one area from the other, while not denying the Southeast Asians the opportunity to employ their customary use of incense.

There is a list of questions concerning the perceptions outlined here in Appendix B: Questions That Might Be Asked.

Editors

SOME BASIC IDEAS OF BUDDHISM

According to Buddhist tradition, Siddhartha Gautama, the Buddha, an ascetic who lived in India during the sixth century B.C., discovered that life is basically unsatisfactory. More important, he discovered a way to transcend this existence—the Eightfold Path. Actions conditioned by a defiled mind full of greed, hatred, and delusion produce suffering and *karma* resulting in repeated rebirths in unsatisfactory worlds. By understanding that all aspects of life are impermanent, and by conditioning the mind with the discipline of the Eightfold Path, it is possible for the diligent person to escape from the continuing cycle of rebirths and to attain enlightenment (*nirvana*). *Nirvana* is not viewed as a heaven, but as an unconditioned state beyond the world of suffering, sometimes called the "other shore." The discipline required to achieve it is very difficult. The Buddha attained it only after hundreds of rebirths during which he developed compassion and mindfulness. The Buddha's teachings address right understanding, right thought, right speech, right action, right livelihood (vocation), right effort, right mindfulness, and right concentration. Teachings on all of these subjects are recorded in Pali sutras.

Other ways of relieving suffering and attaining blissful states were developed long after the Buddha's death, particularly in the Mahayana and Vajrayana traditions. Through faith in a higher being (Buddha or Bodhisattva) one might be saved from this suffering world. Instead of placing confidence in the Eightfold Path discovered by Gautama Buddha, one could have faith in a savior who would do the perfecting work for the believer. The most important of these savior figures are Amida Buddha, the universal Buddha of light, and Avalokitesvara (*Kwannon* in the Orient), the Bodhisattva of compassion. Amida Buddha helps suffering beings perfect themselves by taking them to a Pure Land after death, a kind of heavenly realm. This realm as described in Mahayana literature hardly resembles the vague "other side" resulting from enlightenment. Buddhists in the Vajrayana tradition also place faith in rituals and initiation rites that protect them from suffering and help them attain blissful states.

All of these special forms of salvation can be interpreted metaphorically as representations of mind states. In fact, all the traditions emphasize the mind. However, there are numerous variations in practice. Theravada Buddhism, which concentrates on the teachings found in the Four Noble Truths and the Eightfold Path, is found in the Southeast Asian countries of Sri Lanka, Myanmar (formerly Burma), Thailand, Cambodia, and Laos. Mahayana Buddhism in its various faith and devotional forms is practiced widely in China, Japan, Korea, Taiwan, and Vietnam. Vajrayana, with its emphasis on rituals and initiation rites, is found in Tibet, Nepal, Mongolia, and parts of India.

IMPORTANCE OF THE MIND

Attaining a clear, calm state of mind, undisturbed by worldly events, full of compassion, is the central focus of most Buddhist practice. Skillful actions, deeds that do not cause further suffering for the practitioner and other living beings, will naturally result from this state. An agitated or unclear mind will produce *karma* results that condition rebirth and bring unsatisfactory future life experiences. Killing, stealing, unwholesome sexual conduct, lying, and indulging in drugs or intoxicating drinks will bring bad results. But it is impossible to control these actions without first controlling the mind. In the *Dhammapada* (a summary of the Buddha's teachings), the central importance of the mind is clearly stated:

> All states have mind as their forerunner, mind is their chief, and they are mind-made. If one speaks or acts with a defiled mind, then suffering follows one even as the wheel follows the hoof of the draught-ox.
>
> All states have mind as their forerunner, mind is their chief, and they are mind-made. If one speaks or acts with a pure mind, happiness follows one as one's shadow. . . . (Rahula, 1974, p. 125)

In practice, lay people may consider acts of veneration toward special monks as a way to gain merit. They may believe that observing memorial services for ancestors, building temples, chanting, or performing rituals can be as important for "good *karma*" or merit as the acts of generosity, loving kindness, and compassion that would come from a pure mind. Those seriously involved in meditation and/or mindfulness pay less attention to merit and place more emphasis on the progress of their mindfulness.

GAUTAMA BUDDHA AS AN EXAMPLE

The birth of Gautama Buddha, according to tradition, is interconnected with his mother's death and rebirth. "Seven days after the Bodhisattva (Buddha-to-be) was born, his mother died and was reborn in the Heaven of the Contented." (Nanamoli, 1972, p. 4). As Gautama grew up, leading a sheltered existence, he was allowed to experience only the good life and material luxuries of one born to the ruling caste (Sakya clan) of northern India. But he soon began to realize that this rosy picture was an illusion and became aware of aging, sickness, and death.

When Gautama saw the "serene countenance" of a wandering ascetic, he was encouraged to renounce his life of luxury and go forth in search of the truth. He finally realized enlightenment, according to tradition, by meditating on his breath, which in Buddhism is the simple life-sustaining function that reveals the impermanence of all forms, feelings, and mental constructs. From knowledge of impermanence derived knowledge of the causation of suffering and delusion, and from knowledge of causation derived the Four Noble Truths, including the path to enlightenment, i.e. the Eightfold Path.

At the time of his death, Buddha's final utterance was a challenge to his disciples: "Indeed, *bhikkus* (monks), I declare this to you—it is in the nature of all formations to dissolve. Attain perfection through diligence" (Nanamoli, 1972, p. 317).

The Buddha requested no special rituals or ceremonies, nor any cosmetic tampering with his corpse. Instead he advised his disciples to attend to their own path attainment and to avoid attachment to his earthly personality. Thus, the person of the Buddha and even his particular teachings may be discarded when the other shore is reached. But the reaction of his followers was varied and sometimes inappropriate to the teachings.

His disciples spent the night following his death contemplating the law (teachings) and meditating. But in the morning, lay leaders insisted on a ceremony customarily given to a great king.

> After seven days of ceremonial homage, an iron sarcophagus, filled with oil, was placed on the funeral pyre, made of many kinds of fragrant wood. When the fire had died down, only the bones were left. For seven days the closely guarded bones were honored with dance and song and music, and with garlands and perfumes. . . . That the Buddha was cremated indicates not that this is universal practice among Buddhists but rather his status as a great man. At that time in India, as now, not all dead bodies were cremated; those of children, and of holy men, and of [the] very poor are notable exceptions: these are buried or even left in a charnel field to be devoured by beasts and birds of prey. (Ling, 1972, pp. 124–125)

So even in Buddha's time, traditional cultural practices overlay the starkly realistic Buddhist interpretation of death.

SOME COMMON TEACHINGS ON DEATH AND DYING

During his lifetime the Buddha also instructed his followers to contemplate death as a means of understanding impermanence. One of the most poignant stories in Buddhist literature is of Kisa Gotami, a young widow, who in her grief asked the Buddha to restore her only child to life. Using everyday life experiences, the Buddha led her to realize the universal truth of impermanence and death:

> Kisa Gotami lost her only infant, and she went in search of a remedy for her dead son. Carrying the corpse, she approached the Buddha and asked for a remedy.
> "Well, sister, can you bring some mustard seed?"
> "Certainly, Lord!"
> "But, sister, it should be from a house where no one has died."
> Mustard seeds she found, but not a place where death had not visited. She understood the nature of life. (Narada, 1973, p. 657)

In some Buddhist countries, monks are instructed to meditate on decaying corpses as a way to understand impermanence and free themselves from sensual attachments. The Vietnamese monk Thich Nhat Hanh describes this experience and gives a Buddhist interpretation of it:

> When I was only 19 years old, I was assigned by an older monk to meditate on the image of a corpse in the cemetery. But I found it very hard to take and resisted the meditation. Now I no longer feel that way . . . since then, I have seen many young

soldiers laying motionless beside one another, some only 13, 14, and 15 years old. They had no preparation or readiness for death. Now I see that if one doesn't know how to die, one can hardly know how to live . . . because death is a part of life. . . . Meditate . . . knowing that your own body will undergo [a decomposition] process. Meditate on the corpse until you are calm and at peace until your mind and heart are calm and tranquil. (Nhat Hanh, 1976, p. 50)

Buddhist teachings on death, derived from an understanding of impermanence, reject all cosmetic masks for the realities of death and decay. Ultimately, enlightenment can be gained from a proper orientation to this universal experience. With complete awareness of reality, "we must look death in the face, and recognize and accept it, just as we look at and accept life" (Nhat Hanh, 1976, p. 51).

IMPORTANCE OF THE MIND AT DEATH

The state of the mind of the dying person at the moment of death is thought to influence the rebirth process. Thus, the better the state of mind, the better the chances of a favorable rebirth.

When chanted aloud with sincerity, certain sutras (recorded teachings of the Buddha) are thought to have a calming effect on the mind of the dying person. They also serve to protect the listener by driving away evil influences and directing the mind to the teachings.

The most elaborate preparation tradition is found in Tibetan Buddhism, described in *The Tibetan Book of the Dead*. The purpose of the preparation extends beyond calming and focusing the mind. It serves as an initiation of the dead or dying person to the transition from death to rebirth. Instructions are read to the dying person and later to the corpse to help guide it through the *bardo* (transitional state) between life forms. The goal is to initiate the consciousness of the dying one to the great opportunity of *nibbana* that lies ahead (Evans-Wentz, 1976, pp. 94–96).

Elaborations of this ceremony continue for 49 days until rebirth is assured. In a sense, death becomes the highlight of life, a great opportunity for realizing pure enlightenment through attainment of the Buddha mind.

In Mahayana Buddhism, Bodhisattvas or saviors offer to help suffering humanity when death is near. Knowing that most beings are stuck in the morass of life without hope of attaining enlightenment through their own efforts, Amida Buddha created a pure land (the equivalent of the Western paradise) as refuge for all who have faith in him. By sincerely repeating his name (and believing his vow), the believer's mind is cleared and is assured entrance into Pure Land. The believer finds salvation in the perfect consciousness of the infinite Buddha. The dying person, therefore, should focus his or her mind on the Pure Land and on Amida Buddha.

Funeral and death anniversary customs in Buddhist countries may reflect customary respect for the dead to a greater extent than might seem consistent with Buddhist beliefs. The actual practices may become elaborate, interwoven with non-Buddhist traditions. Ann Crawford describes these practices in Vietnam:

> The Vietnamese strongly believe that a person should die at home and surrounded by his family. It is considered bad misfortune to die away from home and bad luck to carry a corpse home. Many people are carried to the hospital if they are sick, then they are rushed home with all possible haste so that their demise may be made there.
>
> Before the body is placed in the coffin, it is wrapped with strips of cloth and a white silk shroud. The body is wedged in the coffin with reed branches, paper, and other objects. This helps keep the body in place as it decomposes. Embalming is not widely practiced.
>
> The family may gather before the special altar which has been erected for the dead person and make offerings of food for the dead person's soul. This usually is three bowls of rice, three cups of tea, and a few other special dishes. In North Vietnam it may be different. . . . This ceremony is supposed to be repeated three times a day during the entire mourning period.
>
> The ceremony of distribution of the mourning garb is carried out by monks or the eldest son of the deceased who leads the rite. Offerings are made and symbolic votive papers are burned. The mourning garb is made of very low grade white gauze and looks as if it may fall off the person wearing it. Turbans are carelessly wrapped around the head with straw crowns and a sash placed on top of this. Mourners use walking sticks made of bamboo and act as though they are groping their way along. . . .
>
> [An elaborate procession is described.] The eldest son, the monk, or funeral attendants throw a symbolic handful of dirt into the grave and then pass on their respects to the rest of the family. Relatives leave the grave but wait a short distance away until the grave is completely covered before they go home.
>
> Later, a special altar that had been previously set up for the dead member is lighted with candles continuously and incense sticks burned for 100 days.
>
> Regular ceremonies are held for the dead person after that time, especially on the death anniversary, the lunar New Year period (Tet), and often on the first and 15th days of each lunar month.
>
> Families normally have dinners on the 49th and 100th day after the death and also on the first anniversary. They may also have a dinner every year after that on the death anniversary.
>
> When the body is exhumed three years later and the bones are cleaned and rearranged in proper order and reburied in a small earthenware coffin, only relatives and close friends are in attendance . . . (Crawford, 1961, pp. 124–130)

Reverence for ancestors is also supported by Confucian notions of filial piety and the proper observance of rituals. Practices in countries that have not been penetrated by ancestor worship and Confucianism may vary significantly.

Oriental Buddhist temples usually have two prominent altars. One bears the image of the Buddha; the other has pictures of deceased people from the community. Two altars are also present in most Buddhist homes. Incense is burned and offerings of fruit and flowers are made both in the temple and at home, especially on anniversary days and on special memorial days.

In the Jodo Shinshu sect (Japanese believers in the Pure Land), funeral services have become very much like Western memorial services. They are held for the benefit of the living, as it is believed that the deceased has already been reborn in the Pure Land due entirely to the grace of Amida Buddha, not through any good works or ceremonies on the part of the living.

> As in Christianity, the funeral service is held for the memory of the deceased. Friends and relatives of the deceased are expected to attend to share the sorrow and memory. However, it must be noted that the funeral service had nothing to do with Buddhism originally.
>
> A Buddhist name is given to the deceased at the funeral service . . . i.e., those who are not yet given a Buddhist name by the time of their death will be given Buddhist names by the officiating minister at the time of the funeral service. It has been the tradition of Buddhists to send the dead body to the crematory and cast the ashes in the river after death.
>
> It has been believed that there was a 49-day interval between this life and the next. Every seventh day is believed to be the day on which the destination of the deceased will be decided. Nowadays only the 7th and the 49th are usually held. It is supposed that the body, in case it was buried, will be reduced to earth and dust 100 days after it was buried. (Hanayama, 1969, pp. 39–42)

Despite efforts to eliminate non-Buddhist customs such as these, it seems likely that some of these practices will endure even in the Western world. They apparently meet basic needs: to honor the dead and to help the survivors show publicly that they have done everything possible to assist the departed ones in the next life.

DEATH EDUCATION

Death is so integral to Buddhist tradition that special education regarding death and dying is hardly needed. There is a saying in China: If you want to know about living, study Confucianism; if you want to know about death and dying, study Buddhism. Knowledge about death and dying comes from family experiences, attendance at death anniversary celebrations, lectures given by religious notables, and Buddhist literature.

Nevertheless, there is a good deal of discussion and disputation regarding doctrines associated with death and dying. Buddhists are constantly concerned about the no-self or no-ego doctrine and how it fits with the continuation of life after death. (If there is no self, but only a collection of *karma*, then what is reborn in the next round of the cycle of life?) This is also difficult for Amida Buddhists who may like to think that their family members will be reunited in some heavenly realm. If there are no selves, what is reunited? Moreover, the ultimate destination, *Nirvana*, is not satisfying because it is described only by negatives, i.e., it is neither this nor that. Religious teachers spend a good deal of time answering questions about these matters. Sometimes a series of lectures will be held at a local temple or meeting place, followed by questions and answers. It is likely that many younger people, influenced by Western life-styles, are less interested in these matters and must be forced to listen to lectures and attend appropriate ceremonies.

EXPRESSIONS OF EMOTION

Although Buddhist doctrine views death as an opportunity for improvement in the next life, filial piety and local family customs require a display of grief. So family members, particularly the surviving spouse and children, still wear the traditional white cloth and openly show grief, even wailing at times. It may be particularly important for a surviving spouse to display emotion in order to demonstrate loyalty to the family members of the departed. As in Western traditions, friends and relatives comfort the bereaved and say kind things about the deceased. In turn, the spouse and children may describe how calm and good-humored the departed one was just before death.

SOME PRACTICES OBSERVED IN AMERICA

Everything is done to ensure a calm and peaceful environment for the dying person. Caregivers are concerned about the comfort and state of mind of the one being cared for. It is important to be able to say that she or he died peacefully or was very calm at the time of death. Buddhists generally refrain from using drugs, although in the case of extreme discomfort, drugs or traditional medicines would be accepted as long as they do not affect the state of mind, for example, by causing hallucinations. Chanting in the household might be disruptive and the visit of a monk may or may not be considered beneficial. Traditional chanting at the temple with relatives and friends may be thought to help calm and focus the minds of the caregivers, thus indirectly helping the dying person.

The funeral is planned by family members, usually by the survivor's spouse and/or oldest children, brothers, and sisters. Relatives may come from great distances to be present at this time. The body of the deceased must be treated with respect and care. Embalming is not necessary and is apparently not traditional, since there is no belief in resurrection of the body. Services may be held at a funeral home. Lay persons, with or without monks, chant appropriate sutras. As at the temple, flowers and fruit may be offered and incense burned.

It is traditional to have a large photograph of the deceased on a stand or table near the casket. At the final service, family members may wear white headbands and armbands. They may walk with sticks, symbolizing that their grief has left them in need of support.

Both cremation and below-ground burial are practiced. At the time of cremation or burial, relatives and friends may follow the casket. Chanting may continue at this time. It is customary for close family members to view the cremation and to preserve the remains in an urn or special box. At the cemetery, close family members may remain until the casket is covered with earth.

There are apparently a number of taboos with respect to funerals. We have heard that pregnant women should not attend the services as this might bring bad luck to the baby. There may also be special concerns when the death is a suicide, or is violent, unexpected, or involves a small child. Because the person may not have been prepared for death or perhaps had the wrong mind-set at the time of death, concerns may arise about the future rebirth. Relatives may rely on monks, soothsayers, or special rituals to help overcome such negative factors. In these special situations, families may also want to maintain the integrity of their traditions as much as possible. There may be a need to stress that everything be done in the proper way, so as not to cause any additional negative influences.

PERSONAL ACCOUNTS OF BUDDHIST PRACTICE

In an interview with the authors, a senior Vietnamese monk affirmed many of the descriptions of death and dying found in Buddhist literature. He pointed out that death is a transition from one form to another—not an end, but an opportunity to become something better. The dying person must train the mind, so that before death a favorable consciousness will endure to the next form. Worlds, heaven, hells are in reality creations of the consciousness (the mind). In Vietnam, it is customary to chant at the home of the dying or deceased person or at a nearby temple because it is believed that this will help to support the person in the transition. Various saviors (Bodhisattvas) or even monks may have power to provide such support, but the intention must originate from the mind or consciousness of the believer.

He also noted that most of the customs practiced in Vietnam, such as processions and anniversary ceremonies, had non-Buddhist origins. Many have now been given Buddhist interpretations. For example, the wearing of white at funerals and death anniversaries symbolizes truth and purity. The practice of leaving pictures of the deceased at the temple for anniversary ceremonies helps the survivors feel closer to the entire community. Although lay people believe the monks should have a special role in funeral and anniversary observances, their presence is not necessary; traditions can be carried on by the lay community without the monks' presence. He noted that all dead are remembered on the

Buddhist All Souls' Day in August, when it is customary to perform special services at the temple every year.

In the past few years, two important Buddhists have died in our community. A famous meditation teacher who died recently was cremated soon after his death. His followers showed their respect for him by pursuing their own meditation practice. This reflects the Buddha's admonition that his followers should carry on with diligence in pursuit of their goal. In the Asian tradition, a public funeral ceremony was held 49 days after his death.

A lay leader of the Buddhist community died several years ago and was cremated. Lay people in the community chanted for several days at the funeral home in ceremonies leading up to the final service. Family members wore white clothing, armbands, and headbands in the Asian tradition. The service included saluting the closed casket and the giving of remembrances and statements by members of the community. Several mentioned his good humor and clear mind as the time of death approached. The closed casket was taken to the crematorium with family and friends following in a semi-procession. However, only the family members, who led the way, entered the crematorium with the casket. Later, the family members strictly observed all anniversaries at 49 days and 100 days, some even returning from another state so that they could be together with the local temple community.

Funeral practices vary greatly from family to family in America, but the importance of the anniversary services remains. Most people apparently have a need to maintain these customs, which mark both their cultural and religious identities.

ACKNOWLEDGMENTS

The editors wish to acknowledge assistance with Buddhist materials from Rhoda Gilman, Senior Research Fellow, Minnesota Historical Society.

REFERENCES

Crawford, A. (1961). *Customs and culture in Vietnam.* Tokyo, Japan: Charles E. Tuttle.

Evans-Wentz, W. Y. (1976). *The Tibetan book of the dead.* London: Oxford University Press.

Hanayama, S. (1969). *Buddhist handbook.* Tokyo, Japan: Hokuseido Press.

Ling, T. O. (1970). *A dictionary of Buddhism.* New York: Scribners.

Nanamoli. (1972). *The life of the Buddha.* Kandy, Sri Lanka: Buddhist Publication Society.

Narada. (1973). *The Buddha and his teachings.* Colombo, Sri Lanka: Vajirarama.

Nhat Hanh. (1976). *The miracle of mindfulness.* Boston: Beacon Press.

Rahula, W. (1974). *What the Buddha taught.* New York: Grove Press.

BIBLIOGRAPHY

Conze, E. (1959). *Buddhism: Its essence and development.* New York: Harper Torchbook.

Gunaratne, V. F. (1966). Buddhist reflections on death. *The Wheel, 102–103.* Kandy, Sri Lanka: Buddhist Publication Society.

"Impermanence." (1973). In: *The Wheel, 271–272.* Kandy, Sri Lanka: Buddhist Publication Society.

Khantipalo. (1980). The bag of bones. *The Wheel, 271–272.* Kandy, Sri Lanka: Buddhist Publication Society.

Owen, N. G. (Ed.). (1987). Vietnamese attitudes regarding illness and healing. In N. G. Owen (ed.), *Death and disease in Southeast Asia: Explorations in social, medical, and demographic history,* (pp. 162–186). Oxford: Oxford University Press.

"Suffering." (1973). In: *The Wheel, 191–193.* Kandy, Sri Lanka: Buddhist Publication Society.

Walshe. (1978). Buddhism and death. *The Wheel, 261.* Kandy, Sri Lanka, Buddhist Publication Society.

Chapter Ten

Islamic Customs Regarding Death

Farah Gilanshah

Illustrative Episode

It is Saturday morning. A Muslim father and his daughter have left home for the shopping center where the daughter works. The father has decided to go along to "window shop." Both have arrived at the mall and the daughter leaves for her store. Since the father has used the shopping mall for walking every winter, he knows the area well.

After about half an hour, the father suddenly collapses. The daughter hears her name called on the mall's communication system. She learns that her father has just had a fatal heart attack. She cries and screams, an emotional response pattern very common among Muslims. An ambulance arrives to take the body to a clinic.

Questions then arise regarding what should be done, how, and by whom. The family is Muslim. They have their own system of beliefs, rituals, and ceremonies about the dead. They live in a society that is predominantly Christian. They also live in a community in which no other Muslim immigrants have died recently. All of the immigrants left their countries within the past decade or so. The younger ones have little knowledge about, and virtually no experience with, appropriate rituals. The older ones lack command of the new language. But they know that Christian procedures are wrong according to Islam.

Submitted by Farah Gilanshah

There is a list of questions concerning the episode described here in Appendix B: Questions That Might Be Asked.

Editors

⸺⸺⸺◦◦◊◊◊◊◊◦◦⸺⸺⸺

What are the Muslim customs, beliefs, and expressions related to dying, death, and grief? Will a Muslim community in a foreign land be able to perform Islamic rituals? What insights can be promoted not only for the close relatives of the dying person who are Muslims, but also for doctors, nurses, social workers, hospital chaplains, funeral home directors, and others who have little or no knowledge of Muslim customs? One immigrant group may act like Christians in terms of the rituals they practice, while their relatives may preserve the Muslim rituals along with their Islamic faith.

PRINCIPLES OF ISLAM

Islam is the name of the religion preached by the Prophet Muhammad, who appeared in Mecca around 1,400 years ago. The word "Islam" means peace or complete submission. Technically, when applied in religion, Islam means "achievement of peace with Allah and man, and complete resignation to Allah in thoughts, words, beliefs, and deeds" (Ali, 1962, p. 1).

The most important principle in Islam is the belief in only one God, or Allah. Mussulmen, the people who profess this religion, have to abide by the following guiding principles:

- to believe in one God, or Allah;
- to believe in the Prophet Muhammad and the Holy Koran;
- to believe that there is a day of judgment and a life after death;
- to make a commitment to fast;
- *haj*, to go at least once, if at all possible, on a pilgrimage to Mecca;
- *zakat*, to perform the duty to give generously to poor people;
- *jihad*, to fight for the sake of Allah; and
- to pray five times a day.

According to Imam Ali, (the first Shi'at Imam) the principal object of the Islamic faith is to show the best straight path by which people's faculties may be brought to perfection and the souls of individuals may experience their full self-realization (Ali, 1962, p. 1). The governing of an Islamic state involves the whole community of Muslims, and its law is the law of the Koran. This prohibits slavery; emphasizes charity very strongly; and places great importance on education regardless of sex, age, and race. Prostitution, drinking alcoholic beverages, gambling, robbery, and adultery are prohibited in Islam. Strong attention is given to family life, and the Koran is the guide. Muslims that follow the Koran will have a happy and healthy life in this world and in the afterworld.

ISLAMIC VIEWS ON LIFE, DEATH, AND WHAT HAPPENS AFTER DEATH

Death is frequently discussed within Islamic culture; sometimes a Muslim is taught more about life after death than about life itself! The accepted view is that every Muslim should have a happy life in this world and in the afterworld. Death is considered as a natural part and process of life. According to Dehlvi, "Hazrat Umar reports that the Prophet was asked which is the wisest man and the Prophet replied that he is the man who remembers death more frequently and devotes himself and works in preparing for life after death" (Dehlvi, 1974, p. 53). And it is said that according to Prophet Muhammad:

> If Allah keeps one alive in Islam for 40 years He turns away from him leprosy, insanity, quinsy and the satan and if anyone is allowed to live 50 years his account is made easy for him and if anyone is allowed to live 60 years then it becomes easier for him to turn to things dear to Allah and if one is allowed to live 70 years then the dwellers of heaven begin to love him and if one is allowed to live 80 years then his sins are blotted out and virtues are recorded in their place, and if one is given to live 90 years then all his earlier sins are forgiven and he is Allah's prisoner on earth and his intercession for his household will be accepted. (Dehlvi, 1974, p. 26)

In *Life After Death* by M. H. Tabatabahi (1978), the concepts of death, soul, and day of judgment are explained. According to Tabatabahi, we pass through one phase to another. In Islam, human beings are created to survive, not to vanish. Death is a return to God. Imam Jafar Sadegh said that human beings are created from two things: world and afterworld. Human beings experience the two worlds while they still live in this world. When they die, however, the separation of the two worlds will occur, and then the person lives only in the afterworld. According to Imam Ali, the afterworld has both beauty and ugliness. Death for believers means to be rid of the ugliness of this world and to join the beauty of the afterworld. For nonbelievers, death means to return to the ugliness of the afterworld. According to Imam Ali, death is like a long dream that one experiences. If one has a peaceful dream, one is blessed both in this world and the afterworld. However, if one has no peaceful dreams, it is time to take care of one's sins and guilt in this world.

It was not only Imam Ali who mentioned the analogy between sleep and dreams, but the Prophet also. Muslims believe that the person will leave everything behind in this world and enter the afterworld alone. It is said that human beings are aware of their death at the time of departure from this world. Those who are afraid of death are those who panic when they are aware of entering the afterworld and the hell it probably holds for them.

According to Imam Ali, human beings will see their children and their wealth at the last moments of life. Parents will tell their children, "I loved you all very dearly and I was very protective of you. What do you have for me?" The children will answer, "Nothing"—and they cover the grave. Then the person sees all of his or her wealth and goods from this world, and says to the wealth, "I always liked you and sought you out, and I was never satisfied. What do you have for me?" The response will be "Nothing." Then the person will look at all of his or her actions and tell the actions, "I never paid attention to what I have done, and I always misused you in any way I wanted, wrong and right. What do you have for me?" And the actions will respond, "I will be with you on the grave, in the afterworld, and on the day of judgment." In other words, what we take with us from this world are our actions.

Muslims believe that when the body is buried two angels will come to the grave. They each have a voice like a thunderstorm, and they have eyes like lightning. They will ask the buried person: "Who is your God? Who is your Prophet? What is your religion?" If the dead body answers, "Allah is my god; Prophet Muhammad is my Prophet; Islam is my religion," then the angels will open the grave and pray for the dead person; they will ask that God forgive him or her and take the soul to the beauty and peace of the afterworld. However, the angels will also ask the same questions of a nonbeliever. If the individual responds that she or he does not know or does not have a God, the angels will take the soul to the ugliest, dirtiest place where there are fires and snakes.

It is said that God will send the souls of believers to heaven. There they will eat and drink. When other souls arrive in heaven they will be recognized by features that they had while they were alive. Once they meet the new arrivals they will ask questions about the people that they both used to know. If the newly arrived soul says that a person was alive, it is the sign of his or her arrival in heaven. But if the soul says that the surviving person is dead, that is the sign of his or her entering hell. In other words, the believers are aware of what their family members are doing and can observe them from heaven, but this is not the case for nonbelievers.

If the souls were believers and see that their families, too, are believers and happy, they will thank God and be pleased. If they are nonbelievers, but their families are believers, they will regret their disbelief deeply. A dead person who was a believer and is favored by God will be able to make family visits more often, whether the family members are believers or not. Believers' spirits will appear at the porch of the house as birds and join their family members at meals or other gatherings.

The day of judgment occurs when there are no human beings left in this world. All the dead will appear in front of God, who will ask them questions about all the wrong things they did when alive. Judgment will be based on their good and bad actions, and good actions will weigh more than bad ones. Justice is the most important criterion.

Concepts of death and dying, the soul or spirit, and the day of judgment have been emphasized in Islamic culture. The purpose of the funeral ceremony is to make the dead person ready for the day of judgment. This is a very serious concern for every Muslim, especially for Muslim immigrants who live where Islam is not the dominant religion.

DEATH AND DEATH CEREMONIES

When the dying person is suffering in the last moments, a close relative remains with them. The relative prays for God's blessing and reads the Koran during the last moments, to remind the dying person about the unity of God, the Prophets Muhammad and Immamat, and to teach other tenets of the true religion. It is believed that Satan will be close to the person at the time of death, but angels will be there, too. Though the dying person may not be able to see, talk, or move, he or she can understand what is happening, so it is the relatives' responsibility to pray for the dying person until the last breath is taken.

As soon as the relatives see that the person is dead, they must take the following immediate actions:

- turn the body to face toward Mecca;
- have someone sitting near the body read the Koran;
- close the body's mouth and eyes, and cover the eyes and face;
- straighten both legs and stretch both hands by the sides;
- announce the death immediately to all friends and relatives; and
- hasten to bathe the body and cover it with white cotton.

It is undesirable to leave the dead person alone. If the death happens at home, the body should be taken immediately to the place where it will be bathed. Before the bathing, the relatives should have an assurance from the doctor that the person is not alive. There are always two people who wash the dead body. Males always bathe a male and females bathe a female. It is a sin if females wash the male's body or vice versa. Three kinds of water are used: water with leaves of the plum tree; camphorized water; and pure water. If only one kind of water is available, the caretakers are allowed to wash the body three times in the water that is available.

FUNERAL CEREMONIES

Generally, four people place the four corners of a bier on their shoulders. No one must walk in front of the bier, so while changing shoulders one should pass behind the bier. While carrying the body the carriers repeat *"Allah Akbar"* (God Is Great) and pray for blessing. It is customary to show the face of the deceased to some close relatives before burial. Spouses, daughters, and sons, however, are not supposed to see the face, but sons-in-law may see the face, if they wish. The view is that the death is most tragic for those closest to the deceased.

The man who buries the body should be able to stand or to sit between the body and the side of the grave, and he should not wear shoes. The grave should face Mecca. The burial should take place between sunrise and sunset on the day of the death or the following day.

At the time of burial, all the family members and friends gather with a religious person. They pray and ask God for forgiveness. No discussion goes on, just crying and praying, because it is believed that people should weep and release their sorrow. Some mourners may faint at the time of burial, and for that reason, tea, sugar, and sugar syrup are available. Muslims believe that once sorrow is released by crying, one's body system will be relieved and the process of coping and attaining peace can proceed. The body can tolerate only a certain amount of sadness; so, in effect, people become their own healers. The funeral is both depressing and expressive; even participants who may not know the deceased will find themselves moved to cry.

Following the funeral ceremony, all the friends and relatives go to the house of the deceased's family. Usually a meal is prepared and the guests will remain there for the whole day or night. Close relatives frequently stay for the entire week. During this time there is a good deal of crying, and the deceased's immediate family will talk about their sorrow and the problems of adaptation to their new situation. They will be "social" for the entire week and are not left alone. Socializing is seen as a way of reassuring the relatives of the deceased person.

On the third day after the burial, a ceremony lasting several hours is held in the mosque, when friends and relatives gather to pray. A religious leader reads from the Koran and prays for blessing. The rest do the same. Muslims believe that the more prayers uttered for the deceased person at the time of death, and for days after that, the easier the departed one's life will be in the afterworld. Praying for the first seven days is crucial. After seven days, a prepared stone will be placed to cover the grave and fresh flowers will be put on top. Close relatives are required to wear black clothing for 40 days. After 40 days, they gather in the cemetery or at the house of the deceased to pray from the Koran and ask for God's blessing. Thereafter, everyone, except close relatives, changes their dress to colors other than black, although widows will sometimes wear black for a year.

One year after the person's death, there is another ceremony to pray for and remember the deceased person. All through the years it is recommended to pray for the deceased, give money to the poor, and ask for God's blessing.

ACCULTURATION PROCESS

What do Muslims do in the Western world, living in societies that hold different cultural and religious values? For Muslims, the ultimate goal for living is a death through which a desirable transition to the other world takes place. The goal is to do well in this world and to prepare for the afterworld. The rituals concerning burials are down-to-earth and nonmaterial, with great emphasis on prayers, cleanliness, and purity. No one leaves this world with material wealth or goods. In contrast to the Muslim experience, the most important rituals relating to death and dying in Western culture frequently involve displays of luxury and materialism. The one emphasizes cleanliness and purity; the other emphasizes clothes, "make up" and the conspicuous display of the deceased. The contrasts are many and often stark.

There is a small Muslim community in the Minneapolis/St. Paul area of Minnesota. Muslims have a place for their ceremonies in a western suburb of Minneapolis. Local citizens of both sexes who have been converted to Islam also perform the bathing of dead bodies. The Islamic Center invited Muslims from Saudi Arabia to teach these converts how to bathe the body, and they have imported special waters and the white cotton called *kafan*. A training program is in place so that when there is a need for more help, there will be more than two people available to perform the ritual bathing. As a result, the rituals are almost the same in Minnesota as in Islamic countries.

There have been similar conformances as far as the graves and the burial ritual are concerned. The cemetery used had belonged to Christians, but half of it has been bought by Muslims. The Muslims of Minneapolis are not alone. Many Muslims in the United States have retained their cultural traditions and religious rituals.

DEATH EDUCATION IN ISLAMIC COUNTRIES
AND THE WESTERN WORLD

The reality of life and death has been taught through socialization in Muslim countries. Children's education in Islamic societies has religious values. Life has purpose. It is short, and it ends in death.

Currently, people in Muslim countries have a shorter life expectancy than in the West. As a result, children frequently experience the death of family members. Because of the harsher conditions of life in Muslim countries, people are constantly reminded of death and dying. In the Western world, by contrast, people are not taught to accept death easily. In Muslim societies, death and dying are very common subjects and people learn to talk about them readily, in school and within families. Children born and reared in the Western world do not talk about death and dying as readily as Muslim children do; they do not know how to view them as integral parts of life.

REFERENCES

Ali, A. K. (1962). *Introduction to Islamic culture*. Dacca, Pakistan: Mohammadi Book House.

Dehlvi, A. S. (1974). *What happens after death* (Al-Hashmi, Trans.). Delhi, India.

Syed Muslim, M. (1972). *Death and death ceremonies*. Karachi: Peermahomed Ebrahim Trust.

Tabatabahi, M. H. (1978). *Hayat Pas As Marg [Life after death]*. Kohm, Iran: Azadi Kohm Press.

BIBLIOGRAPHY

Anthony-Z, & Bhana-K, Kastoor. (1988-89). An exploratory study of Muslim girls' understanding of death. *Omega: Journal of death and dying, 19*(3), 215-227.

Brandon, S. G. F. (1970). *The judgment of the dead*. New York: Scribners.

Chittick, W. C. (1987). Eschatology. In S. Nasr (Ed.), *Islamic Spirituality: Foundations* (pp. 378-409). New York: Crossroad.

Chittick, W. C. (1988, January). Death and the world of imagination: Ibnal-Arabi's eschatology. *Muslim World, 78,* 51-82.

Cragg, K. (1983). Finality in Islam. *Studia Missionalia, 32,* 219-230.

Granqvist, H. N. (1965). *Muslim death and burial: Arab customs and traditions studied in a village in Jordan*. Helsinki, Finland.

Islam, K. M. (1976). *The spectacle of death: Including glimpses of life beyond the grave*. Lahore, Pakistan: Tablighi Kutub Khana.

O'Shaughnessy, T. J. (1969). *Muhammad's thoughts on death: A thematic study of the Qur'anic data*. Leiden, Netherlands: E. Brill.

Racy, J. (1969). Death in Arab culture. *Annals, New York Academy of Sciences, 64,* 871-880.

Sicard, S. Von. (1978, July). Marantha: Advent in the Muslim world. *Missiology, 6,* 335-341.

Smith, J. I. (1979, July). The understanding of Nafs and Ruh in contemporary Muslim considerations of the nature of sleep and death. *Muslim World, 69,* 151-162.

Smith, J. I. (1980, February). Concourse between the living and the dead in Islamic eschatological literature. *History of Religion, 19,* 224-236.

Smith, J. I., & Haddad, Y. (1975). Women in the afterlife: The Islamic view as seen from Qur'an and tradition. *Journal of the American Academy of Religion, 43,* 39-50.

Smith, J. I., & Haddad, Y. (1979, December). Afterlife themes in modern Qur'an commentary. *Journal of the American Academy of Religion Thematic Studies, 47*(4S), 699-720.

Smith, J. I., & Haddad, Y. (1981). *The Islamic understanding of death and resurrection.* Albany: State University of New York Press.

Toynbee, A. J., et al. (1976). *Life after death.* London: Weidenfeld & Nicolson.

Tug, S. (1987). Death and immortality in the religions of the world. In P. Badham & L. Badham (Eds.), *Death and immortality* (pp. 86–92). New York: Paragon House.

Vandewiele, M. (1983–1984). Attitudes of Senegalese secondary school students toward death. *Omega: Journal of death and dying, 14*(4), 329–334.

Wikan, U. (1988). Bereavement and loss in two Muslim communities: Egypt and Bali compared [Special issue: Permanence and change in American health care transition]. *Social Science and Medicine, 27*(5), 451–460.

Chapter Eleven

Memorial Services among Quakers and Unitarians

Donald P. Irish

Each of us knows another person only partially, within the given time frame of our acquaintanceship and solely through our specific interacting roles. A "non-traditional" memorial service can aid the survivors of a death to come to appreciate more fully the total self and the many selves of the person being remembered. Some Quakers, Unitarians, and people in noncreedal and relatively nonritualistic faiths use such services to memorialize family and community members. However, this form of commemoration would be found mainly within certain segments of American and Canadian Quakerism. It is not typical of most Quakers worldwide.

ONE MEMORIAL SERVICE

Friends, neighbors, and family members arrived before the appointed hour and sat in contemplation in the concentric circles of chairs. (A church sanctuary with fixed pews would not have provided the face-to-face intimacy and the level of interpersonal sharing offered by this spacious and flexible university ballroom. At its center was a low round table covered with vases of daffodils which the attendees had been invited to bring, as symbols of the early spring. A woodwind trio formed by young family friends provided a soothing background for reflection.

This gathering in honor of the deceased was held on a Sunday afternoon, two weeks after her death. The time lapse allowed the family to prepare the personalized features of the service—special Latin American music and a slide show of her life. The body had been cremated promptly after her death. Her ashes were scattered in subsequent months in places especially meaningful to her in the states where she had lived. The traditions of Quaker simplicity and dignity precluded embalming, "body preparation," viewing, a casket, limousines and hearse, and the many other accouterments typical of modern American funerals. Memorial services tend to be do-it-yourself events.

Most celebrations of life in this form are designed specifically to highlight the life of the deceased and do not follow a mainline church pattern. Each such occasion of remembrance is unique to the person being cherished and is unlike any other in specifics of form and content.

An eight-page folder was given to each attendee upon arrival. The cover photograph showed a vibrant, smiling image of the deceased in the prime of her life. Inside, the sequence of the program was listed, four pages provided a resume of her 65 years, and the words to a song, "The Rose," were included as well. A final page expressed the family's gratitude to the 126 persons who had donated blood to her credit, the 10 friends who remained always available for leukophoresis, her two physicians and eight devoted nurses, many friends who had provided fruit, food, and flowers, and all who had conveyed messages of concern and love. The names of agencies that represented her commitments to peace and justice were listed for those wishing to commemorate her with a donation.

Orientation to the Service

After the trio finished a Bach piece, and allowing for a brief period of quiet, the woman who was clerk of the Friends (Quaker) Meeting opened the service. The program was conducted in a spirit of worship and in a quite unprogrammed way. On behalf of the Meeting and the family, she welcomed everyone who came for the celebration of this life. Their presence was deemed to be a personal tribute to the deceased and an indication of the love she had given and received from all the different communities in which she had participated. For those unfamiliar with the "manner of Friends," the clerk explained what they might expect to occur:

> We sit in silent worship and, when an individual feels moved to speak, that person arises and delivers their message as appropriate to the occasion. Every message is

important, comes from the spirit of life, and should be heard by all those present. [Microphones were placed in the several aisles.] We ask that you share so that all of us may benefit by learning about the deceased's life from one another. The offering might be a song, poem, selection from Scripture, a specific remembrance of her, or something distinctly your own that you may wish to say. We also believe that silence has its own eloquence; so we ask that messages be kept short, allowing "spaces" for reflection between presentations.

Family and Friends "Speak Out of the Silence"

Altogether during the entire program 22 people spoke, interspersed with musical interludes. The initial segment included commentaries from the deceased woman's sister and from two friends, "speaking out of the silence," with pauses between.

Then three friends presented "The Rose," one singing, another playing viola, and the third providing piano accompaniment. The season was early spring, and the words epitomized their friend's life and spirit.

From the silence that followed, her middle daughter, and three more friends spoke. A young friend who had served in the Peace Corps in Paraguay then accompanied himself on guitar and sang the Spanish song *Gracias a la Vida* (Thanks to Life). Six more individuals followed, with "spaces in their togetherness." Following another brief period of reflection, eight more people offered their heartfelt thoughts.

At this point, someone began to sing the Shaker hymn, "'Tis a gift to be simple, 'Tis a gift to be free," and the entire gathering took up the song. Young friends from Paraguay played their national instrument, the harp. The widowed husband then shared some concluding thoughts.

Closing Moments

The movement "Spring" from Vivaldi's "The Four Seasons" was played while the youngest daughter projected slides from her mother's life, without commentary. Her many roles and endeavors were portrayed from her infancy to the final months: as daughter and sister, wife, mother, grandmother. She was shown cycling, swimming, mountain climbing, camping, driving a tractor, and in Africa, Asia, Europe, Latin America, and Canada. She appeared in her hospital dietitian's uniform and in her gown as a hospital patient. A final happy picture showed her on a Nova Scotia shore amid flowers, with a sparkling blue sea behind, displaying a winning smile, a twinkle in her eye, and the tilt of her head that conveyed her customary joy in the present and an anticipation of adventures yet to come.

All those gathered then clasped hands and closed the service. A reception for the family followed.

CONCEPTS AND BACKGROUND
OF MEMORIAL SERVICES

The holding of memorial services, instead of funerals in the common pattern, is more often found among Quakers, Unitarians, humanists, and others whose religious faith is less creedal (or devoid of creeds) and minimal in ritual. However, an increasing number of families of more orthodox faiths are adopting some of the features of memorial services and incorporating them into their ceremonies.

How do funerals differ from memorial services in aura and focus?

> In a funeral the center of attention is the dead body; the emphasis is on death. In a memorial service the center of concern is the personality of the individual who has died, and the emphasis is on life. In addition, a memorial service generally involves less expense and can be held in a greater variety of locations. . . . The distinctive thing about memorial services is that they stress the ongoing qualities of the person's life individuality rather than his death. Each service can be worked out to meet the needs and circumstances of the particular family (Bender, 1974, p. 139).
>
> A funeral service is, by definition, a service held in the presence of the body. The casket may be open or closed. A memorial service is . . . held after the body has been removed. Both serve the same purpose. Each has something to recommend it (Morgan & Morgan, 1988, p. 50).

Dignity, simplicity, and economy characterize memorial services—though economy is the least important concern. To aid individuals who are oriented toward these concepts, the Continental Association of Funeral and Memorial Societies (USA) and the Memorial Society Association of Canada were organized. These nonprofit, consumer-cooperative organizations operate democratically. They assist members through advance planning, advice, and contractual agreement with funeral establishments for inexpensive services appropriate to each perspective. There are memorial societies in 200 cities in North America with a combined membership of about half a million people. The People's Memorial Association of Seattle, Washington, the first such group in the United States, was organized in 1939. The Canadian Memorial Society Association was formed in 1971. (Morgan & Morgan, 1988, pp. 67–70, 117–124).

PHILOSOPHICAL/THEOLOGICAL ORIENTATIONS
AND VARIATIONS

Religious Society of Friends (Quakers)

George Fox (1624–1691) "founded" the Religious Society of Friends in England about 1652. The term *Society of Friends* came to be used in the late 18th century. Though they arose out of the Christian tradition, the early Friends differed considerably from the major Protestant denominations in that continuing direct revelation took precedence over traditionally evolved belief and practice. Quakers seek firsthand experience of Christ's teachings and the immediacy of leadings from God, and they endeavor to apply them to the whole of life. They accept the "priesthood of all believers," believing that it is the individual responsibility of each and every member to contribute to the group ministry. Traditionally, they have supported equality between men and women and among all races. They have formulated no standard creeds or liturgies and practice no sacraments. They believe that creeds "tend to crystallize thoughts in matters that cannot be embodied in language" and restrict a search for truth that is more adequately experienced through waiting upon the Light within. However, their meetings follow distinctive customs and language. No days, places, or buildings are viewed as distinctly holy—because every day and any site has this potential. Traditionally, Quakers oppose all war and participation in it as un-Christian and inhumane, for there is that of God in every person. The Quakers, along with the Mennonites and the Church of the Brethren, have been considered the traditional "peace churches."

There is considerable variety within the Quaker tradition—and a tolerance of these differences. Three principal traditions arose in America, which have been labeled "Gurneyite" or pastoral, "Conservative," and "Hicksite." The spectrum includes quite theologically conservative evangelical groups, not unlike some Protestant denominations. Isolated Friends on the frontier sometimes adopted the pastoral form from their non-Quaker neighbors. They have paid clergy, follow a formal pattern of worship, and are often called Friends' "churches" rather than "meetings." These pastoral Friends grew out of the "Great Awakening" revival of the late 18th and early 19th centuries.

The Conservative Friends have maintained the traditional unprogrammed (silent) form of worship, and they have often remained faithful in adhering to the traditional testimonies such as pacifism, older customs of speech and dress, and simplicity.

The Hicksite Friends also hold unprogrammed silent meetings, but they more often include members who are intellectually oriented, frequently found in university communities, and tend to be more influenced by modern schools of thought. In many instances they are close to Unitarianism-Universalism in philosophy, being both universal and humanistic in their views. They are often more inclined toward action on social issues, more concerned with "works" than with a focus upon faith.

Thus, Quakers may range all the way from those that are quite Christocentric to those members that are humanistic or agnostic. Each orientation (and there are more than these three) has its own inheritances from the era of George Fox and its own national association of meetings or churches. The Quaker "denomination" has no hierarchical authority figures or structures. Each meeting is fully autonomous. Unprogrammed meetings are presided over only by a clerk, selected from among its members.

The world membership of Friends exceeds 216,000, the majority of whom (108,000) are in the United States. Canada and the rest of the Americas account for 25,000 Quakers, half of them in Bolivia. Africa has 57,000, mainly in Kenya. About 21,000 Friends live in Europe and the Near East; and the Asia-West Pacific area has 5,300. (Friends World Committee for Consultation, 1988, pp. 130–131). The vast majority of North American Friends are middle class and of European extraction.

Unitarian-Universalist

Statements from two Unitarian groups provide a succinct introduction to the philosophical/theological orientation of this denomination:

> Unitarian-Universalism is based on the conviction that each of us evolves religious beliefs from our own personal life experience. As we have a variety of contrasting experiences throughout our lives, we find it undesirable and impossible to lock ourselves into one creedal statement. We joined together in religious community to support one another in our personal quest, to bear witness in the world to our commitment to every individual's unique potential growth, and to seek communion with the infinite (Unitarian Universalist Church, 1989).
>
> The First Unitarian Society of Minneapolis . . . was founded . . . to unite people in intellectual, moral, and religious culture and humane work; to support and develop freedom of individual belief; to promote the continuous search for truth; and to foster democratic relations and concern for all humanity.
> Rather than looking to outside authority or mysterious revelation as the ultimate center or source of all power and goodness, we strive to deal with reality by relying on rational thought, science, the democratic process, and our human spirit.
> The humanist vision toward which we strive is a better world of freedom, peace, dignity, love, and tolerance of diversity. At the same time we strive to develop as thoughtful, compassionate, ethical human beings. We alone are responsible for ourselves and our world. We choose to pursue our vision through this Society—a vital, caring community. (First Unitarian Society, 1990)

In 1568 the only Unitarian king in history, John Sigismund of Transylvania, issued the Western world's first edict of religious freedom; and in a small Transylvanian community is to be found the world's oldest Unitarian congregation. By 1600 there were more than 400 Unitarian congregations in that area. Later, in England, John Milton, Isaac Newton, and John Locke advanced liberal views of religion, and the denomination began to take an organizational form. Early in the 18th century, such views began to be heard in American pulpits. In 1760 the Methodists excommunicated John Murray for his liberal views; and in 1770 he helped to found the Universalist churches in America. The first churches in the United States that were named as Unitarian were founded by Joseph Priestley in Northumberland, Pennsylvania, in 1794 and in Philadelphia in 1796. In Boston, William Ellery Channing stimulated the founding of the American Unitarian Association in 1825.

Although there was no strong urging for the Universalists and Unitarians to join in the last century, there was a growing awareness of an affinity between the groups. Resolutions for union were issued on a gradual basis, culminating in a complete merger in 1961. A statement of principles issued in 1984 sets forth the basic philosophy of the Unitarian-Universalist churches and fellowships (Mendelsohn, 1985, pp. 12–14). The Unitarian Universalist Association now has a membership of about 1,000 congregations in the United States and Canada.

James Luther Adams has enunciated five precepts of Unitarianism-Universalism:

1 Revelation is continuous; nothing is complete; and everything is open to criticism.

2 Relations between persons ought to rest on mutual free consent and not on coercion.

3 There is a moral obligation on every member to work toward a just and loving community: "salvation by character."

4 "The decisive forms of goodness in society are institutional forms." Even though individual virtue is necessary for social virtue, faith cannot be placed in individual merit alone. Freedom and justice are impossible without expression in societal forms.

5 The divine and human resources available justify an attitude of ultimate optimism regarding the achievement of meaningful change (Adams, 1987, pp. 1–13).

Life and Death Commonalities

Unitarian–Universalists and the majority of North American Quakers have much in common both philosophically and organizationally. Both traditions tend to focus on the here and now and their members' moral obligations to commit themselves to work for peace and justice and a loving community. Both tend to stress "salvation by character" and social responsibility, with little concern for a fear of hell or hope of heaven, although some individuals may believe in personal immortality.

Regarding issues of life and death and health care, those decisions by principle and practice are left to the individuals and families most involved, with support and advice provided by their religious communities. Neither group objects to the therapeutic use of drugs, vaccines, or blood. They do not oppose biopsies, organ donations, or organ transplants. Both find autopsies acceptable, and Unitarians may even recommend them. Neither group is opposed to passive euthanasia, and each supports the "right to die," though Unitarians tend to be more positive and to favor "non-action" when death is imminent. Although both leave the disposal of bodies to individual preferences, Unitarians consider cremation to be customary, with occasional donation of a body to a medical school for study. Both traditions generally accept all forms of birth control, tests for sterility, and artificial insemination, but the Unitarians are more explicit in favoring those actions as human rights. Both usually accept therapeutic abortions and those by choice, with Unitarians strongly favoring the right of the woman to decide (Catholic Hospital Association, 1978, pp. 55–56, 61–62).

Whereas the majority of Unitarian-Universalists tend to be humanists, Quakers range from the more traditional members who believe in a personal God, to others who phrase the entity more in terms of an impersonal cosmic force, to yet others who would merely say "I don't know" when asked to characterize a Supreme Being. While both Quakers and Unitarian-Universalists generally view suicides as personal and social tragedies, they recognize that desperate personal situations bring individuals to hopelessness, and that even a loving support system, when it exists, may be inadequate to prevent self-destruction. Members of both religious groups are more apt to empathize with than to stigmatize such events.

DEATH EDUCATION

American middle-class white culture's traditional reticence in confronting human mortality somewhat parallels its avoidance of discussing human sexuality. Yet the general religious philosophy of those who favor memorial services leads them, perhaps more often than other denominations, to accept the reality of death as part of life. Unlike many Christian churches that focus once a year upon Easter as their prime consideration of death—and a very atypical one—those accustomed to memorial services are apt to maintain a more year-round concern.

Many Quaker meetings and Unitarian-Universalist groups have developed materials (pamphlets, manuals, audiovisuals, checklists) that relate to dying, death, and mortality for the guidance of their members. Since many within these constituencies also belong to memorial societies, they have ready access to information of this nature (cf. Morgan & Morgan, 1988). Becoming an individual or family member of a memorial society in itself indicates recognition of the fragility and uncertainty of life. By so doing, arrangements are made well in advance through a society with a cooperating mortician for the disposal of the body through a contract specifying one of several options, with different costs, that are consistent with dignity, simplicity, and economy. The form to be completed and filed with the mortician (as well as with family, attorney, and religious group) asks the applicant to specify the kind of body disposal desired, which may include cremation (the usual choice), burial, or donation of the body to science (usually to a nearby medical school). The process also provides an opportunity to consider the content of the service that will be wanted—music, poetry, spokespersons, site, the designation of recipients for memorial donations, and the like. Included also would be an expression of desires about autopsy and organ donation.*

Since in law the next of kin are generally the final arbiters of what is to be done at the death of a loved one, discussion and agreement beforehand with one's family is essential if one's wishes are to be followed.

"Living wills" are utilized. When properly worded, witnessed, and processed, these are being given legal status in many states. Extensive checklists are available to aid people in "getting their houses in order" for the information and benefit of their survivors. Included are data to be provided regarding one's will, insurance policies, debts, mortgages, investments, safe-deposit boxes, bank accounts, retirement pensions, Social Security benefits, real properties owned, disposal of personal possessions, specified memorial funds, information for the obituary, and so on.

For example, the Death and Dying Study Group of the Langley Hill Friends Meeting in Virginia developed a checklist "to prepare themselves for their own deaths and to free themselves to aid others at such occasions" (Langley Hill, 1978). Included were items related to specific roles and tasks at the time of death—notification of members, visiting the family and offering aid and support, help with the obituary, decisions on funeral or memorial service and body disposal, notification of distant relatives and friends, provision of food and child care, housecleaning, helping with ready cash, transportation, answering the phone and door, meeting emotional needs, and numerous other items. The Meeting created a packet which is taken by a trained member of the Meeting to the household where a death has occurred, to help with the many concerns. Included in it is a copy of the Morgans' *Manual of Death Education and Simple Burial* (Morgan & Morgan, 1988) and reference to a book, *I Never Know What to Say,* (Donnelley, 1990). A bibliography, "Mourning Our Losses," has been prepared which makes reference to a Grief Recovery Handbook. A practice is suggested in which paired persons meet to talk about, review, and assess their lifelong gains and losses. The Philadelphia Yearly Meeting, too, has revised its guides for funerals and memorial services, and suggested ways of dealing with grief.

The resource handbook published by the Pacific Yearly Meeting, *When Death Occurs in the Meeting* (1975) is quite extensive. Its concerns include: preparation within Meeting (death education); what to do when death occurs (22 items); and special needs at time of death (arrangements, emotional and social needs, expression of grief, accepting the reality of death, situational variations, rehabilitation, re-establishing relationships, relief of guilt, death of a child, and affirmation of values). A major section deals with interpreting death to a child;

*Arrangements with a genuine memorial society and cooperating mortician should not be confused with commercial contracts of "preplanning" offered by other funeral homes that are not in accord with memorial society principles and practices. Nor should a mortuary calling itself a "cremation society" be viewed as a legitimate consumer-cooperative membership organization.

another with caring for those who mourn. There are materials related to suicide, euthanasia, "last rites," and books for children. A form is provided, to be filed with the Meeting, so that the deceased person's wishes may be carried out.

A Brotman-Marsh-Field copyrighted unit for parents and church school leaders (provided by the Unitarian-Universalist office) builds a program around two books by Rabbi Earl Grollman (1969, 1976), which adults may use with children in orienting them to human suffering and life and death issues, focusing on naturalist and existentialist perspectives. A film, *The Day Grandpa Died*, which portrays the loss of a beloved grandfather by a Jewish boy, is also incorporated in the program.

ACTIONS BEFORE OR AFTER THE DEATH

There are no prescribed actions that are standard before or after a death for those who utilize memorial services. Specific patterns tend to arise within given meetings or congregations in response to the needs of their individual and family members and to the sensitivity and resources of that community. Memorial services tend to be ceremonies that the family and friends prepare and conduct themselves, with little involvement of professionals. Sometimes they may benefit from suggestions provided beforehand by the deceased. Minimally, the sole involvement of a funeral director might be to transport the body to a crematorium. The remainder of the services would be arranged and carried out by the religious community itself.

DISPOSAL OF THE BODY

Those who utilize memorial services as their means of closure generally have the body cremated promptly after the death or provided to a nearby university for educational and scientific purposes. Thus, the body is almost never present during the service. Some families may transport the body of their loved one to the crematorium themselves, where this can be appropriately and legally arranged. By agreement, they may remain for reflection during the cremation process. Of course, there is no "body preparation"—no embalming or cosmetic work. Nor is there a casket, hearse, procession of cars to a cemetery, or the other usual accouterments of a "standard American funeral," critiqued by Harmer (1963) and Mitford (1976).

The ashes can be disposed of in any legal manner that is appropriate to and desired by the deceased and the survivors. They might be scattered in places beloved by the deceased—a flower garden, mountain glen, bird sanctuary, favorite haunt, or retreat site. They might be buried in a cemetery plot or placed in a mausoleum niche; but these alternatives would be rare.

ACCULTURATION

Since the vast majority of North American Quakers and Unitarian-Universalists and others who prefer memorial services are white, middle-class, majority-group persons, they have not felt constrained to adapt their practices to a "dominant" group's tradition. They have not had to change any ingredients of their traditional ceremonies simply because they are not available. Rather, the memorial services are consciously chosen and conducted on the basis of belief in simple, economical, and dignified body disposal, in contrast to the more typical "commercial" funerals. The latter employ practitioners to perform most of the services and often involve conspicuous consumption and elaborate rituals.

ACKNOWLEDGMENTS

The author wishes to acknowledge the assistance provided by the staff of the Unitarian Universalist Association, Boston, and by the Reverend Khoren Arisian, First Unitarian Society of Minnesota; by Frank and Raquel Wood, Prospect Hill Friends Meeting, Minneapolis, and Robert Tatman, Administrative Assistant to the General Secretary, Philadelphia Yearly Meeting.

REFERENCES

Adams, J. L. (1987). *The five smooth stones of liberalism* (Pamphlet, pp. 1–13). Boston, MA: Unitarian Universalist Association.

Bender, D. L. (Ed.). (1974). *Problems of death: Opposing viewpoints* (Vol. 8, pp. 127–135, 136–144). Anoka, MN: Greenhaven Press.

Catholic Hospital Association. (1978). Religious Society of Friends (Quakers); Unitarian-Universalist. In *Religious aspects of medical care: A handbook of religious practices* (2nd ed., pp. 55–56, 61–62). St. Louis, MO: Catholic Hospital Association.

The Day Grandpa Died [Film].

Donnelley, N. H. (1990). *I never know what to say.* New York: Ballantine.

First Unitarian Society. (1990). *The First Unitarian Society of Minneapolis* (Pamphlet). Minneapolis: Author.

Friends World Committee for Consultation. (1988). *Finding Friends around the world* (9th ed., pp. 130–131). London: Author.

Grollman, E. A. (1969). *Explaining death to children.* Boston: Beacon Press.

Grollman, E. A. (1976). *Talking about death.* Boston: Beacon Press.

Harmer, R. M. (1963). *The high cost of dying.* New York: Collier-Macmillan.

Langley Hill Friends Meeting. (1978). *Death and dying packet.* Langley Hill, VA: Author.

Mendelsohn, J. (1985). *Being liberal in an illiberal age* (2nd ed.). Boston: Beacon Press.

Mitford, J. (1976). *The American way of death.* Boston: Beacon Press.

Morgan, E., & Morgan, J. (1988). *Dealing creatively with death: A manual of death education and simple burial* (11th Ed., pp. 67–70, 71–82, 117–124).

Pacific Yearly Meeting, Religious Society of Friends. (1975, January). *When death occurs in the Meeting* [Resource Handbook]. Palo Alto, CA: Author.

Philadelphia Yearly Meeting, Religious Society of Friends. (1959). *Shadow and light in bereavement: An anthology.* Philadelphia: Author.

Philadelphia Yearly Meeting, Religious Society of Friends. (1979, July). *The conduct of funerals for Friends; Beauty from ashes, strength and joy from sorrow,* and *Facing one's own death* by E. G. Vining (Pamphlets). Philadelphia: Author.

Unitarian Universalist Church. (1989). (No title) (Pamphlet). Urbana, IL: Author.

BIBLIOGRAPHY

Religious Society of Friends (Quakers)

Brinton, H. H. (1965). *Friends for three hundred years.* Wallingford, PA: Pendle Hill.

Comfort, W. W. (1949). *Quakers in the modern world* (pp. 64–201). New York: Macmillan.

Jones, R. M. (1949). *The faith and practice of the Quakers* (7th Ed., pp. 36–159). London: Methuen.

Keene, C. (1977, January). Simplicity in funerals. *Friends Journal, 23*(2), 41.

Taylor, P. (1984). *A Quaker look at living with death and dying.* Philadelphia: Philadelphia Yearly Meeting, Religious Society of Friends.

Unitarian Universalist

Adams, L. A. (1986). On being human religiously. In M. Stackhouse (Ed.), *Essays* (2nd Ed.). Boston, MA: Skinner House.

Cassara, E. (Ed.). (1984). *Universalism in America.* Boston, MA: Skinner House.

Lynn, E. C. (1985). *Come join us* (Pamphlet). Boston, MA: Unitarian Universalist Association.

Marshall, G. (1987). *Challenge of a liberal faith* (3rd Ed.). Boston, MA: Unitarian Universalist Association.

Mendelsohn, J. (1987). *Meet the Unitarian Universalists* (Pamphlet). Boston, MA: Unitarian Universalist Association.

Parke, D. (Ed.). (1985). *The epic of Unitarianism.* Boston, MA: Skinner House.

Robinson, D. (1985). *The Unitarians and the Universalists.* New York: Greenwood Press.

Seaburg, C. (1968). *Great occasions: Readings for the celebration of birth, coming of age, marriage, and death.* Boston, MA: Unitarian Universalist Association.

Memorial Services and Societies

Black, A. (1974). *Without burnt offerings: Ceremonies of humanism* (pp. 135–215). New York: Viking.

Continental Association of Funeral and Memorial Societies. *A multitude of voices: Funerals and the clergy* (Packet). Washington, DC: Author.

Green, B. R., & Irish, D. P. (Eds.). (1971). *Death education: Preparation for living* (pp. 45–67). Cambridge, MA: Schenkman.

Irish, D. P. (1976). *Awareness of death: Preparation for living* (Pamphlet). Philadelphia: Friends General Conference.

Part Three

Reflections and Conclusions

Chapter Twelve

Reflections by Professional Practitioners

Donald P. Irish

What might be the relevance of the foregoing materials for people in professional practice, for those who in their daily occupational roles must confront death and relate to dying or bereaved individuals? What individual attitudes might be affected? What insights might be gained? What might heighten sensitivities and impel practitioners to change? What personal experiences and creative responses to cultural differences might such professionals share? What meaning might the materials have for their professions?

What aspect of the institutions in which professions function militate against the full application of such learnings? Are there collective routines that make difficult the expression of sensitivities to multi-cultural differences within the systems? Are there ways by which a diversity of cultural perceptions might be introduced through broader staff recruitment, on-the-job training, meetings of professional associations, realignment of decision-making boards and committees, rewriting of policies in pertinent areas, and through other, similar means?

We sought commentaries from numerous colleagues across the country, asking them to peruse the manuscript and to provide us with their reflections upon the materials as they might have an impact upon their own roles and within their institutional settings and structures. Those to whom we wrote represent some diversity in their personal backgrounds, professional training, institutional settings, and practical day-to-day experiences with dying, death, and grief. While some religious diversity is also represented among those who responded, we were not successful in securing much diversity of racial minority backgrounds, although the attempt was made. The proportional rarity of such professionals in part accounts for that lack, and the relative absence of racial minorities in several of these professions attests to the wider systemic racial problems in our North American societies.

Certainly the few excerpts from the following groups cannot be considered as views that necessarily represent the professions in general. We can present here only a compilation of the thoughtful commentaries offered by a few of our respondents.

PHYSICIANS

Barbara Meyer, M.D. (Resident physician, family practice, St. Paul-Ramsey Medical Center, St. Paul, MN)

Much has been made in medical literature and the popular press in recent years of the importance of cultural values to patient compliance and to healing. Patients who have confidence in their physicians have been shown to have higher cure rates, even when given treatment programs similar to patients with less confidence. Community health organizers have discovered that trusted members of an established community are much more effective agents of change in the health practices of that community than are outsiders, however well trained [or well intended].

Assumptions by . . . service professionals that a "melting pot" . . . means that dominant American cultural ways of dealing with health problems will serve all those within our borders are not borne out by experience with people. If the beliefs and understanding of *individuals* on issues of health shape the effectiveness of our attempts to serve them, surely the centuries-old, well formulated understandings of *cultural groups* also demand consideration.

Unfortunately, it is my experience as an inner-city physician that little practical account actually is taken in most hospital situations of a patient's individual or cultural health beliefs. There is no standard training of physicians on this subject. . . . Time and energy constraints frequently discourage individual health-care providers from actively seeking opportunities to educate themselves or to raise their own awareness of ways in which issues of cultural values are impacting their practices.

Some examples impose themselves on practitioners' awareness. A Southeast Asian family denied autopsy permission for a patient with an unusual illness on the grounds that they feared organs would be taken for experimentation or for use with other patients. Diagnostic procedures involving the collection of blood or spinal fluid may be denied for the same reason. Rumors can circulate in an ethnic community and cause continuing suspicion and patient "noncompliance," as they have in at least one city community in which I work.

On several occasions medical teams at a hospital were denied permission to perform potentially life-saving operations on patients . . . because the relationship between the health-care provider and the community was one of only partial trust and understanding—and actual differences in values *did* exist. In one instance, a woman suffering from a ruptured tubal pregnancy with sufficient internal bleeding refused surgery on the grounds that it might make her sterile, in which case her husband might divorce her. It required significant time and work with a translator from her ethnic group for us even to uncover this basis for her refusal.

In another instance, perhaps a little more sensitivity and awareness on the part of hospital personnel resulted in an invitation to a local ethnic healer to visit a young girl in the hospital in an attempt to keep her parents from taking her out of the hospital to seek such help.

Mainstream health-care providers have been unable to avoid the ramifications of cultural differences. . . . Our cities . . . include increasing numbers of ethnic groups, some more recently arrived and others with communities of long standing, yet frequently underappreciated in terms of their cultural differences and richness. We will continue to "miss the boat" with these groups [if] we refuse to learn their values. . . .

"Missing the boat" means economic loss to our health-care system, as we work at cross-purposes with patients and their families, through ignorance and prejudice. More importantly, it means failure in the main goal of health care: the assistance of all people in an effort to attain their highest level of well-being. . . . Beliefs about death and dying are integral to beliefs about life and health.

There is value in hearing each other's stories, learning each other's beliefs, and respecting each other's community understandings on a basic level.

Gary L. Grammens, Ph.D., M.D., FACP (Private practice in hematology and oncology, Group Health, Inc., Minneapolis, MN)

Dr. Grammens shared his experiences as a physician who feels he has come to grips with death and dying. He comes from a middle-class, white, second-generation American family. He recognizes that he has lacked prior experiences with funeral customs, dying, and bereavement among diverse cultures.

No one ever prepared me to tell another human being that they are dying and then to manage that process to the end. Medical school training places heavy emphasis on the technical knowledge base needed to form the foundation of every doctor's skill. In my day, freshman medical students were almost exclusively undergraduates with a strong science background. Students with a humanity degree were rare and thought to be at a disadvantage. . . . Even now, conventional wisdom acknowledges that this core of factual information must be continuously upgraded lest . . . one becomes obsolete. Hence, the "science of medicine" is an exponential fight to stay on the cutting edge of technical progress.

Conversely, the so-called "art of medicine" . . . focuses mainly on intangibles such as the hunches or personal experience of the astute clinician who uses these to make the difficult diagnosis. Proper bedside manner was essential to establish the patient-doctor relationship to gain trust and confidence in the treatment plans proferred by the physician. Such lack of professional training concerning cultural differences will affect patient-physician relationships, diagnosis, and treatment.

For most freshman medical students, their first hands-on contact with any human is a dead one—a . . . startling beginning. . . . Frequently I wondered how he lived, what he enjoyed, how he died.

The inevitable visit to the morgue to witness an autopsy occurs. This happened . . . when one of the patients on my service expired. . . . Somewhere between the bedside and the autopsy table I missed an education in talking with the patient about his death. As a student, no one expected that type of intimacy between them and a patient. . . . There was an unwritten taboo against dwelling on death. Patient rights regarding cardiac resuscitation, intubation, and other such heroic and often futile efforts in the terminally ill patient were not even considered. . . . Patients almost had to *earn* their way out of this life by enduring a barrage of mechanical and chemical insults. . . . Between then and now, a tremendous change in public attitude and physician awareness has had to happen.

Nowhere in any medical school course, postgraduate residency, fellowship training, continuing medical education class, or self-directed readings is there to be found the secret success of looking into another human's eyes and with compassion and sensitivity explaining what the end of their life will be like and offering physical and emotional support until the very end.

The dying person doesn't fear death as much as they do the sense of abandonment and loss of control over body functions and pain. These fears are universal and cut through all social, racial, sexual, and economic strata. . . . Each dying person requires a tailored approach.

The major emphasis of most, if not all, of the contributors [to this volume], deals with the rituals and customs after death and the ways various cultures and faiths approach the funeral. I found these chapters very enlightening, especially since I have not attended many nontraditional American funerals.

Nancy Laraby Groves, M.D. (Anesthesiologist, Abbott-Northwestern Hospital, Minneapolis, MN)

Dr. Groves is one of those rare physicians who was not a science major as an undergraduate. She majored in sociology, and that social science training has aided her in medical practice.

I see the issues of cross-cultural differences in attitudes toward death intersecting with medical-care decision-making all the time.

Jehovah's Witness patients demonstrate this in a very specific way—no use of blood products. We have developed good means to get most Witnesses through even major surgery in compliance with their wishes. Cross-cultural differences that impact on medical decision-making in non-religious [groups] are just as important.

The living will language requires people to address very specific items: e.g., development of a terminal condition or diagnosis, use of one's organs for donation, and so on. Cross-cultural differences clearly play a role in how individuals write their living will. These are everyday issues.

Dr. Groves provided another example of a cross-cultural situation. However, the lack of full candor suggested by the Latin American physician in this case is shared by many North American health practitioners as well.

I was discussing a case of exploratory laparotomy and hemicolectomy for colon cancer with one of the surgery residents from a South American country. The diagnosis of cancer was made at surgery and removal was accomplished. The Latin American surgery resident said that if his own mother had this done, the report to her would be that it was a *benign* tumor. . . . *We'd* say the *malignant* tumor was removed, but that there is always a chance that it could recur or appear elsewhere. This presents a much less optimistic picture. The surgery resident said his mother would go into a deep depression from an accurate report and never recover. The optimistic report would allow her to go on living normally.

Of course, this reaction could reflect the resident's inability and/or unwillingness to confront death himself, especially with his mother, a not uncommon trait among our health-care professionals as with the general public.

Lillian Burke, M.D. (Researcher, National Institute of Diabetes, Digestive, and Kidney Diseases, National Institutes of Health (NIH), Bethesda, MD).

Dr. Burke has had seven years' experience in upper New York State with diverse ethnic groups, among African Americans in Alabama, and in work with the

NIH. She indicated that her "experiences have been broadest in relating to older immigrants and first-generation Americans who were Italian or Polish, poor people in the South, both black and white, as well as [Midwest] Scandinavians." Yet she indicated that there are two inter-related aspects:

The first is the obvious relationship of the patient's culture to his or her death. The second is the physician's culture and its impact on that death and the decision-making which precedes it. In dealing with people from many cultures and social backgrounds . . . there is marked variation within cultures while people from very different cultures can be remarkably similar in their reactions to particular situations. In other circumstances their reactions may be very different.

At every step, the patient's culture affects the medical decision-making process and the patient's reaction to it. Culture includes not only the nominal ethnic identification of a person, but also his location within a particular subculture of our society. The important determinants of this person's culture might include his college, his regional location, his profession, and his religion.

Patients respond to the diagnosis and dying experience in a way that is intimately connected to their beliefs in a God as well as according to their beliefs about what is going to happen to them after they die.

One day a patient who was dying of cancer looked quite despondent. She shared with me her belief that she got breast cancer because God was punishing her for trying to lose weight. She should have accepted that He wanted her to be fat. . . . Some of the feeling which patients experience in their dying process may be related to unresolved guilt from other areas of their lives. How common are these thoughts? What is their cultural basis? How do they affect the patient's relation to their death?

One area of marked differences between cultures is the discussion of who talks to the doctor. Among Italians, the women were most involved in the day-to-day discussions with the physician. However, once a critical decision regarding . . . whether the patient was to have an operation, or whether resuscitation was appropriate, men, who had previously been invisible, mysteriously appeared. In addition, daughters and wives seemed less willing than sons and husbands to make a final decision regarding a "do not resuscitate" order. There is sometimes a need among the children . . . to await the arrival of the oldest child, whether male or female.

Other areas of cultural differences among patients include who takes care of the dying patient. It seems that people who are closer to their immigrant roots are more likely to feel comfortable taking care of a patient at home. They will also respond differently to the burden of caring for a dying person. . . . It is rare for a spouse to be able to care for a person at home without assistance from the children. Daughters, in general, seem more likely to be willing and able to assist their parents in their dying. The daughter's role is sometimes taken by daughters-in-law and only rarely by sons. . . . What cultural beliefs and experiences allow a family to care for the dying person at home and to watch that person's suffering with acceptance? Any generalizations about a culture are likely to be incorrect for a particular family within that culture. . . . How does a person's gender affect their interaction with the medical care system? Are decisions made differently for men and women? How does the power structure within families from different cultures affect the medical decision-making process?

One knows that the person is really dead, but he just doesn't look dead. He also doesn't look dead to the family. . . . My hand turns the switch; the chest stops rising; the beeps of the heartbeat monitor slow and finally stop. There is a feeling that I have killed someone, no matter how intellectually I know that this is not so. I have seen physicians leave patients on ventilators knowing that they were legally dead, and disappear for the weekend without commenting. . . . Such denial may be culturally based.

In the first year after death it is common to see relatives shortly before important holidays. Usually the relative comes with a physical complaint. . . . Sometimes the complaints have been quite confusing until I realized that there was an important anniversary or another holiday which was pending. . . . Many of these symptoms miraculously disappeared after the holiday.

The ritual of the official year of mourning seems to have disappeared from general cultural awareness. . . . This is unfortunate because people are often unprepared for their feelings during this time. . . . The wearing of black . . . also serves to indicate that this person might be more fragile. . . . Different kinds of holidays and anniversaries would tend to be important within different cultures.

Certain cultures . . . seem to encourage relatives to deny their feelings and reinforce the person for their "strong" appearance. . . . This culture may fail to give the person a socially acceptable outlet for their grief. In my experience the person who outwardly seems to fall apart at the time of death may be the person who resolved her feelings the best six months later. The strong person may be angry years later.

I was taught as a child that a person who commits suicide would go to Hell. I no longer have this belief. . . . Rather, such a death is tragic because the work that the person was meant to do may be left undone. . . . Relatives who believe that the suicide of a person condemns that person to eternal punishment have an additional burden to bear above and beyond the guilt which is commonly shared by survivors of a suicide. . . . What are the beliefs about suicide among different cultures? Why do people deny that a suicide has occurred? What do various religions teach about the fate of the person who completes a suicide?

Physicians and nurses who care for the dying share common perceptions. We can talk . . . in a certain way and sometimes laugh in ways that might not be understood by those who don't share our perceptions. In this way we share a culture. One of the purposes of this culture is to protect ourselves from the thoughtlessness of those "outside," who forget that we are people too.

This group of people who care for the dying is a definite subculture. . . . We have shared experiences, perceptions, and rules of behavior. We also notice, consciously and unconsciously, how people from different cultures are likely to react to certain experiences of illness.

In regard to her medical training, Dr. Burke indicated that it did include some lectures on the "psychology of dying." However, she cautions against the tendency to "judge the quantity or quality of education . . . by the number of hours of lectures which are allotted to that subject."

She contends that "we must not fall into the trap of believing that just because a culture is 'traditional' that its teachings are necessarily beneficial. Reinforcing traditional attitudes can be destructive if the culture forbids open grieving and the person needs to grieve. People from 'stoic cultures' may be able to grieve adequately once they are given permission to do so."

Concluding her lengthy essay, Dr. Burke stated:

Every step of the medical decision-making process is affected by both the patient's and the physician's cultural background. In the emotionality of life-and-death decisions, cultural beliefs are likely to be perceived as absolute beliefs about what is right and wrong. . . . There is a need for systematic documentation of different cultures and their beliefs regarding death, including the meaning of death, what is considered an appropriate grieving process, the afterlife beliefs, as well as the reactions to the unexpected death. . . . Anniversaries and holidays which hold particular significance within a culture need to be [studied].

That challenge is, of course, one to which this volume is directed.

NURSES

Cynthia Bartoo, R.N. (Public health nurse; Home Health Care Services, University of Minnesota, Minneapolis, MN

Bartoo served for 11 years as a nurse in a university hospital and has also been director of a neighborhood home care project. She shared her views in recognition of the role of culture for others.

Within our own culture, each of us finds different meaning in our life and different meaning in our death. It is useless, indeed even harmful, for me . . . to assume anything about what life's events mean for another person. But with the understanding of the culture of which the other person is a part, I can put in context and interpret some of what that person tells me . . . of the meaning they find in the events of their life.

I believe that the final work of our lives is to make meaning of our life and come to terms with our death. . . . As a hospice nurse, I am in a privileged position in the home to observe and support these processes. If I understand how my client's culture answers the questions of the meaning of life, how grief and other feelings may be expressed, and what behaviors are appropriate at the time of death, then I can offer counseling and succor effectively. If I know that the Hmong fear the "ghost" of their departed under certain circumstances, or that there is more acceptance of outward signs of grief in one culture and less acceptance in another, or that a certain kind of death can be a good thing in another culture, then my mind is open to wider interpretations of people's actions and words than if I operated only with an understanding of my own culture.

As a health professional, I depend on cues from my client and my client's family to tell me how much information they can absorb or want, what issues they are ready for or needing to discuss, and what kind of support I can offer. . . . Unfamiliarity with another culture can cause misunderstanding, missed cues, and bring communication to an end, leaving the health-care person a stranger, an outsider, instead of a trusted friend and counselor.

Marjorie O. Larson, R.N. (Obstetrics nurse, retired, University of Minnesota Hospitals, Minneapolis, MN)

Like Bartoo, Larson's reflections inter-relate her own reactions to the need to be sensitive to cultural differences, based on 12 years of experience.

As a nurse for several years in a hospital setting, occasions arose dealing with cultures with which I was not familiar. . . . Occasionally, an in-service workshop was held in the hospital explaining the beliefs and ceremonies of one group of patients of a different culture; but there was not readily available a comprehensive source for reference.

Certainly as nurses we try to be non-judgmental and open to beliefs and practices which are not our own. We try to put ourselves in the place of the other, to understand his world view, and to respect his values. But the more knowledge we can have of the other's culture, the better we can serve that person and the family.

We all have expectations of what our own and others' behavior will be under given circumstances. We are comfortable when the rituals and ceremonies are familiar to us and fulfill these expectations. We may even rehearse our behavior in our mind when a crisis such as death is about to occur. To have these expectations frustrated by . . . medical personnel or other staff, and to have our rituals seen as unimportant, or even foolish, is very unkind and can lead to anger.

I was impressed by the importance of *community* that seems to be universal to all cultures. The support of family and friends cannot be overemphasized.

Eunice Peterson Johnson, R.N. (Staff development coordinator, Lyngblomsten Care Center, St. Paul, MN)

Johnson orients new personnel and coordinates the in-service programs for the 300 persons on the center staff. From her experience in these roles she shared the following insights.

We have very few minority residents here, and I didn't think it would enter into my day-to-day work. . . . Almost immediately, however, I did see a correlation between the book and my job. Many of our employees—about 30 percent of our nursing assistants—are minorities, from Southeast Asia and Africa primarily. I was never aware of the extent of the cultural differences they were encountering coming here to work . . . sometimes with a dying resident. How hard this must be for them, especially when we don't address some of these beliefs and practices more fully.

Last summer our institution and the International Institute were awarded a grant to provide instruction for refugees in the field of nursing assistants in long-term care. This is a wonderful opportunity for us to work more closely with other cultures.

I do address death and dying in orientations but have never focused on anything but the common beliefs of our residents. . . . I intend to have special in-services where our employees can share their beliefs and backgrounds and we can discuss different ethnic practices related to death.

HOSPICE CHAPLAINS

James A. Vogt (Oncology hospice chaplain, Hennepin County Medical Center, Minneapolis, MN)

My first experience . . . deals with a Native American family. Their infant child was brought in with difficulty in breathing. In the ensuing time in the emergency room the child died. The . . . grief process was a touching experience for which I shall never lose my sense of awe. The family had a Native American friend help with the burning of sage. He brought eagle feathers for the grieving process that is part of the Native American culture. Their pastor from a Protestant church was also present. Each of us was given the honor of holding the child while the smoke from the sage was stirred around us with the eagle feathers. It was striking to see the support and comfort that was afforded to the family when they were allowed to grieve in their own fashion and how they honored those who helped them to grieve in what was an appropriate manner for them.

Another situation dealt with an African American family. Staff people involved were interpreting the "hyperactivity" and constant movement by family and friends as excessive anxiety. . . . This was a family that lost a loved one in a violent death, and they were expressing their grief and anger in the way they had learned. They were overwhelmed by the grief and loss and their emotions needed release. Their movements, loud moaning, and wailing gave them the needed outlet for the beginning of their grief process. . . . This was a "grief process in action."

A third situation dealt with a Southeast Asian family. This family came from Thailand, and the husband had just died of cancer after a very long hospital stay. Many times I have talked with staff of various institutions who felt uneasy around Southeast Asians because of their lack of understanding of the Buddhist faith. Yet this experience has allowed me to see that we who are of a Judeo-Christian faith do have pastoral care to offer . . . by being their friend and seeking to understand what they would appreciate . . . to experience their grief and loss within their faith. Allowing the family dynamics that are part of their culture and faith to flow naturally here in the hospital is our desire. . . . They were not in need of doctrinal/faith conversion. . . . It was made easier for them by experiencing a nonthreatening relationship here in the hospital.

Edward Holland, M. Div. (Coordinator of hospice spiritual care and grief support, Methodist Hospital, St. Louis Park, MN)

My "subcultural context" is white, Scandinavian, liberal, Methodist, college-educated, and middle class. Most of the people we serve are white, probably 95 percent, upper- and middle-class, well-educated Christians (Catholics and Lutherans) and Jews. . . . There is no doubt that our patient population will be more culturally diverse in the future. The sooner we become better educated and sensitized to and accepting of differences, the better in terms of quality of patient-family care with which we can meet the needs of those we serve (and learn from).

Just as your colleagues advocate understanding the dying and grieving processes from the individual's cultural perspective, I would argue that, regardless of culture, each person's dying and grieving experiences are unique to that individual. Just as we should not assume that all cultures understand dying, death, and grief in the same way, neither should we assume that all individuals experience "stages" of dying and grieving. . . . There are no prescriptions or recipes. . . . Our challenge is to be open to learn from the person who is dying/grieving. Each of them is "expert" about their death/grief process.

SOCIAL WORKERS

Marion McNurlen, M.S.W. (Oncology Department, St. Paul Children's Hospital, St. Paul, MN)

McNurlen daily confronts others' life-threatening situations, occasionally with the death of a child.

As a hospital social worker, I find death is a relatively frequent occurrence. . . . The events surrounding the death of a loved one provide an opportunity for a social worker to use a variety of skills . . . [to help] the family.

When an individual has had a long illness, the professionals involved have most likely gained some knowledge of the family's coping style, traditions, and wishes. In some instances, desires regarding handling the loved one's death have been discussed in advance. It is often the hospital social worker, along with the chaplain, other clergy, and at times nursing staff, who initiate and assist this discussion.

It is always easiest for us to assist others who share our basic values and views of the world. If we know a family well, or they seem "like us," the process of making decisions regarding the death of a loved one is relatively smooth for the professional helper. However, it is important to understand that each person views this situation in a different way. No one really is just "like us." We each come to death with a deep history of family tradition . . . cultural expectations, ethnic and class background, religious belief, and personal relationship issues. Paul Rosenblatt stated that "it pays to treat everyone as though he or she were from a different culture." This is a critical issue in the health-care professional's work of helping families with death.

Social workers are trained to be empathic, to see situations from the point of view of the other. We are also trained in crisis intervention and assisting people with decision-making. Many of us do not have training in dealing specifically with death; and even fewer social workers are formally educated in working with cultural differences. We often know the process of helping others, but we do not always know the content of the issues. It is extremely helpful, then, to have resources . . . to assist us in understanding the specific cultural and religious issues regarding death in various cultures.

It is fascinating to understand the variations from culture to culture regarding such aspects as the meaning of death, the rituals surrounding death, dealing with the body of the deceased, celebrating the life of the deceased. How to make sense of life in the midst of death?

Whenever a family hears the diagnosis of cancer in their child it is a time of crisis, psychologically, physically, and spiritually. The cultural sensitivity raised by understanding more of the background of the family's culture will make me a more sensitive and competent care provider. . . . I may never fully understand the context a family places this crisis in, but I can be increasingly sensitive to the issues the crisis raises. It will help me ask better questions, look at the situation with less of my own cultural baggage, and be more sensitive to the unique aspects of the situation for each family.

Fremont Williams, M.S.W. (Clinical social worker, Minneapolis Children's Medical Center, Minneapolis, MN)

Belonging to a minority group may be somewhat like being left-handed in a right-handed world. . . . As a social worker in a children's hospital we have daily contact with several minority groups. Social workers throughout their history have championed the rights of smaller, less powerful groups, and this value of fairness seems particularly important when it comes to death, funerals, and grief. The way in which people are treated in health care and funeral home settings at these times will be remembered for a lifetime.

Sometimes . . . support can be expressed simply through removing obstacles. I remember the morning a Native American child stopped breathing and was transported to our emergency room. After many attempts to revive the child failed, he was pronounced dead. The family requested that their medicine man be allowed to come to the hospital to perform a sage-burning ceremony for their son. The hospital staff was concerned about the presence of fire near large supplies of oxygen. Inquiry with the maintenance staff revealed that the central supply of oxygen to the emergency room could be shut off temporarily and portable oxygen in other rooms would serve as a backup. The family was allowed to have their religious ceremony in the emergency room and were grateful that the hospital was willing to make an exception for their customs. That day we did honor to the life of that young child and his family. That was a good feeling in the midst of such a loss.

Hospitals, nursing homes, and mortuaries may not always be able to accommodate every wish a family may have; but the willingness to consider each request and to be as flexible as possible goes a long way toward letting the family know we respect them and their unique traditions.

Gail A. Noller, M.A. (Social worker and certified grief counselor, Health One, Mercy Hospital, Coon Rapids, MN)

She functions in two roles: as a grief therapist who facilitates grief support groups and provides counseling for children and adults, and as a therapist who offers home counseling for dying people and their families through a hospice program. She has learned through the years "the hard way that the dying and grieving are our teachers. If we listen, they will tell us what they need in order to resolve their loss."

Each individual's story is richly told, sprinkled with signs of unique family traditions. Each individual, even those who look "just like us," has a unique perception of the world and what's "right" for him or her in grief or dying.

Two incidents early in my career caught me off guard in relation to unusual cultural traditions in death and grief. The first occurred when I visited a young black mother whose six-year-old son had recently died. She had several photographs surrounding the hospital bed of her son in his casket, each photo from a different angle. I wondered what this "aberration" meant: Was she denying death? Was she . . . obsessed with his death? Was she feeling guilty about her mothering, thus carrying on in such a "strange" way after his death? I discovered later that this practice is not unusual, especially if there are relatives who are unable to come into town for the funeral, who would appreciate a copy of the picture to help "realize" the death. . . . I learned to encourage photos, audiotaping, and even videotaping if families desire.

The second experience relates to the privilege of having been the director of a program concerned with death and dying at a Jewish hospital . . . when a local synagogue developed a startlingly new practice. Members of the congregation volunteered to be trained to be present after the death of one of their members in order to wash and shroud the body. These volunteers then sat with the body so it was never alone, illustrating the reverence this Jewish congregation had for the physical body. While sitting with the body, the volunteers often would read materials related to dying, death, and mourning. Initially this practice was seen as rather radical, and it was interpreted by some as a threat to the Jewish funeral home in the area. The special instructions for contacting these volunteers had to be made clearly with the nursing staff, since this was a practice "out of the ordinary" and thought by some to be rather morbid.

It is always inappropriate to prescribe what grief ought to be for an individual. Each person's journey through grief is unique. As long as there are rituals, as long as there are traditions, as long as families have taught their members the family's way in dying and grief, I work to understand and respect their uniqueness. However, in this melting pot of cultures, many have lost contact with tradition and ritual and find themselves without guidance when death and grief occur. These are the ones who struggle greatly. There are no guideposts, there are no rules, no expectations, no frameworks in which to move. It becomes the task of the family, often with guidance from caregivers, to define and establish tradition, to discover rituals, to give a framework to an unanticipated experience.

MORTICIANS

Paul V. Johnson, M.A. (Director, bereavement services and education, Bradshaw Family of Funeral Homes, Twin Cities, MN)

Johnson was trained in sociology and taught for a number of years at the college level. His firm has had extensive experience in providing funeral services for families from the Southeast Asian community. They were concerned that these families were not being served as well as they could be, because of cultural differences that were compounded by language difficulties. There were often misunderstandings of what those families wished to include in their funeral rituals. His firm became motivated to find ways to minimize those problems:

A Hmong group arrived at the funeral home with a rented trailer containing a cow. It was their intention to sacrifice the cow as part of their funeral ritual. Since we could not allow that anywhere on the premises of the funeral home, we arranged to tie a rope around the cow's neck and run the rope into the funeral home and tie the other end around the wrist of the deceased individual. That seemed to satisfy their need to have a cow present.

One evening at one of the visitations a Hmong man came to the funeral home. As he came into the room where the viewing was occurring it became apparent that there was something moving inside his coat. Upon further examination by our staff person, it was found that he had a live chicken . . . which he intended to kill and place with the deceased individual.

As might be expected, our staff found these practices somewhat different. A number of conversations about these "strange" customs took place within our staff. We felt that if we understood the reasons for these particular activities, we would be better able to serve these individuals. As a result of our lack of knowledge of Southeast Asian funeral practices . . . we formed our Southeast Asian Committee and attempted to educate ourselves about their funeral rituals.

Included in our activities was the surveying of our entire staff (funeral directors, secretaries, funeral home attendants, support staff) about their ideas related to serving members of the Southeast Asian community. . . . We invited the chair- [person] of the Board of the Lao Family Community . . . to make a presentation at one of our regular staff meetings about Hmong funeral practices. . . . We learned what is represented by the sacrificing of the chicken and the cow.

Members of the Hmong community would like to have at least one 24-hour period during the visitation time when they can stay with the body. We have tried to accommodate this request even though it means having a staff person available during what would otherwise be quite untraditional hours. In addition, during the time of visitation there is often a flute playing as well as continual beating on a drum. When the funeral home is not busy with other funerals, these practices do not pose much difficulty. On the other hand, when there is another visitation occurring . . . we have had to request that doors be closed and that drums and instruments playing not be done at times that would interfere with the funeral services of the other families being served.

Some families being served simultaneously with a Hmong family have indicated that they were distracted by the Hmong funeral activities going on within the building. However, it has been more common that families have expressed an interest in the Hmong funeral customs and wanted to learn more about them. [T]he deceased individual in one family had been a missionary in another culture. They were especially pleased that a funeral for an individual from a different cultural group was occurring within the funeral home at the same time as the funeral for their loved one. They had no difficulty at all with the two cultures "blending" within . . . the funeral home.

Our . . . committee continues to function, and we continue to be in touch with members of the Southeast Asian community. There has been some effort to help Hmong community members purchase their own funeral home . . . where they could continue to practice some of their cultural activities which cannot be done in a traditional funeral home. Another thought has been to offer a scholarship for a member of the Southeast Asian community to study with a mortuary science program to prepare the individual to serve as a funeral director within a local funeral home and help bring these cultural groups together.

Robert C. Slater (Professor and director emeritus, Program of Mortuary Science, University of Minnesota, Minneapolis, MN)

After considering the prospectus of our material, Slater's comments reinforce the spirit of Paul Johnson's responses:

Having been active for over four decades with professionals involved in dying, death, and bereavement, especially those in caretaking roles, I learned early that any response to crisis would be influenced by the race, religion, and ethnic culture of those intimately involved in the crisis. These features will influence not only one's reactions to the event but also the way in which the responders to the crisis will function with caring and sensitivity.

Now with qualified professionals, we have the opportunity to face the diversity as well as the universality of death. Perhaps no one in a community is as conscious of cultural diversity as the funeral director, because when death enters a family he or she is most concerned about serving the family in those ways which are most meaningful and significant. . . . Funeral service as an institution will be well served in being knowledgeable and expert in providing those services to the various cultures.

HEALTH CARE ADMINISTRATOR

Michael D. Resnick, Ph.D. (Associate professor, School of Public Health; director of Research and Demonstration Programs, Adolescent Health Program, Department of Pediatrics, University of Minnesota, Minneapolis, MN)

As an educator Resnick prepares graduate students who will be practitioners in public health and health services administration.

There are varied ways that communities and cultures provide connectedness and support to families and individuals. There is at once great divergence in these pathways to connectedness between members of a community and an underlying common denominator that has to do with our human needs for belonging.

For students, it is an easy fallacy to assume that death is only of concern to those who are going to "specialize" in hospices and nursing home services. A far different perspective assumes that death is part of the journey from birth through life, to the mysteries beyond, with an accompanying acknowledgement and humility about the limits of medical technology and human intervention, and the fact that different groups and cultures approach and understand inevitable death in very different ways. Absent from most students' understandings is that their professional work in public . . . health services will invariably involve their direct and intimate contact with death and loss, culture, and community.

It is accepted in our program of study that medical sociology and medical anthropology provide valuable insights and sensitivities toward cultural variation in health and illness behavior. Our sanitized approach to death in this country has meant that academic study of social support and cultural norms has produced an intellectual appreciation of how those forces make contributions to the health and well-being of populations. But our literature and teaching usually does not integrate these dynamics with healthy dying and an understanding of the experiences of life after loss for different people.

I have seen this in discussions with students following viewing of films . . . on various aspects of dying or death in the United States. Observation of loud emotional outbursts or expressions of grieving create chagrin, even contempt among some students. (Why can't "those people" be more stoic, more circumspect?) Those typically accustomed to methodical, routinized funeral services involving formal signs and prescribed musical sounds are often stunned or amused that our human senses might be used otherwise: e.g., through the use of brightly colored shrouds or burial garments, the burning of sage or incense, or the rituals of chanting or wailing.

We need to take the richness of human cultural variation and place it in a framework grounded in the universality of human experience *and* the particularity of its expression.

Chapter Thirteen

Conclusions

**Donald P. Irish, Kathleen F. Lundquist,
and Vivian Jenkins Nelsen**

The editors of this book have had considerable experience working with organizations and colleagues involved in terminal care and hospice work, death education, and health-service institutions. We have concluded that there is an urgent need to enhance the quantity and quality of services rendered to culturally diverse patients and clients who are responding to the universal experiences of dying and grieving.

Ethnic Variations in Dying, Death, and Grief: Diversity in Universality has been compiled to meet this need, which several factors render even more pressing:

- Given current ethno-demographic trends, professionals who hitherto have had little opportunity to confront and serve culturally different individuals will, in the future, need to serve that expanded client base.
- Existing curricula in disciplines that serve the dying and bereaved are still giving scant attention to cultural differences.
- Changing public policy surrounding cultural diversity, as well as increasing litigation in that domain, mandate that services related to death, dying, and

grief must become both more sensitive and more accountable to a client base that is becoming ever more culturally diverse.

Throughout this work, we have documented numerous authentic instances where health-care professionals in their institutional settings have encountered cultural differences when serving patients or clients. We have encouraged professionals and volunteers alike to reflect upon their personal attitudes and beliefs concerning death, grief, and multi-culturalism. Finally, by responding to a framework of seven specific aspects, representatives from selected ethnic communities have provided extensive information about the attitudes, beliefs and behaviors that surround the experiences of death and grief within their given culture.

DIVERSITY IN PRESENTATION

Wishing ourselves to be sensitive to cultural differences, we resisted imposing any rigid format for the content of each cultural representative's contribution. Writing styles will differ among individual authors of any compendium and a strictly parallel sequence of topics did not seem to accommodate the discussion of dying, death, and grief for authors as diverse as ours. There are bound to be cultural differences in the telling. A format with fixed categories might have stultified and perhaps precluded a holistic approach. Thus, the eight "ethnic" authors present their segments in their own manner, although, since all were Western-educated, in whole or in part, the writers' stylistic differences are minimized.

DIVERSITY WITHIN A CULTURE

There is, of course, considerable diversity within some ethnic entities—for example, Hispanics may be Cuban, Mexican, Puerto Rican, or from another Latin American background. Thus, generalizations for all who fall within the popularly used categories or census rubrics cannot properly be drawn. Second, even though the authors endeavor to describe in-group variations, we editors could not assume that they as individuals represent a modal point for their culture group. Finally, there remain intragroup differences not only because of ethnic background contrasts but also due to socioeconomic positions and educational attainments. Middle- and upper-class people and those who are better educated within ethnic communities may tend to behave and believe differently in numerous ways from those who are poor and relatively uneducated.

Therefore, in summarizing major points from all the material collected here, we will not attempt to place entire ethnic groups on a spectrum of behaviors or beliefs, although we do alert readers to some of the contrasts—extremes and/or middle-range features—for particular aspects that have been presented. Nor do we claim to place whole cultural groups "objectively" on a scale for any particular trait. Our basic goal has been to inform practitioners about *some* cultural features that distinguish *certain* communities. We trust those professionals to be sensitive to *other* features when serving those whose culture is different from their own.

CHALLENGES ENCOUNTERED

While preparing this volume, some unanticipated challenges arose. First, there has been a continual concern that we be "multi-cultural" ourselves. From the beginning we were such a team—a Native American, an African American, an Anglo Quaker, and a Minnesota Scandinavian—though, regrettably, our Native American colleague was unable to remain active for the full period of collaboration.

Second, we were determined that materials about selected ethnic communities would be provided by people from those backgrounds. With but one exception, that has been accomplished. Most of the major contributors, however, reside in Minnesota. Yet despite the somewhat narrow geographic range of the authors, illustrative episodes, and professional respondents, we still are confident that the concerns we share are widespread social issues. The concentration of authorship and examples should in no way diminish the validity of the content.

Third, problems of terminology had to be confronted. We wanted to use terms for cultural groups which they preferred when identifying themselves. However, changes in group consciousness, along with the diversity within major ethnic groups, make for difficulties with rubrics. We have tried to be fully respectful of each ethnic community.

Fourth, the project evolved over two decades. The original impetus came from conferences of the Minnesota Coalition for Death Education and Support in 1979 and 1989, which were chaired by Irish, which shared the same theme as this volume. While a few segments stemmed directly from those occasions, a number of additions were made to the original design of the volume in order to include:

- an opportunity for readers to reflect upon their personal attitudes and beliefs concerning death, grief, and multi-culturalism (Chapter 3);
- a broader representation of cultural groups (Chapters 4–11);
- reflections from professionals in health-care disciplines (Chapter 12); and
- 1990 Census data concerning ethnic trends in the United States and Canada (Appendix A).

CONTRASTS OF DYING, DEATH, AND GRIEF
WITHIN THE FRAMEWORK

Each of the eight "ethnic" chapters focused on seven aspects of dying, death, and grief. Those were set forth in the Introduction and will be distilled in this chapter, as distinctive, though not exclusive, contrasts.

Experiential Features

All the "ethnic" materials characterized the "feel" or aura of their cultural expressions. One strand appears in the fabric of all the cultural groups in relation to death: the importance of community or group support. Whether the ingathering is of a black church, Hmong community, Jewish congregation, Mexican parish, Native American band, or Quaker Meeting, a strong sense of community participation is manifested through mutual aid with tasks, emotional support, and sharing of ritual. Native Americans will often return to their reservations, and blacks in the North will "return home" to their native South for funerals. A sense of obligation is felt but there is also the pull of desire.

Community participation seems more evident among the Hmong of our "urban villages," within some Jewish congregations, and among Quakers, in contrast to the more commercialized and professionalized rites found among mainline denominations. The folk-urban contrasts appear with Southern rural blacks in contrast with their Northern and urban counterparts and urban Native Americans compared with those on the reservations. Professionalization of "death and dying"—even aid in grieving—will be found more frequently among the urban, educated, affluent, and secularized segments of our societies. Their loved ones will more often die in hospitals. They will use a funeral home more frequently for services and employ professionals to "take care of all the details" more often than will those who are more rural, who more often die at home surrounded by family, and who are buried in the local churchyard. Certain groups still rely considerably on folk medicines (e.g., Hmong), while others find modern medicines both acceptable and preferable.

Philosophy/Theology of Death and Dying

Only bits and pieces of complex philosophies can be alluded to in this summary. Fatalism regarding life and death is more common among poor and dispossessed peoples. They more readily accept events as "God's will" rather than as the results of natural processes or human endeavors. Afterlife expectations are more prominent among the less powerful and oppressed than among the privileged, who tend to focus more upon this life. Historically that has been the case for African Americans in the United States, but oppression has not been the only factor. Traditional Latin Americans, Buddhists, and Muslims also have prominently focused on after-death expectations. Islam strongly prepares for the next life as a process; and Buddhists seek perfection for a state of Nirvana. Jews, Quakers, and Unitarians tend to stress the here and now. The Lakota assume that an afterlife is automatic for every tribal member, not something that needs to be earned.

The body is viewed as a receptacle for the human spirit within all groups. However, some Christians believe in a physical resurrection of the body after death. The Hmong traditionally believed in the ongoing presence of people's spirits and those of their relatives, who have influence upon the survivors. Caribbean *santería* followers assume a realm of spirit forces. When the body is viewed as inviolable or venerated, autopsies are avoided—as they are among the Jews, Hmong, and others. Whereas most of the groups presented use burial for the deceased (Mexican American, Muslims, Hmong, Native Americans, Jews), some cultures use public funeral pyres (Buddhist, Hindu), while others very frequently utilize professional cremation (Quakers, Unitarians). The horrors of the Holocaust deter Jews from using cremation; and that means of body disposal is also rare among Catholics (including Mexican Americans), Lakota, and others.

Islam, Christianity, and Judaism have highly developed concepts of a single Deity—whether it be called Allah, God or Yahweh—whereas the noncreedal Quakers and Unitarians minimize such elaborations, and Buddhists lack that particular concept. Mysticism is strongly present in Buddhism as well as among some Catholics, Quakers, and Native American traditions. Ancestor worship appears among traditional Hmong and in some segments of Buddhism; and the Buddha, though not a deity, is an object of veneration. Both Christians and Muslims accept notions of a day of judgment.

Death Education

Much of death education is "caught" rather than "taught," as children and youth observe the actions and reactions of the adults. Within traditional folk societies and contemporary rural areas, children acquire their attitudes and beliefs about life and mortality through direct observation of and participation in most community activities. They are not so sheltered from the events of birth and death as are most children in the urban or suburban areas of our countries. However, children in urban ghettos, in rural Appalachia, in the Mexican American communities of the Southwest, and on Native American reservations will grow up witnessing death—both natural and violent—with considerable frequency. As integral to their philosophy, Muslims and Buddhists have accepted death as an inherent part of life, and there is a strong focus on preparation for it.

A death and dying education movement was greatly advanced by the writings, lectures, and workshops of Elisabeth Kübler-Ross and others. They have stimulated the development of more formal death education within North American school curricula and church materials during the past more than two decades. Even so, death education is still seldom a regular and significant part of formal schooling, even in higher education, or within most religious denominations. As Cytron indicated, death education has been incorporated by some Jewish congregations, and it is also not uncommon among Quakers and Unitarians. Regrettably, the mass media and films provide abundant informal death education for many youth in our societies, often negative: violent deaths, brutal killings, life-threatening risk-taking, and a general insensitivity to the value of human life.

Actions, Rituals, and Emotional Expressions Regarding Death—Before, After, and Later

In some cultural groups, traditional rituals, actions to be taken, and appropriate emotional expressions are prescribed in considerable detail. Among the groups examined, this is more the case for the Hmong, Muslims, Jews, Buddhists, and Christian groups. Quakers and Unitarians will be found at the other end of the spectrum. Strong emotional expressiveness, publicly manifested, is deemed appropriate within Islamic, African American, Native American, and Hmong groups, and for some traditional Jewish segments; Quakers and Unitarians tend to be more reserved. However, emotional expressiveness is often linked to the socioeconomic-educational status of the bereaved community.

While awaiting death, keeping a vigil is common as family and friends gather at the bedside of the dying person. This is more feasible with patients at home in their own community than in the sterile confines of a hospital or nursing home. Among Jews, there are farewell rites, times for confession, forgiveness, and expression of hope. Buddhists focus upon the mind-set of the dying, chanting sutras and pursuing other rituals to initiate the dying person into the transition from life to death. Muslims read the Koran and believe that Satan and angels are also present at death. Last rites are standard within the Catholic tradition.

Some groups have more rituals than others for the period immediately after a member's death. Memorial services found frequently among Quakers and Unitarians are the least ritualized, simplest, and most open to variety. However, the Hmong, Jews, Muslims, and others have elaborate ceremonies of very considerable complexity concerning the care of the body of the deceased, including vigils to protect it, and so on. The funeral ceremonies of the Hmong are perhaps the most elaborate among those included here. Following death and burial the novena is standard for Latin-oriented Catholics, in which a prayerful vigil is maintained for nine days. The Jews sit shiva for seven days after a death and schedule remembrances again 30 days after a death. Wearing black is still customary within some traditions. Muslims, Jews, Buddhists, and the Lakota, among others, recognize anniversaries with ceremonies a year after the loved one's death.

Acculturation

Each of the ethnic groups (omitting the Quakers and Unitarians, who are principally within the majority culture) has had to modify its ways of dealing with dying, death, and grieving within North American society. African Americans, Mexican Americans, and Native Americans, to a greater or lesser degree, have been able to retain many traditional ways. They have remained nearer to their "indigenous sources," the Deep South, Southwest, and Indian reservations, than have recent immigrant groups. The Hmong and others with small and scattered populations have had more difficulty in maintaining their traditional ways.

Now, burials at the neighborhood churchyard are less frequent. Simple pine boxes have been replaced with commercial coffins. Funeral homes have more often been the sites of wakes, viewings, and funerals. With a mobile society, family burial plots have become less appropriate. Prescribed rituals are abbreviated, attenuated, or omitted in the more secularized, highly scheduled urban life.

Abandoning many funeral rites causes stress within the Hmong community. Certain customary items are not available, and their use of animal sacrifices creates misunderstanding with the dominant society. Some Hmong and many Native Americans have become Christian, while often maintaining a strong identification with traditional concepts and ways. (There has been in recent years a resurgence of interest among Native Americans in traditional religious practices and beliefs.) Muslims have difficulty securing the proper cloth and special waters for bathing the body. They and other small religious minorities often lack personnel who are knowledgeable enough to act as officiants.

CONCLUDING INSIGHTS ABOUT DEATH AND GRIEF

Death and grief, though they are universal, natural, and predictable experiences that occur within a social milieu, are deeply embedded within each person's reality. When examining death and grief in a multi-cultural context, the myths, mysteries, and mores that characterize both the dominant and nondominant groups directly affect attitudes, beliefs, practices, and cross-cultural relationships.

Some insights concerning diversity in death and grief practices can be gleaned from information gathered over the course of this project. First, although the topics of death and grief have taken on new life in recent decades, specific changes concerning those universal life experiences have been minimal when assessed within the parameters of multi-culturalism. Granted, countless books have been published on those topics, support groups abound in churches and hospitals, talk-show hosts focus on grief and loss, and individuals are less apt than formerly to speak euphemistically about death and dying. All those actions have had a positive effect in reawakening society's awareness and acceptance of death and grief. Yet a concern exists that the processes of dying and grieving will be culturally stereotyped as a result of the tendency to generalize Euro-American theories about the stages of death across diverse cultures.

Second, death and grief engender different reactions from members of the dominant group when they occur among those groups that lie outside the mainstream. Gang-related homicides, drug-related suicides, AIDS-related deaths, and the deaths of non-American combatants in war all tend to be depreciated. Indeed, because of the low status ascribed to members of "outside" groups, some representatives of the white, male, "Christian" mainstream seem to ignore, minimize, or give silent acquiescence to their sufferings and the grief of those who survive them.

Third, grief is a normal reaction to the death of a loved one, but individuals from culturally diverse groups in our countries may be grieving for significant losses on a *chronic* basis. Such populations may be dealing simultaneously with the loss of their homeland, personal belongings, family members, economic status, professional identity, cultural traditions, language, and sense of self. The chronic and deep-seated nature of such unresolved grief may complicate the bereavement process in terms of intensity and duration. Not only will culturally diverse populations grieve differently over the death of a loved one but they may be grieving for other significant losses at the same time.

Fourth, based upon the incidences described in this volume, lack of cultural understanding and sensitivity to cultural diversity in death and grief appear to have caused more problems than language barriers.

CONCLUDING STATEMENTS
ABOUT CULTURAL DIVERSITY

Diversity has become a "hot" topic in the 1990s because of demographic changes taking place worldwide. Government studies indicate that women and racial minorities will predominate in the workplace of the future, beginning early in the 21st century. Service organizations and educational institutions are facing major changes in mission, public policies, staff training, and organization structures in order to acknowledge and serve a newly expanded and differentiated client base. Business organizations, too, are being encouraged to reassess their structure and policies in order to compete effectively in the delivery of services to the culturally diverse population who will make up both the work force and the consuming public.

Some conclusions concerning the implementation of policies and the assessment of practices around issues germane to a multi-cultural patient-client base can be drawn for the benefit of organizations and personnel that care for the dying and bereaved.

First, service providers need (a) to understand and respect values reflected in members of nondominant culture groups, and (b) to enhance their communicative effectiveness with such people by providing interpreters and/or on-site language instruction.

Second, organizations that discriminate will be under increasing scrutiny, prodding them toward greater fairness.

Third, an organization that does not acknowledge and reach out to a multicultural consumer base will not be able to compete with those that do.

Fourth, business organizations, educational institutions, and service agencies must embed accountability for cultural diversity into their operational structures in order to remain viable and socially acceptable.

Fifth, ethnic and other underserved groups are challenging unfair treatment and employment practices through litigation under equal-access laws.

CONCLUDING QUESTIONS AND ISSUES

The editors have consulted extensively with physicians, nurses, medical social workers, clergy, hospital administrators, hospital chaplains, and morticians on issues concerning death, bereavement, and multi-culturalism. Thus, we raise the following questions and issues. We trust our colleagues in those disciplines and structures to seek the solutions:

1. What content should be included within the curricula of professional schools that would better prepare future practitioners to meet the needs of the less-common cultural patterns in society? How might scholarships and internships assist them?

2. What programs might be developed for inclusion in annual professional meetings, disciplinary journals, special workshops, and in other ways, to enhance the sensitivities, knowledge, and skills of current practitioners to relate more effectively, respectfully, and compassionately to members of minority groups seeking their services?

3. What structural arrangements and administrative regulations need to be reviewed to minimize intercultural strains and personal affronts within the pertinent institutions?

4. What in-service training might be introduced for staff members of each social institution to humanize more fully their professional attitudes and practices?

5. How might members of these smaller cultural groups be involved initially, and directly, as advisory or full members of institutional boards and committees, as apprentices or interns in the workplaces, and, most desirably, as fully credentialied practitioners working within the various systems to change them?

6. What research should be conducted that would (a) validate recognized theories of death and grief from a multi-cultural perspective, (b) identify points of potential conflict concerning death and grief among individual family members and professional personnel from both dominant and nondominant cultural groups, (c) examine the long-term impact of death and grief on the family, school, organization, and community, and (d) document attitudes, beliefs, and practices surrounding death and grief within culturally diverse groups?

7. How might diversity training be designed so as to (a) encourage the exploration of personal attitudes and ethnic prejudices, (b) incorporate death education, (c) redefine the term *family*, (d) integrate information about life-style, history, values, and traditions surrounding death and grief among diverse groups in society, and (c) analyze institutional strategies to achieve both change and fairness in the treatment of multi-culturalism and people from minority backgrounds?

8. What short- and long-term consequences may prevail as a result of an organization's failure to reflect and serve a multi-culturally diverse work force and patient/client base?

9. What societal values are evidenced by how health-care organizations and educational institutions (a) determine which individuals are given access to the system, (b) process individuals out of that system, and (c) allocate funds and resources in serving a culturally diverse patient/client base?

A FINAL STATEMENT

The goal of this project has been to be helpful to those in the health-care professions and, through them, to benefit culturally diverse clients and patients in dealing with death and bereavement. We respect the general competence of our colleagues and believe in their genuine desire to provide the best services possible in a not-ideal world. Although we have presented examples of misunderstanding, ignorance, and prejudicial actions on the part of some people, in no way has it been our intention to denigrate our colleagues, embarrass individuals or institutions, or add to the difficulties they already confront.

While we have provided a broad framework that begs for more detailed investigation, we hope that others will extend what we have initiated to include a greater number of diverse groups. We also hope that our work will serve as a catalyst for research, education, and training in the areas of death, grief, and cultural diversity. Finally, our primary guiding principle for professionals working with multi-cultural populations is that they acknowledge and appreciate different ethnic norms while cherishing the absolute uniqueness of each individual.

Ethnic Population Data and Trends—United States and Canada

Donald P. Irish

UNITED STATES—SUMMARY

The U.S. Census failed to count up to 6 million people in 1990, a 2.1% deficit. The racial composition of the country changed to a greater degree between 1980 and 1990 than during any other decade in this century. One in five American residents were members of "ethnic minorities" in 1980, compared with one in four in 1990, with a total increasing to between 61 and 62 million people. "Whites" comprised about 80% of the nation's population.

Within each ethnic group there are considerable cultural contrasts. Within the Asian minority group the largest subgroups are of Chinese (one quarter), Filipino (one fifth), or Japanese extraction. Registering the fastest growth rates were those of Vietnamese (135%), East Indian (126%), Korean (125%), and Laotian-Hmong (1600%) origins. Immigrants accounted for most of the growth among both Asians and Hispanics, with more than a third of the past decade's increase resulting from that influx.

Ethnic and Religious Minority Populations in the United States, 1990 and 1991

	Population (in millions)	Percentage total population	Percentage increase since 1980
Ethnic minorities[a]			
African Americans	30.0	12.1	13.2
Asian Americans	7.3	2.9	107.8
Native Americans	2.0	0.8	37.9
Hispanics	22.4	9.1	53.0
Others	9.8	3.9	45.1
Religious minorities[b]			
Jews	6.0	2.4	NA
Muslims	4.0–6.0	1.6–2.4	NA
Buddhists	0.1	NA	NA

Total U.S. population, 1990: 248,709,873.
[a]Whites, including many Hispanics, differently classified, equalled 80.3%.
[b]Data from 1991.

Among Hispanics, the Mexican American, Puerto Rican, and Cuban American groups have had the largest numbers in the past, but their increases are now exceeded by migrants from Central and South America. Within the total U.S. population there were 13.5 million Chicanos or Mexican Americans (5.4%), 2.7 million Puerto Ricans (1.0%), 1 million plus Cuban Americans (0.9%), with other Hispanics constituting 2.0%.

Of the 2 million Native Americans, Inuit, and Aleuts, only 35% live on their tribal or band lands, with 1.3 million living outside Native American areas.

For two centuries, U.S. race relations have focused upon a white majority and a black minority; Native Americans have tended to be ignored. Now, at the end of the 20th century, there are at least three major minorities—African Americans, Hispanics, and Asian Americans—and they have grown to constitute about 20% of the population. Language, culture, and religion are having resurgent significance. Race no longer is the sole differentiating factor.

With regard to religious affiliations, a plurality of Jews belong to Conservative congregations. The number of Americans identifying themselves as Jews has increased slightly in recent times. Since 1985, however, fewer than 50% of marriages that included Jews have been between couples both of whom were born into a Jewish family; and in only a small fraction of these "mixed marriages" does the partner convert to Judaism. Thus, Jewish communal life is weakened.

Islam is gaining adherents through immigration, high birth rates, and a steady influx of conversions. By the 21st century, Islam may become the second largest major religious faith in the United States. The nation is moving toward a Judeo-Christian-Muslim society.

Roman Catholics continue to be the largest single Christian denomination. All evidence indicates a decline in members among mainline, liberal to moderate, ecumenical Protestant denominations. The Southern Baptists are the only such group showing significant numerical growth. The fastest-growing religious bodies are the Mormon Church, Buddhism, Islam, and various New Age sects. The proportion of the non-church going population has also been increasing, with regional differences.

CANADA — SUMMARY

Canada is a multi-ethnic country that is becoming more diverse. Its 1986 Census registered about 25 million residents, a population one tenth that of the United States. Ontario and the western provinces gained proportionately more than Quebec and the Maritimes. Canada's population density is one of the lowest in the world.

Race, language, and ethnic origins continued to be socially significant. About three fifths of the population are English-speaking; one fourth are French-speaking; and the remainder speak Italian, German, Chinese, Native Canadian, or other languages. Many people, of course, are bilingual. About three quarters of all Canadians recently claimed at least one British ancestor. Their 1981 Census reported over 50 immigrant groups, a sixth of whom had been born outside Canada. During the 1971–1981 decade, the proportion of Canadians of European background declined from four fifths to only two thirds, due largely to declining birth rates and changes in the composition of immigration.

The "First Nations" (Native Canadians, Métis, Inuit, Aleut) have recently gained greater attention in Canada through their increased consciousness of their identities and historic rights, challenging the dominant majority in a number of arenas. What is now Canada had about 200,000 non-Inuit indigenous people in the 16th century, along with a few thousand Inuit, who were rather evenly distributed. By 1990 estimates, there were about half a million "native peoples" in the country, affiliated with about 600 different bands or tribes and related to 2,250 reserve areas. Altogether, they comprise about 2% of the Canadian population.

Data from 1990 indicate that more Canadians belonged to the Roman Catholic (11.4 million) or Anglican (800,000) faiths. The proportion of the former has grown to be more than 47% of the population, while the Protestants have declined to about 41%. The United Church of Canada (864,000), Lutheran (297,000), and Presbyterian (157,000) constituted the other principal Protestant affiliations. Estimates indicated that there were about 350,000 Muslims (1.4%

of the population), more than 300,000 Jews (1.2%), and about 250,000 Sikhs (1.0%) in the country.

Note: Data in this appendix were drawn from *Census of Canada, 1981 and 1986*; *Commonwealth Yearbook, 1991*; *Europa World Yearbook, 1990*; *Yearbook of American and Canadian Churches, 1991*; *U.S. Census, 1990*; and the *World Almanac of Facts, 1991*.

Questions That Might Be Asked

Donald P. Irish

CHAPTER 4: AFRICAN AMERICANS

What should the local police have done differently at the scene of the shooting? At the hospital? How might the hospital staff have handled the situation better— for example, the administrator who asked the gathering to leave or "be removed" or the security staff who asked other police units to come to the area? What may have prompted them to react so strongly? Should the hospital have given prompt medical aid to those bitten by the police dogs?

What might African American leaders within the community—pastors, agency workers, teachers, among others—have been able to do, beginning with the scene after the shooting?

Were hospital staff and police sufficiently acquainted with, and sensitive to, grieving patterns within the African American community? Should the ambulance drivers have been directed instead to the county morgue rather than to a hospital, given that the young man was already dead? Could added materials in the training of police and/or hospital staff have helped avoid the aftermath of the shooting and its divisive consequences for the entire community?

The incident having occurred, what might be expected by the African American community and the general public from the mayor, city council, NAACP, Human Rights/Relations Commission, and the like? What might the hospital governing board consider grounds for a special meeting?

CHAPTER 5: HISPANIC AMERICANS

What role may the differences in education levels between those of the priest, social worker, and physician, and that of Ramona, have played in their definitions of the situation? Might the priest's perception have, perhaps, resulted from the threat which *santería* as a folk faith presented to his Catholic orthodoxy? To what extent might ignorance of *santería* have been a likely influence on the conclusions formed by professional practitioners? What role might their own cultures have played in the inability of the "Anglo" professionals to accept Ramona's beliefs and practices as normal within her culture or as useful adjuncts to their practices?

If ill and/or dying persons in such Caribbean culture areas request the presence and aid of *santeros* at their bedsides, should health-care institutions assist in satisfying their desires? If so, in what manner? If not, why not? How might the professionals have reacted differently, more humanely, perhaps also more effectively, in aiding Ramona? What changes in professional curricular and/or institutional polices might have avoided Ramona's loss of her children, extended institutionalization, and personal trauma?

CHAPTER 6: HMONG

How might this cultural misunderstanding, the psychic injury to the Hmong families, the bewilderment of the teacher's family, and the embarrassment for the school possibly have been avoided? Was the funeral director at fault? What about any involved clergy? How might the Head Start supervisor have best responded initially and subsequently? Was a three-week delay necessary? Were the school personnel prepared to deal with the pupils—Hmong and others—on the subjects of death and the loss of a teacher? Could the Hmong children have been expected to return to Head Start with equanimity and an eagerness to learn following the exhumation?

Will the other children in the school be helped to understand and appreciate their schoolmates' contrasting cultural beliefs and emotional responses? Are the Hmong families likely to feel some additional alienation and separation from the dominant community? Is a Christmas tree a neutral symbol to convey parallel sentiments across cultural boundaries?

What further in-service training might have been helpful for funeral directors, ministers, and school personnel in raising their consciousness of cultural differences? Should the Hmong be expected to adapt or to give up their distinctive patterns?

CHAPTER 7: NATIVE AMERICANS

What examples of cultural insensitivity are revealed in these episodes? How might the reactions of the physicians, nurses, and security personnel have reflected perceptions of the dominant society? What would have been appropriate responses to these divergent views of the situation? Why might the admitting physician have presumed that Tom Bear needed treatment for alcoholism when the 911 call had been made for severe chest pains? Why would the physician walk away from her when Alice challenged the treatment given her husband upon entrance? How might the behavior of the nurse be explained, when she called the security personnel to remove the sons from their father's bedside? How might the matter of the customary autopsy request have been better handled?

What could these several episodes in the case indicate about the hospital's on-the-job training and orientation programs? What might the hospital administration and board be expected to do in reaction to these incidents? Are there other faith traditions that involve singing, chants, or rites at the point of death that might seem strange or disturbing to others? If *you* were one of the involved personnel (physician, nurse, security guard), how would you hope to have reacted?

CHAPTER 8: JEWS

What is the *primary* multi-cultural issue involved? What is the implicit definition of "interfaith?" Which of the orientations best represents cross-cultural sensitivities? Which of them may best reflect the values of the dominant communities in which the hospital and chapels are located? Would the situation distress a community citizen of Jewish faith? Someone of Muslim faith? A traditional Native American? How might one of these people have proceeded to bring about change in the plans which the minister says have been completed? What roles might other Catholics, Lutherans, and Protestant clergy or parishioners in the community play in trying to resolve the disagreement? What modifications might be suggested to satisfy non-Christians with loved ones in the hospital? Do you think the presumably completed plans adequately reflect the broader constituency to be found within the wider community?

Were the hospital's patient clientele, medical personnel, administrative staff, and board likely to be representative of all community segments? Were representatives of other faiths probably involved in the planning committee, or on the hospital board? Would contentions be different if the hospital were totally independent of public funds or oversight? That is, if it were strictly a private, denominational institution? What might the hospital administration be expected to do in this situation now? How would *you* have proceeded had you been a member of the planning committee?

CHAPTER 9: BUDDHISTS

Can a mortuary staff be expected to know in advance the many possible idiosyncratic differences among cultures? If not, how might the mortuary personnel have been able to take advance steps to avoid such a distressing situation? By a more thorough inquiry regarding the nature of each occasion? By modification in room and wall construction and locations? By not scheduling two viewings in the same area at the same time?

Under the circumstances, was the dilemma resolved quite reasonably, or satisfactorily?

CHAPTER 10: MUSLIMS

Who is going to take care of all the rituals? Does anyone in the dominant culture know about Muslim ceremonies? Will the Muslim survivors be subjected to Christian patterns or be able to follow their own? As a young person of Islamic faith in America, not very familiar with behaviors appropriate to the situation, what counsel might the daughter seek, and from whom? How can Muslims explain to "the Americans" that Muslims cover their dead with a special kind of cloth, or that special water to wash the dead body, is needed? Where are the facilities to wash the dead body according to the ritual? If the body is not buried according to the Islamic way, how will the survivors feel about the events? If, as is quite likely, some of the family members have converted to Christianity, how might the mourning, funeral, and cemetery ritual aspects be conducted?

Without knowledge of the Islamic view of life after death, the philosophy of death and dying in Muslim culture, and the rituals associated with grief, Euro-Americans will be unlikely to understand Muslim immigrants and respect their values. In preparation for such relatively rare incidents involving persons of faiths that are currently unusual in America and Canada, how might ambulance personnel, hospital staffs, morticians, ministers, cemetery staffs, social workers, and others be aided to deal with them? Given that autopsies are taboo for those of Muslim faith, what provisions (exceptions) might be made by states or provinces in cases of death in which no criminal aspect is involved? Would there be mortuaries that would accommodate the unusual requests for the use of special facilities and the performance of distinctive rites? Cemeteries? Hospitals?

How might a more informed public respond helpfully to the screaming daughter? Would it be appropriate in the mall setting to try to "quiet" her? Or might some other response have been better? What role might an available Christian pastor or Jewish rabbi have in such circumstances, given that the deceased is a Muslim and an Imam would be wanted to officiate at the services? Although no professionals can be expected to have an exhaustive knowledge of the beliefs and customs of many other faiths and cultures in detail, how might they be prepared attitudinally and in procedures to take better care of the needs of such patients or clients?

Personal Reflections on the African American Experience

Juan L. Turner

Through our close association with other groups, blacks share many similarities in relation to death, dying, and grieving: areas of residence, ages of persons, religious beliefs and practices, educational levels, and family patterns. However, the socioeconomic factor does not play as large a role for African Americans.

Death in general is an awesome state. The spirit is extremely important, and the body houses the spirit. We believe that life is a bridge, a transition, and that death brings us to a better place. Most African Americans believe in life after death: immortality is a given. We refer to funerals as "home-going services," as celebrations. We may fear death and not want it to come; but also at times it is welcomed.

Until the recent past, suicide was not a common African American experience, unless it was used to escape oppression. The act was then viewed as an appropriate and unjudged means of release. My grandmother would say, "They had every reason, I don't blame them." Sometimes unusual deaths will be "related" to a sin the deceased has committed, something the person "did wrong," perhaps harking back to African beliefs that displeasing the gods precipitates misfortune.

The person who is dying is not feared but treated with an almost reverential awe. A tradition of taking care of our own deceased person involved some people taking responsibility for washing the body and sitting with it. Death education occurs within the family, the community, and the church. Children are included in every aspect of the dying, death, and grieving processes. They are encouraged to look at and touch the body, to say "goodbye," to cry, and to share in the joy of the memories. We teach them appropriate behavior simply by the way we adults act. The children are encouraged to do small tasks, and they can become acquainted with relatives that they have not known before.

Many times, death is a mixture of joyful mourning. Funerals provide opportunities to relate to people we have not seen for a long time. Further, there can be joy in seeing someone who has been ill and who has lived a good life going on to something better. In my church we often say, "If this is all there is, God forbid! We're ready to go!" We want something better; so there can be joy when a person dies, although we know we will miss them.

When death is close, the extended family is called. We try to assemble everyone. If a close relative can't afford the cost, we may put money together to pay for the trip. If a minister is called, it's usually the one who has known the family's life experiences. If the deceased is a member of a fraternal organization, there are added ceremonies to be conducted. We have some African American fraternal groups that are very pompous and tradition-conscious. Costly funerals, unfortunately, often are a norm for African Americans, regardless of economic level, some believing that they show how much they care for the loved one in that way.

The preferred method of body disposal is to have the deceased buried "back home." Because we believe in the sanctity of the body and spirit, there is a common resistance to cremation. African Americans will travel long distances to decorate graves at a particular time.

How can African Americans be best served by professional practitioners? Don't assume anything! Ask the family what they want; then leave and give the family an opportunity to decide. Don't hover over them, for some feel threatened when that is done. Just let the bereaved know that you care and want everything to be "right" for them.

Personal Reflections on the Hispanic Experience

Marcial Vásquez

While growing up in Belize, I awakened one night to discover that my grand-father had died. Old age was not considered a factor in his death; rather, it was a consequence of witchcraft. My mother had discovered a toad in the *escusado* (a toilet hole in the yard, enclosed by pimiento trees). The toad's eyelids were sewn together with a black thread. She had mentioned the night before that several snakes had made their way through our house. Witchcraft and *curan-derismo* were very much a part of our community. Due to a lack of medical facilities, *curanderos* were a necessity. A *curandero* was summoned to help us dispel the curse of the witch. He was the one person who could lift curses and also heal people of their illnesses.

This death erupted into my life and left me in a state of confusion and fear. My grandfather's body was taken to a Catholic church for the funeral; but we had no priests in the village. A rosary was said; the haunting song sung at the service stays in my head. It was a sad, cold day, and everyone was crying. After the unfinished pine coffin was lowered into the grave, the site was crossed seven times to ward off the evil spirits that had driven my grandfather to his death.

Features of my informal death education as a child included rumors and stories of spirits and *animas*, which shaped my life and dreams. (*Animas* are souls in purgatory; but the word may also denote souls in general.) They drove me to panic whenever I passed the village cemetery. My parents did not talk about death. We just lived with it and tried to cope as best we could.

Many Hispanics in the United States have problems with its welfare institutions, which are often experienced as dehumanizing, although they are established to provide assistance. The tradition of taking care of our elderly parents does not depend on whether we grew up in Latin America or in the United States. We endeavor to retain our *religiosidad* wherever we may be.

Most Hispanics are Roman Catholics. Generally they have representations of the saints and the Virgin in their homes, and they light candles and pray to them. Their Catholic beliefs are sometimes mingled with indigenous traditions. They place emphasis on holy places, miracles, and emotional experiences. They feel a need for penitence and other forms of sacrifice.

For Christian Hispanics, there is no finality in death. Dying is seen not as an end but as a beginning, a passing from one state to another. Yet the meaning of death is different for different groups. For those of Catholic background, death brings a passage to heaven if their actions have warranted that and if their sins have been forgiven, or if they have received the last rites. Protestants focus more on the Resurrection, especially those who are Pentecostals. Among the mainline denominations, a closer balance is maintained between the present life and the one beyond. Their emphasis is less future-oriented than that of the Pentecostals.

Many Hispanics believe that illness is associated with being good or bad. For them, the devil is often mentioned as a primary cause of illness and death. When some Hispanics are hospitalized, they cover their gowns with crosses to ward off the devil and evil spirits.

For those who are mainstream rather than believers in *santería* or *espiritismo*, whatever God wants is expected to be fulfilled. God makes a way, a course for them to follow. People may pursue devious routes, but they will ultimately be subject to what God wants for them.

Souls are part of God; and God is within us. Some believe that the soul becomes part of a person at the moment of conception. Thus, no matter how small a fetus may be when there is a miscarriage, there will be a sense of great loss because the soul of the fetus has already been recognized by God. When miscarriages or stillbirths occur, the reason lies with God to know. God knows why, and that must be accepted. Within the Catholic tradition, abortions generally are not sanctioned, with some permitted exceptions.

Some Hispanics cannot separate the reality of old age from being sick from an illness. They believe that no matter how old people are, there should be some medicine that can enable them to recover their strength.

When a Hispanic dies, many of the same traditions apply now as in Euro-

American or Canadian funerals, whether Catholic or Protestant, because some customs have been lost through acculturation. Interment is usually utilized; but those who bury their dead may spend many hours at the cemetery speaking to their loved ones. One woman reported that some of her children refused to take her to the cemetery again because they say that all she does is cry. She recalled: "We placed his body in a cold, wet tomb and closed it. I felt badly for him because he was all alone in the dark. I wanted to be there for him all the time, but my children did not understand me." For her, and many others, the past still remains in the present.

General Bibliography

Kathleen F. Lundquist

Anderson, B. G. (1965). Bereavement as a subject of cross-cultural inquiry: An American sample. *Anthropology Quarterly, 38,* 181–200.

Aries, P. (1974). *Western attitudes toward death: From middle ages to the present.* Baltimore: Johns Hopkins University Press.

Badgam, P., & Badgam, L. (1987). *Death and immortality in the religions of the world.* New York: Paragon House.

Bardis, P. D. (1981). *History of thanatology: Philosophical, religious, psychological, and sociological ideas concerning death from primitive times to the present.* Lanham, MD: University Press of America.

Bengston, V. L., Cuellear, J. A., & Ragon, P. K. (1976). *Group contrasts in attitudes toward death: Variation by race, age, occupation, status, and sex.* Unpublished manuscript.

Berger, A., et al. (Eds.). (1989). *Perspectives on death and dying: Cross-cultural and multi-disciplinary views.* Philadelphia: Charles Press.

Bloch, M., & Parry, J. (1983). *Death and regeneration of life.* Cambridge, England: Cambridge University Press.

Bowlby, J. (1961). Processes of mourning. *The International Journal of Psycho-Analysis, 42,* 317–340.

Chunn, J. C., Dunston, P. J., & Ross-Sheriff, F. (Eds.). (1983). *Mental health and people of color: Curriculum development and change.* Washington, DC: Howard University Press.

Counts, D. R., & Counts, D. A. (Eds.). (1991). *Coping with the final tragedy: Cultural variation in dying and grieving.* Amityville, NY: Baywood.

Eisenbruch, M. (1984). Cross-cultural aspects of bereavement I: A conceptual framework for comparative analysis. *Culture, Medicine, and Psychiatry, 3,* 283–309.

Eisenbruch, M. (1984). Cross-cultural aspects of bereavement II: Ethnic and cultural variations in the development of bereavement practices. *Culture, Medicine, and Psychiatry, 4,* 315–347.

Fabian, J. (1972). How others die: Reflections on the anthropology of death. *Social Research, 39,* 543–567.

Feifel, H. (1971). The meaning of death in American society: Implications for education. In B. Green & D. Irish (Eds.), *Death education: Preparation for living* (pp. 3–12). Cambridge, MA: Schenkman.

Feifel, H. (1977). Death in modern America. *Death Education, 1*(1), 5–14.

Fulton, R. (1965). The sacred and the secular: Attitudes of the American public toward death, funerals, and funeral directors. In R. Fulton (Ed.), *Death and identity* (pp. 89–105). New York: John Wiley.

Grof, S., & Halifax, J. (1977). *The human encounter with death.* New York: Dutton.

Grollman, E. (1974). *Concerning death: A practical guide for the living.* Boston: Beacon Press.

Habenstein, R. W., & Lamers, W. M. (1960). *Funeral customs the world over.* Milwaukee: Bulfin.

Hafferty, F. W. (1991). *Into the valley: Death and the socialization of medical students.* New Haven, CT: Yale University Press.

Harwood, A. (1981). *Ethnicity and medical care.* Cambridge, MA: Harvard University Press.

Huntington, R., & Metcalf, P. (1979). *Celebrations of death: The anthropology of mortuary ritual.* Cambridge, England: Cambridge University Press.

Kalish, R. A. (Ed.). (1979). *Perspectives on death and dying I: Views from many cultures.* New York: Baywood.

Kalish, R. A., & Reynolds, D. K. (1981). *Perspectives of death and dying IV: Death and ethnicity: A psychocultural study.* New York: Baywood.

Kamerman, J. B. (1988). *Death in the midst of social and cultural influences on death, grief, and mourning.* New York: Prentice-Hall.

Kastenbaum, R. (1977). *Death, society, and human experience.* St. Louis: Mosby.

Kavanagh, K. H., & Kennedy, P. H. (1992). *Promoting cultural diversity: Strategies for health care professionals.* Newbury Park, CA: Sage Publications.

Kleinman, A. (1980). *Patients and healers in the context of culture: An exploration of the borderland between anthropology, medicine, and psychiatry.* Berkeley: University of California Press.

Kübler-Ross, E. (1977). *Death: The final stage of growth.* Englewood Cliffs, NJ: Prentice-Hall.

Leming, M. R. (1991, April). *Funeral customs in Thailand.* Paper presented to the Midwest Sociological Society, Des Moines, IA.

Leming, M. R., & Dickinson, G. E. (1990). *Understanding dying, death and bereavement* (2nd ed., pp. 93–137, 295–322). Ft. Worth: Holt, Rinehart, & Winston.

Locke, D. C. (1992). *Increasing multicultural understanding: A comprehensive model.* Newbury Park, CA: Sage Publications.

Mathison, J. (1970). A cross-cultural view of widowhood. *Omega, 1,* 201–218.

Mitford, J. (1963). *The American way of death.* New York: Simon & Schuster.

Pine, V. R. (1969). Comparative funeral practices. *Practical Anthropology, 16,* 49–62.

Putsch, R. W. (1988). Ghost illness: A cross-cultural experiment with the experience of a non-Western tradition in clinical practice. *American Indian and Alaska Native Mental Health Research, 2*(2), 6–26.

Reynolds, F. (1977). Natural death in myth and religion. *Hastings Center Report, 7*(3), 38–44.

Romanucci-Ross, L., Moerman, D. E., & Tancredi, L. R. (1983). *The anthropology of medicine: From culture to method.* New York: Praeger.

Rosenblatt, P. C., Walsh, R. P., & Jackson, D. A. (1976). *Grief and mourning in cross-cultural perspective.* New Haven, CT: Human Relations Area Files Press.

Rubin, N. (1990). Social networks and mourning: A comparative approach. *Omega, 21*(2), 113–127.

Savishin, J. S., & Wimberley, H. (1974). The living and the dead: A cross-cultural perspective in Jewish memorial observances. *Jewish Social Studies, 36*(3–4), 281–300.

Sokolovsky, J. (1990). *The cultural context of aging: Worldwide perspectives.* Newbury Park, CA: Greenwood.

Templer, D. I., et al. (1971). Death anxiety: Age, sex, and parental resemblance in diverse populations. *Developmental Psychology, 4,* 108.

Bibliography for Children

Kathleen F. Lundquist

Currently, there are not many books for children and young people that present death and grief from a multi-cultural perspective. Those few that reflect a nondominant tradition are listed below, with a note of the age group for which they are written.

Bunting, E. (1982). *The happy funeral.* New York: Harper, (5–8, Chinese American.)

Clifford, E. (1985). *The remembering box.* New York: Houghton Mifflin. (3–5, Jewish American.)

Clifton, L., & Grifaiconi, A. (1983). *Everett Anderson's goodbye.* New York: Holt. (5–8, African American.)

Coerr, E. (1977). *Sadako and the thousand paper cranes.* New York: Dell/Yearling. (8–14, Japanese.)

Daisaku, I. (1991). *The cherry tree.* New York: Knopf. (Japanese.)

Kaplan, B. (1978). *The empty chair.* New York: Harper. (6 + , Jewish American.)

Prepared with the assistance of Grace Sulerud, Reference Librarian, Augsburg College, Minneapolis.

211

Miles, M. (1971). *Annie and the old one.* Boston: Little, Brown. (5 + , Navajo.)

Pomerantz, B. (1983). *Bubby, me, and memories.* New York: UAHC Press. (5 + , Jewish American.)

Simon, N. (1989). *I am not a crybaby.* Morton Grove, IL: Albert Whitman & Co.

Walker, A. (1987). *To hell with dying.* New York: Harcourt Brace. (10 + , African American.)

Index